Frontier America
1800-1840

Immigrants En route to the Frontier by Water
Courtesy, Illinois State Historical Library

FRONTIER AMERICA
1800-1840

A Comparative Demographic Analysis
of the Settlement Process

by
JAMES E. DAVIS

THE ARTHUR H. CLARK COMPANY
Glendale, California
1977

LIBRARY OF CONGRESS CATALOG CARD NUMBER 77-077031
ISBN 0-87062-120-3

To my wife,
Joanna

Contents

Illustrations

The maps are based on Charles Paullin's "Atlas of the Historical Geography
of the United States." They were drawn by Clifford Donahue.

Acknowledgements

It is not possible to acknowledge properly all of the assistance I have received in the course of this study. Credit for retrieving much of the census data and for much of the initial planning must go to Professor Jerome Clubb and Mr. Eric Austin of the Inter-University Consortium for Political Research at The University of Michigan. Moreover, Mr. Austin, always available for patient consultation concerning various strategies for using the computer, provided innumerable bits of excellent advice which kept me from becoming permanently ensnared by the wily computer. The personnel in the Computer Assistance Program, The University of Michigan, also helped me to prod the computer.

Giving invaluable direction to this work while it was in the dissertation stage at The University of Michigan was my dissertation committee. Professor Donald Deskins, Jr., provided fine ideas concerning the geographical aspects of the investigation and some bibliographical suggestions pertaining to black people, all of which were of considerable help. Professor Reynolds Farley assisted greatly in analyzing some of the technical facets of demography, steered me away from pitfalls, and provided advice in constructing the tables. Professor Sam Bass Warner, Jr., contributed suggested readings and useful insights concerning relationships between independent and dependent variables. To Professor Shaw Livermore, Jr., the chairman of the committee, must go immense credit. The study benefitted greatly at every stage of development from his skillful and conscientious guidance. His encouragement was constant and his enthusiasm infectious.

For the historian financial assistance is quickly translated into an even greater resource: time. Considerable amounts of financial assistance were provided by the Department of History and the Horace H. Rackham School of Graduate Studies, The University of Michigan. Additional grants purchased vast quantities of computer time, thereby saving years of work. Travel for the purposes of research was also made possible by a grant from the Shell Companies Foundation, Inc., a grant extended to me by Illinois College. The college also granted me a hefty sum from the Faculty Summer

Development Fund, and this defrayed the costs associated with revising the manuscript for publication. Providing either additional funds or blocks of time in which to work, or both, were the following: my parents, William Franklin and Mabel Corley Davis, also Mildred Ildza, and Penelope M. Mitchell. My sincere appreciation to these institutions and individuals for donating time, resources, and encouragement.

The staffs of various other institutions also rendered courteous and efficient assistance. The Clements Library made available numerous maps and other materials relating to early America, making it possible to identify and classify counties. The Michigan Historical Collections supplied me with manuscript censuses, works which were valuable in the formative stages of this project. The National Archives was of immense assistance in providing census manuscripts from which it was possible to gather data pertaining to household size and household composition. Information was gleaned from hundreds of diaries, journals, travel accounts, and other primary sources located in many libraries: University of Michigan, Illinois State Historical Library, Illinois College, University of Illinois, Wayne State University, Library of Congress, Newberry Library, MacMurray College, Chicago Public Library, St. Louis Public Library, State Historical Society of Wisconsin Library, University of Pittsburgh, Michigan Historical Commission, Missouri Historical Society Library, and the Detroit Public Library. Of the many competent people who lent assistance at these institutions, Dr. Roger Bridges, Director of Research at The Illinois State Historical Library, was especially helpful.

My colleagues, past and present, at Illinois College have taken an interest in this effort. I appreciate the comments, advice, and encouragement from the members of the History and Political Science Department: Richard T. Fry, Ernest G. Hildner, Wallace Jamison, Donald R. Tracey, and Elizabeth Zeigler. William Cross, Chairman of the Department of Sociology, helped greatly in ironing out problems pertaining to the study of the institution of the family.

The greatest debt I owe is to my family. My children, Kathy and Mary, displayed buoyant interest and great understanding. My wife, Joanna, was heroically patient and encouraging. Her confidence in me and interest in my work never flagged in spite of delay and setback.

JAMES E. DAVIS
Illinois College
September, 1976

CHAPTER I

Purpose, Methods and Constraints

It was a time of movement and a time of hope. The nation was young and its spirit youthful. Those who were young in spirit joined those who were young in years, and in the first four decades of the nineteenth century the American frontier pushed out of the hills of the western Appalachians, rolled across the forested Mississippi River basin, and lapped onto the prairie country. Scores of thousands—hundreds of thousands—ventured westward and the result was that much of the nation's territory was settled and the American character drastically altered.[1]

But who were they? What were they like, those who trekked into the unknown, who devastated forests and Indians and carved farms and communities from the wilderness? We know something about their triumphs and failures and the impact of the frontier experience on them. Yet we know little about some of their characteristics.

This study has one basic purpose: identify and analyze some of the demographic characteristics of the individuals, households, and groups that were lured or shoved into the West. More specifically, seven demographic variables for the years 1800 through 1840—household size, household composition, age, sex, race, condition of blacks, and occupation—were measured and analyzed in order to reveal the American frontiersman and understand something of the interplay of forces between him and his natural and cultural environments.

The significance of the frontier is an old point of contention. Attack and counterattack have swept across the academic plain over the issue. Long before the frontier vanished, Americans and others knew that both the western experience and the ideas and myths concerning the western experience were altering American life.[2] The thesis presented by Frederick Jackson Turner heightened this awareness at almost the precise moment the frontier flickered out of existence. Quickly acclaimed and widely accepted, the thesis held sway for decades, the first heavy barrage of

---

[1]For the numbers of pioneers present on the frontier at various points in time see App. C.

[2]Herman Clarence Nixon, "Precursors of Turner in the Interpretation of the American Frontier," *South Atlantic Qtly.*, xxviii, pp. 83-89.

criticism being fired only after Turner died in 1932.[3] Since then, frontal and flank attacks, some missing the mark and some landing telling blows, have been launched from a score of directions against the thesis. Leaping to the defense, Turner's disciples parried some of the thrusts and revised, expanded, or abandoned parts of Turner's arguments, trying to make the core of the thesis more tenable. Neither side plucked decisive victory from the swirl of academic endeavor, nor did synthesis or consensus emerge from the conflict. Instead, the conflict did chip some of the salient features from the positions held by both detractors and defenders of the thesis and make plain the fact that the frontier controversy is highly complex.

Since so many scholars have trod onto the field of conflict and entered the fray, why again examine the frontier? The following chapters constitute neither another foray against the frontier thesis nor an attempt to defend it. (In fact, the study addresses itself only tangentially to the ideas espoused by Turner.) Rather, it is an attempt to examine and analyze an aspect of frontier life which has lacked a full-scale, systematic examination and analysis.

Whatever the nature of pioneer life and whatever impact the western experience had on the nation and on other nations, people were involved. Conditions and events in the wilderness influenced the demographic traits of the settler; the demographic traits, at the same time, created conditions and influenced events in the new lands of the West.[4] For these reasons, demography in this study was analyzed as both a dependent variable and an independent variable in the development of the frontier and nation, a fact of some importance for the following chapters.

One persuasive reason for investigating frontier demography is essentially academic. Over the years professional historians, amateur historians, and genealogists have explicitly and implicitly ascribed to settlers certain demographic characteristics. Although some of these references consisted of rank conjecture posing as researched evidence, others were rigorous attempts to discover and evaluate something of the demographic composition of the frontier. Speculative or carefully researched, the claims addressed themselves largely to the seven demographic variables under consideration in this study. (Examples of the claims appear at the beginning of each of the following chapters.) These

---

[3]One of the opening shots fired in the frontier feud came in 1925 in John C. Almack, "The Shibboleth of the Frontier," *Historical Outlook,* XVI, pp. 197-202. Most of Almack's comments, however, pertain to the post-1840 frontier.

[4]For example, as will be seen, evidence indicates that conditions associated with the westward trek and with western life kept some women of all ages out of the West. This shortage of women, in turn, helped to insure to single women and widowed women in the wilds that they could easily marry if they so desired. Numerous other instances in the following chapters illustrate the fact that various physical, social, and economic conditions associated with the frontier experience influenced demography; demographic conditions at the same time influenced social, economic, and even political aspects of western life.

references, whether unfounded generalizations or sound conclusions, require either refutation or confirmation by means of a systematic and thorough methodology.

There is another and more profound reason for investigating frontier demography: the process of western settlement affected the very essence of American life. So many people scrambled after so much land for so many decades in such comparative freedom and against such relatively ineffectual human opposition that regional and national institutions, customs, and attitudes were either created or altered in the process. Many of these ensuing acts of creation or alteration persist to the present. In large measure, current social, economic, political, and even diplomatic conditions and attitudes spring from the western process, and demography was part of the process as both a dependent and independent variable.

The West lavished onto generations of pioneers spacious tracts of inexpensive land. The newcomers found the land unexploited, void of dense human settlement, full of forests and game, and generally willing to return to the investment of modest capital and tedious labor a reasonable profit, eventual ownership, and great satisfaction. The Vikings plundered wealth from coastal regions, Francisco Pizarro pillaged Peru, and the Americans ransacked the resources of the wilderness. Settlers decimated wild animals, vanquished forests with fire and the ax, extracted minerals from the ground, and drained nourishment from the soil.[5] Frontier plenty offered to many prosperity and, to many more, the reasonable hope of prosperity. Past natural wealth and the largely private, unregulated manner by which it was tapped account in large measure for historical economic abundance and possibly present shortages.

Although a variety of demographic types either gravitated to the wilderness or sprang into existence there, some people failed to share in the western riches. The significance of the distribution essentially hinges on one question: did everyone in the nation have a fairly equal opportunity to venture into the new lands, invest some capital and much labor, and reap the rewards from the land? Obviously not. Many strangers to success were precluded from sharing in the abundance of the West. Most blacks, for example, were slaves throughout the early national era and had no legal right to go anywhere, invest anything, or keep any gain from their toils.[6]

---

[5]The roles played by the continent's wealth in shaping American life are discussed in David M. Potter, *People of Plenty: Economic Abundance and the American Character.* Lending considerable support to Potter's thesis is an account from the 1830s, Godfrey T. Vigne, *Six Months in America.*

[6]The extent to which the lives of slaves were circumscribed is depicted very ably in Kenneth M. Stampp, *The Peculiar Institution: Slavery in the Ante-Bellum South.* Included in this work are various forms of slave resistance to restrictions. A view that effective resistance was rare and that the conditions of slavery and their effects on the slaves were somewhat analogous to the conditions and results of the Nazi concentration camps is found in Stanley M. Elkins, *Slavery, A Problem in American Institutional and Intellectual Life.* A more recent work indicates that

What of the aged, women, single people, young couples, female-headed households, households in which adults were outnumbered by children, and large households? Were they on the frontier in numbers roughly proportionate to their representation in the national population? If they were present, were they *products of* western conditions or were they *attracted to* the backwoods? In addition, were conditions in the wilds conducive to those who lacked capital, formal training, or past accomplishment?

Essentially, two types of individuals apparently entered the wilderness: those who were largely satisfied with their lives and who wanted to perpetuate and extend the attitudes, social arrangements, and opportunities found on the east coast or in Europe; and those who were dissatisfied and who wanted to purge the past of previous failures and plunge into an emerging society in which social flux, cleansing chaos, and generally unsettled conditions augured well for those who sought a new deal and social regeneration.[7] For the former, the wilderness represented a chance to enlarge upon past successes; for the latter, it was one last chance, a place in which a burst of will (sustained by a measure of luck) could overwhelm memories of defeat and heal raw economic, social, and political wounds.[8] Although many of the utterly crushed never managed to scrape together enough capital, knowledge, or nerve to reach the unsettled backcountry, some dejected and beaten households from both Europe and America did trod onto fresh western soil.[9] It was for the buffeted and

slavery was neither extremely restrictive nor damaging: Robert W. Fogel and Stanley L. Engerman, *Time on the Cross.* Sharply critical of this work is Herbert G. Gutman, *Slavery and the Numbers Game: A Critique of Time on the Cross.*

[7]The unfinished nature of the frontier and eastern traditions combined to dictate that thousands of newly-created political, economic, and social positions had to be filled if fledging societies in the wilderness were to survive and function. For example, whatever the origin of state laws in the West, they usually demanded that the new frontier counties join eastern counties in having auditors, treasurers, recorders, prosecuting attorneys, coroners, surveyors, commissioners, clerks of the court, assessors, sheriffs, and a myriad of other county and other local offices.

County histories, although often monuments of plagiarism and inaccuracies, usually give an accurate picture of the growth and relative importance of various public offices in pioneer counties. Many of the county-level governmental positions required by law in early Illinois are found in Francis S. Philbrick, ed., *Pope's Digest, 1815,* II.

[8]Frequently, the western lands served as a safety-valve for both the United States and other nations. The Burlend household, for instance, fled wretched conditions in England and came to Pike County, Illinois: "From the despairing, beaten, tenant family which fled Yorkshire in 1831, the Burlends had become transformed into the confident possessors in fee simple of an extensive acreage in an agricultural region as fine as any in America." Rebecca Burlend, *A True Picture of Emigration,* ed. by Milo M. Quaife, p. xxiv. Additional examples of the safety-valve operation follow, especially in the chapters concerning household size and composition.

[9]The literature of the safety-valve concept is reviewed skillfully in Ray Allen Billington, ed., *The Frontier Thesis: Valid Interpretation of American History?,* pp. 120-21. Visitors to the nation observed what they believed to be a safety-valve in operation: "the western settlers are of incalculable advantage to the government; for not only is by their means the population of

marginal households that the opportunities, hopes, and myths associated with the West had especially critical importance; the question of *who* was on the frontier is highly pertinent to these households.

Amid the bustling construction, bubbling hope, and numerous examples of regeneration in the new lands, other forces were at work. Mixed in with countless stories of personal success were immense social costs. Even for those who emerged victorious from the unsettled conditions the cost was great. Material accumulation and social advancement, however exhilarating and liberating for the individual, sometimes occurred in such a disruptive manner as to slash and tear the fabric of society. Paradoxically, as individual settlers piled up success after success the result was often a net loss in terms of social cohesion, commonly-held values and goals, and a sense of place and purpose in society. The upward surge of thousands of scrambling individuals in the unstable West produced not only feelings of accomplishment and self-esteem but also pangs of doubt and uncertainty as to *relative* gain and *relative* place in society. Success in the new lands was measured almost solely in terms of private gain and personal liberation, not in terms of contributions to social cohesion, justice, or cultural enrichment. Private, competitive efforts in a generally unsettled setting did much to promote social disorder and disruption, conditions in which individual and group tensions and anxieties often found expression in spontaneous, private, and sometimes unthinking acts of violence.[10]

---

the Atlantic States relieved of its annual increase, but new sources of wealth opened to the nation at large, which increases the occupation of those who remain." Francis Grund, *The Americans in Their Moral, Social, and Political Relations*, II, p. 13.

[10]A recent work that analyzes the role of violence in the American West is David Abrahamsen, *Our Violent Past*, pp. 18, 24, 25, 188-201.

Perhaps this work and a host of similar recent works have exaggerated the degree of violence in the nation. Compare, for example, the amount of violence—as measured by deaths, injuries, destruction, and general injustice and inhumanity—present in the nation over the last century to the amount present over the last century in the ten other largest nations in the world, most of which have populations smaller than the population of the United States. The differences are astounding: lacking in the United States are gas chambers, pogroms, civil war, religious war, rebellion, coups, purges of impure elements, orchestrated starvation, and firing squads. Standing in even greater contrast is the virtual absence of a national police force, detention camps, walls and wire to prevent peaceful emigration, and such subtle forms of violence as governmental censorship, governmental control of place of residency and occupation, internal and external travel restrictions, internal passports, and national spy systems in which block and building captains keep close watch on everyone, including movements and visitors. Furthermore, evidence shows conclusively that most of the violence in the nation is of a private, usually spontaneous, and non-ideological nature involving acquaintances—friends stabbing each other, neighbors shooting each other, and relatives slipping poison into each other's tea. It is this *private* spontaneous violence that *is*, it appears, a direct legacy of the frontier experience and the loose, unsettled nature of American society, and which stands in vivid contrast to the much more hideously destructive forms of planned violence periodically wreaked on people by various governments.

In any case perhaps "frontier violence was primarily the result, rather than the cause, of our violent society." W. Eugene Hollon, *Frontier Violence: Another Look*, p. ix.

Just as it is important to know who was on the scene to enjoy the economic abundance of the West, so it is important to know who was present to witness social flux and social upheaval. Many westerners succeeded in amassing considerable *economic* security, an accomplishment which sometimes led directly to a scarcity of *social* security. Economic gain was impressive; social loss was sometimes even more impressive.

The desire to corroborate or refute claims concerning frontier demography constitutes a worthy reason to analyze western population traits. The desire to learn who was in a position to seize western opportunities and experience dynamic social conditions constitutes another reason. But there is a third and more universal reason: to provide some of the evidence by which aspects of the American frontier experiences can be compared to aspects of other frontier experiences.

Other societies have confronted frontier conditions, but the results and mechanics of these confrontations have varied greatly. Some migratory efforts have been calamitous, some have been as successful as the American endeavor, and perhaps a few have enjoyed even greater success. Some frontier societies have been tightly-organized affairs, affairs which display a great degree of social cohesion, disciplined unity of purpose, and militaristic methods; each pioneer in these settlement efforts is made to feel responsible for the safety and well-being of all, and individual options are minimized to enhance the larger effort. Other settler societies have been rather haphazard affairs, permitting individuals and parochial groups much latitude to rattle about, bumping into each other, and solve their own problems in a largely unplanned, catch-as-catch-can manner. Some settlement schemes have employed massive amounts of technology to transport the settlers, subjugate or displace native populations, and subdue and tap the wilderness; such efforts are often international in scope and carry with them the prospects of regional or even international war. Other schemes have relied on relatively little technology, received little international backing, and proceeded virtually unnoticed.[11]

The reasons for settlement, the amount of success, the degree of social

[11]Much of the literature concerning various frontiers is reviewed in Marvin Mikesell, "Comparative Studies in Frontier History," *Annals of the Assoc. of Amer. Geog.*, LX, pp. 62-74. Also, certain aspects of settlement on three frontiers are discussed in John Andrews, ed., *Frontiers and Men*. For a discussion of numerous settlement efforts see W. L. G. Joerg, ed., *Pioneer settlement: Cooperative Studies by Twenty-Six Authors*. Additional comparisons of the American frontier to others are found in Paul F. Sharp, "Three Frontiers: Some Comparative Studies of Canadian, American and Australian Settlement," *Pac. Hist. Rev.*, XXIV. Exploring a number of areas of migration is Isaiah Bowman, *Limits on Land Settlement: A Report on Present Day Possibilities*. For a skillful comparison of two frontiers see H. C. Allen, *Bush and Backwoods: A Comparison of the Frontier in Australia and the United States*. An interesting and valuable approach is Martin T. Katzman, "The Brazilian Frontier in Comparative Perspective," *Comparative Studies in Society and History*, XVII, pp. 266-285.

organization, the extent of personal latitude, the relative role of technology, and the scope of world-wide ramifications—these factors and others affect the settlers and the indigenous people. They influence the type of people who trek to the frontier, their motives and values, and their relative satisfaction after settlement, which, in turn, influence the nature of the frontier and the larger society. Demography, both a cause and an effect of the total settlement process, can suggest some of the workings of frontier societies. A comparison of the demographic traits in one frontier society to those in another can point to significant differences between the two pioneer efforts. This work provides information for such comparisons.

Clearly, few frontiers were ever as large as the early American frontier; fewer still were as quickly laced with networks of transportation, booming communities, and productive farms; perhaps fewer still received or relied upon as little central direction and control, settlers in America basking in both liberty and license in their dealings with each other and with the Indians. Hundreds of thousands of square miles between the Appalachians and the Great Plains were inundated with humanity in only four decades. The combined populations of just three states hurriedly carved from this wilderness (Ohio, Illinois, Indiana) today exceed the total population of all of Soviet Siberia, a frontier for centuries.[12]

This astounding surge was due in part to the relatively ineffective Indian resistance encountered by those who trudged westward.[13] Although the frontier often wavered and buckled in the face of desperate Indian onslaughts, this resistance was slight compared to those accompanying other pioneer efforts. Russia prosecuted full-scale wars in pushing its frontiers eastward and southward. Germany met military disaster in its drive for land in the east, and few Germans now live east of the Oder River. France learned that the peoples of North Africa were quite capable of frustrating settlement efforts, Portugal has been ejected from Africa, and Spain found that the peoples of the western Sahara could thwart economic, cultural, and military penetration. Other settler societies are currently faced with a quickening of effective resistance, a fact which may lead the beseiged populations to resort to nuclear arms. Perhaps only Canada and Australia enjoy massive frontiers on which there has been less conflict than that experienced by the Americans. Pioneers in both of these nations, however, face severe physical challenges, challenges which have doubtlessly modified frontier demography, culture, and attitudes.

---

[12]In 1967 the population of Soviet Siberia was slightly over 25,000,000. In 1970 the combined populations of Ohio, Illinois, and Indiana totaled nearly 27,000,000.

[13]Francis Grund realized the relatively ineffectual human opposition to the westward thrust: "What is termed 'The Indian War,' is nothing but a succession of skirmishes with a few of the neighboring tribes; and is only protracted because it is deemed too insignificant to warrant a general armament on the part of the United States. The case is very different with the French colony of Algiers." Grund, op. cit., II p. 51.

Those venturing into the American West clearly experienced comparatively sustained triumph, especially after the War of 1812. Virtually unbroken success nurtured several legacies. Both pioneers who penned their reactions to their western adventures and those who traveled among the backwoodsmen and observed them at work generally indicate that those who were on the cutting edge of white civilization were rarely lacking in confidence, however misplaced. Landgrabs elsewhere in the world have produced different results: the Algerian conflict did little to invigorate Frenchmen, and warfare in eastern Europe during World War II hardly produced elation among Germans. Conceivably, current pioneer projects in China, Australia, Canada, Brazil, the Soviet Union, and elsewhere are promoting individual and national confidence, but this is a matter of conjecture. Confidence is possibly the prime prerequisite for democracy, and confidence, in turn, is largely a product of feelings of success and security. The nature of the American westward thrust certainly permitted, and possibly fostered, the growth of vigorous democratic impulses and strong traits of economic, social, and political mobility; the effects of present frontiers in other societies on democracy and mobility are still uncertain. If those societies which now possess frontiers meet stiff resistance, garrison states and totalitarianism may result. Indian opposition, including stinging victories, never really struck at the nation's basic security. Rather, the relative ease with which Indians were overcome or dispersed did much to nourish national confidence.

There was another distinguishing feature of the early American westward thrust: nearly everyone lived in a family unit or household unit with others, practically no one lived alone. And the household unit, owning and operating most of the means of production and distribution, was the basic economic unit on the frontier.[14] American pioneer families owned and operated farms, mills, inns, ferries, wagons, and other forms of production and distribution. In other settlement efforts, both past and present, the large, cohesive, and externally-directed group is the unit by which wilderness obstacles are overcome. Such groups vary from society to society but include farming collectives, work brigades of school-age youngsters, forced-labor camps, and international corporations. China, for example, is managing to push its frontier into its remote west against ineffectual opposition. But the social organization, political controls, scope of economic activities, and technological thresholds accompanying the settlement process in present-day China conspire to deny to the Chinese

---

[14]This feature became less pronounced with time. Tens of thousands of families, for example, hacked farms out of the forests of Ohio, but descendents of these families discovered later in the century that the family unit was frequently insufficient to establish and maintain ranches, mines, and railroads in the West. Eventually, the increasing scale of economic activity demanded more capital, knowledge, and organization than most families could muster.

household the opportunity of being the basic, self-sustaining unit of production. Furthermore, the likelihood of any pioneer activity ever again having the household as its basic economic building block appears remote, for technological thresholds, economic interdependencies, and even diplomatic and military imperatives dictate larger pioneer units and tightened social and economic controls. Finally, conditions in nineteenth-century America—in many ways at sharp variance with conditions in most of the nineteenth-century world—contained sufficient social and economic fluidity, suspicion of government as an engine of progress, and belief in privately-sponsored enterprises to make the household, perhaps largely by default, the fundamental social and economic institution in the drive west.

Quite clearly, two facts tend to distinguish the American frontier of the early nineteenth century: American settlers met with almost uninterrupted success for so many years, and the household, the spearhead of the success, enjoyed the triumph in relatively enormous freedom. (These two facts may be somewhat interdependent.) These aspects were distinguishing features of the American frontier; perhaps the consequences of these aspects, both beneficial and detrimental, were equally distinguishing.

METHODS AND CONSTRAINTS

Seven distinct and sequential steps marked this study:

1. Several words were defined to obtain workable and consistent concepts.
2. The scope of the study was explicitly delineated.
3. Many impressionistic notions concerning frontier demography were formulated into hypotheses.
4. Questions were then devised by which the hypotheses were tested.
5. Various methods and techniques were investigated by which frontier history was researched.
6. Pertinent historical evidence was gathered, systematized, and analyzed and the questions were answered.
7. The answers, in turn, were analyzed and the hypotheses were accepted or rejected.

The spatial unit of investigation in this study was the county. It was the smallest, most precise, and most functional unit for which federal census data and written information were readily and consistently available. Counties had to meet several criteria to be classified as frontier in nature:

1. They had to increase in population from under two people per square mile to between two and six people per square mile.
2. They had to do this within the ten years between federal censuses.
3. They had to lie adjacent to large blocks of land uninhabited by whites.

In addition, a county could be in a frontier condition for a period of only ten years unless the population density sagged to below two per square mile and the county, at a later time, again met the first three criteria.

However, if a county contained virtually no white people at one census but contained up to eighteen per square mile by the next census and was adjacent to open land, it was classified as frontier, for it had very recently experienced pioneer activity. Moreover, virtually the entire area within the county had to meet all of these criteria. If a county averaged between two and six people per square mile but contained a sizeable area in which there were fewer than two people per square mile, it failed to meet the criteria. In like manner, if a county averaged between two and six people per square mile but contained a sizeable area in which the density was very great (perhaps reflecting a cluster of towns), it was excluded as a frontier county. Simply stated, for a county to be considered a frontier county, it had to grow at a prescribed speed, contain the stipulated density per square mile, and these conditions had to be met fairly uniformly throughout the county.

Two additional terms were defined: North and South. Southern counties were those in Delaware and those south of the Mason-Dixon Line, the Ohio River, and the current Iowa-Missouri state line. (This is the Census Bureau's definition of the South with Missouri added to it.) Essentially, in order to facilitate demographic measurements, especially those pertaining to race, the South was defined as those states in which slavery by 1840 was doing reasonably well or had done well in recent decades.

Finally, the term "household" refers to all free people listed by the federal census takers as living with the head of the house, including relatives, friends, and employees. Such members were quite free to work for their own gain, voice objections to household activities, and depart to lead their own lives. Because slaves were at the beck and call of their masters, because they raised grievances only with considerable peril, because their unauthorized acts of migration were often foiled by snarling dogs and irate patrols, and because slaves contributed little if any input into the decision-making processes of white households, they were excluded from the study of western households. Be that as it may, their presence was felt demographically. Blacks made it possible for some white households to survive harsh conditions in the wilderness. The fact that white households owned slaves often influenced *where* the households settled, not many slaveowners wanting to risk expensive investments by nesting next to abolitionist Yankee pioneers, for example. Also excluded from consideration as households were groups of people, often thirty or forty in number, who lived in boarding houses and other dwellings in which no household structure was apparent. On the other hand, individuals living alone were counted as separate households, as were small groups of people of the same sex.

The chronological constraints of the study were determined by several factors:

1. The first four decades of the nineteenth century witnessed the early, and probably formative, stages of westward movement.

2. The era was a time of sweeping and fundamental inventions and innovations in transportation—the new forms of transportation radically altered frontier and national development—and the remainder of the century was largely a time of improvement of these innovations.

3. Largely as a result of these early transportation revolutions and the resulting increases in economic range, by the 1840s the settler was being drawn irrevocably into the market economy, abandoning in the process both the reality of considerable self-sufficiency and even some of the myth of sturdy self-sufficiency.

4. After the 1840s the nature of the changing economy—especially increased technological thresholds, increased scales of production, and increased knowledge requirements—made it progressively difficult for the average settler to firmly root himself and his family in frontier soil. By the time of the cattle and mining frontiers after the Civil War, many pioneers were little more than laborers, hardly more independent than wage earners in the shops and mines of Pennsylvania.

5. By the late 1840s the American frontier and the old Spanish frontiers had conflated, producing a situation in which conquered Hispanic people were faced with a heavy influx of largely Anglo settlers, settlers who displayed little appreciation for Hispanic culture as they scurried about looking for gold and other means of wealth.

6. By the 1840s pioneers were probing into the uncertainties of semi-arid lands and leaving behind the relative security of familiar shady forest and lush prairie. Problems associated with water, fencing, plowing, wind, and transportation were part of the new environment.

7. By the late 1840s the steadily advancing frontier, normally a rather contiguous ribbon of recent settlement, hurtled westward in bits and pieces.[15] Some of these islands of settlement landed adjacent to and even in the midst of isolated Hispanic settlements; others were found miles from the nearest European influence.

---

[15]Mormons sought refuge in remote desert, Forty-Niners flooded into California, wagon trains snaked to Oregon, and by conquest the nation acquired numerous Spanish-speaking islands of inhabitation throughout the Southwest. These settlements often reflected distinct and specialized frontier activities and represented homogeneous economic and demographic groupings quite unlike the pre-1840 frontier; the California gold fields at mid-century are perhaps the best example of this development.

8. Between the islands of settlement there was often nothing, not a soul. By the 1850s the population density gradients tapered off to virtually zero at the edges of settlements. Beyond the edges of the communities were stretches of arid and semi-arid country, not small farms. This stood in sharp contrast to the pre-1840 settlement process, a process which saw very few relatively large spaces on the frontier completely void of white settlers.

9. By the 1840s the purposes of many of the settlement efforts had become very specialized, a fact which sometimes increased their relative isolation. The Mormons, for example, sought out isolation for specific reasons. Also, some of the mining and cattle activities of the post Civil War era produced settlements in which the small, comparatively independent yeoman had no real place.

10. Perhaps partially as a result of the above factors, the demographic composition of the frontier underwent a huge change during the 1840s. Although before 1840 male settlers outnumbered female settlers, the imbalance was not very pronounced. After 1840, however, the imbalance was severe.[16] In addition, the settlement process prior to 1840 was almost wholly a family activity, the family sometimes being altered a bit by the process. After 1840, however, thousands of individuals (mostly male) roamed around the gold and silver fields, worked on ranches, labored in construction, and in general led a life quite different from the earlier settlers. True, these loners often teamed up with others for specific purposes, but such acts of community were very much different from the more or less normal family life enjoyed by the vast majority of the earlier pioneers.

11. Finally, the nature of the federal censuses provide an additional reason for breaking the study at 1840. Compared to the census of 1850 and later censuses, those from 1800 through 1840 are uniform. The questions asked by the censuses from 1800 through 1840 are identical or very nearly so. Not so with the census of 1850, a census which goes into great detail and uses a completely revised set of questions. To have continued the study to 1850 or beyond would have introduced many knotty and perhaps insoluble problems involving the comparison of data.

It is difficult to overstate the importance of the years between roughly 1845 and 1870 as a pivotal era in frontier history. The vegetation, soil, climate, topography, and other natural conditions confronting frontiersmen in the last half of the nineteenth century were markedly different from the relatively uniform, predictable, and hospitable natural

---

[16]Typical of this post-1840 imbalance were some counties in California, places where in 1850 males outnumbered females by 30 to 1.

conditions prevailing east of the Great Plains. Unlike the bulk of the earlier settlers, those who ventured westward during or after the 1840s were likely to find semi-arid land, vast wind-swept expanses of treeless land, elusive Indians on horseback, awesome mountains, searing desert, fickle rivers, and drenched rainforests in the Northwest. The natural differences between the two eras were enormous; even greater, however, were the social, economic, and technological differences. Those who managed to survive harsh natural conditions increasingly found themselves threated by new and sometimes harsh economic conditions, not the least of which were problems accompanying the growth of technology. In the last half of the century, technology became vital for success in the West. This was true in mining, ranching, transportation, communication, and other spheres of human activity. Capital was needed to finance the creation of railroads, efficient mining operations, and similar projects, and the amount needed was far greater than was ordinarily available to the average pioneer. The result was that many individual pioneers went to work for remote economic interests, interests promoting mines, ranches, and railroads. Very likely, the economic, technological, cultural, demographic, and psychological differences between the pioneer of 1800 and the pioneer of 1840 were slight compared to the differences between settlers of 1840 and 1860.

The terminology and chronology employed in this study are precise constraints. The gathering of evidence by computer, federal manuscript censuses, and traditional primary and secondary sources imposed additional constraints which are explained in greater detail in Appendix A.

Preliminary research in traditional primary and secondary accounts led to some rather general notions, which were then stated precisely as hypotheses. (Some are found at the beginning of each chapter.) Questions were then constructed to test the hypotheses, and evidence was marshalled in each chapter to answer the questions.

Using data from the decennial federal censuses from 1800 through 1840, the seven demographic variables mentioned earlier were measured. The data obtained from each of the five census years were used to make three comparisons of frontier demography: the five northern frontiers were compared to each other; the five southern frontiers were compared to each other; and, the northern and southern frontiers for each census year were compared to each other.

But the frontiers were not compared in isolation. Instead, in order to provide perspective for the comparisons of the various frontiers over the four decades, control groups were established for each decade's comparisons. The control groups were the settled areas of the nation, those having at least eighteen persons per square mile. They were measured, using the seven demographic variables. The northern settled area and the southern settled area were identified for each census year. Each census year, demographic data for the northern settled area and the southern settled area were compared to data for the northern frontier and the southern frontier, respectively.

In short, five demographic measurements of both northern and southern frontiers were compared not only to themselves but also to the five measurements of their respective settled areas (see Fig. 1). Comparisons of the five measurements of the seven demographic variables drawn from records for frontier and settled areas provided data with which frontier demography could be analyzed and from which conclusions could be drawn.

Several problems cropped up in the course of this study. First, as was noted earlier, it was necessary to exclude blacks from this study for the simple reason that their freedom of choice, including the choice of where to live, was severely limited. This exclusion was unfortunate but necessary. Secondly, this study was essentially a macrostudy of hundreds of thousands of people and hundreds of counties located in vast areas over four decades. Census records provided data by which questions concerning the macrostudy could be answered. But traditional source material from literary sources was also employed, and this presented problems. The information gleaned from diaries, travel accounts, memoirs, directories, guides, and other prosaic primary accounts was unquestionably less representative, less objective, and possibly less valid and reliable than census data. A census taker who asked a pioneer certain questions could easily determine the person's sex; a traveler who attempted to establish the causes or results of migration might encounter considerable difficulty in drawing conclusions that were representative, valid, and reliable. The census taker asked specific questions, and the answers elicited were placed into measurable categories; questions posed by travelers, on the other hand, were far less systematic, probably less specific, and almost certainly elicited fewer precise and reliable answers—sometimes settlers did not really know why they had migrated from one area to another—and the answers were neither numerical nor ordinal.

To be sure, certain forces prompting migration are reasonably clear. Household size, for example, was often the stated reason for migration. Also, some women and some elderly folk refused to budge from the East, giving security as the primary concern. Migration, then, was obviously selective. The nature of frontier demography was also influenced by such factors as the methods of migration, types of transportation used, and the attitudes of whites toward blacks. However, when these influences are evaluated in conjunction with other influences—custom, law, availability of good land, topography, anticipatory talk, ignorance concerning the frontier, and the sources of migration—then there emerges from the mass

Fig. 1.—Three Comparisons of the Northern and Southern Frontiers

Comparison 1.—Northern and Southern Frontiers Were Compared to
Previous Northern and Southern Frontiers

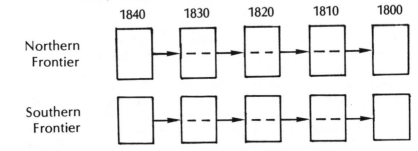

Comparison 2.—Northern and Southern Frontiers Were Compared to
Their Respective Settled Sections

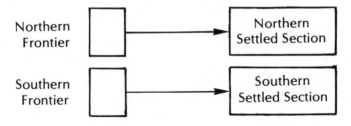

Comparison 3.—Northern and Southern Frontiers Were Compared to
Each Other

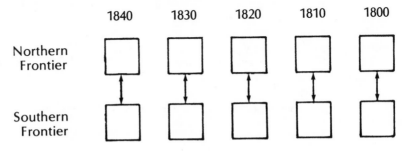

of factors no precise, easily-analyzed, definitive equation of forces that shaped western demographic patterns. Moreover, even if some accurate equation could be formulated for the frontier of 1800, one which would take into account the uncertainties and irrationalities that were inherent in the westward thrust, the equation might be valid only for the frontier of 1800, not for subsequent frontiers. New factors might enter into the equation and the relative importance of each factor would undoubtedly change over time, making the equation invalid for other frontiers.[17]

Instead, what does emerge from the mass of influences is the awareness that the West, far from being a place where a few simple independent variables operated openly to create demographic patterns, was in reality a difficult-to-define region, one which was always in motion, and one in which numerous forces—some internal, some external, ever-combining and ever-changing in relative importance—were part of a process that operated in an organic fashion over space and through time. Simply stated, the numerous influences governing the creation of some demographic patterns must presently be judged to be less perfectly understood than the nature of the patterns themselves.

The difficulty of trying to incorporate into this type of macrostudy evidence from traditional literary sources was partly solved by amassing voluminous stores of evidence from the traditional sources, including many diaries and travel accounts. However, no attempt was made to secure statistically valid samples of information from such sources. Even if such samples had been obtained, they might not really reflect frontier conditions. Instead, they might merely reflect the migrations of those settlers who could and did write or who were subjects of other people's writings, settlers who were possibly far from typical.

Difficulties aside, this study attempts to reveal and analyze demographic features of the American frontiersman and understand something of the interplay of forces between him and his environment. But it does much more than that. It attempts to determine whether a study involving hundreds of thousands of pioneers in 252 frontier counties over four decades could, by means of computerized data, manuscript censuses, and traditional sources, clarify assertions concerning frontier demography, answer questions pertinent to American life, and provide a basis for comparative studies with other frontier societies.[18]

---

[17]It is apparent that some stochastic, dynamic model is needed to explain the frontier experience.

[18]All of the frontier counties used in this study are found in App. B.

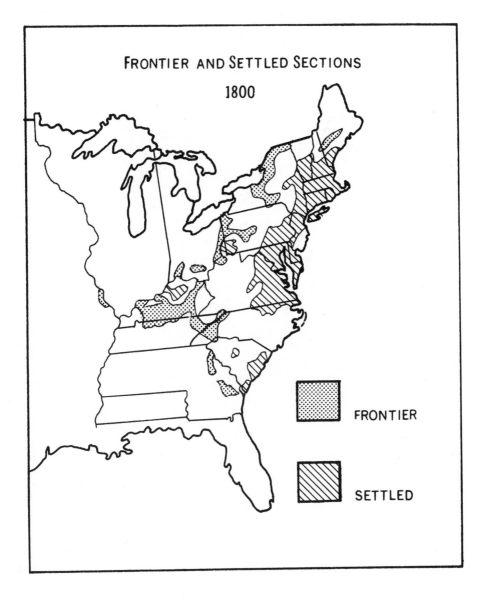

FRONTIER AND SETTLED SECTIONS

1800

FRONTIER

SETTLED

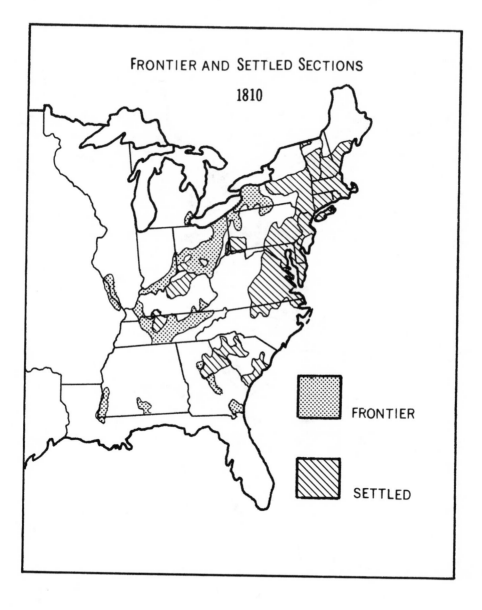

FRONTIER AND SETTLED SECTIONS

1810

FRONTIER

SETTLED

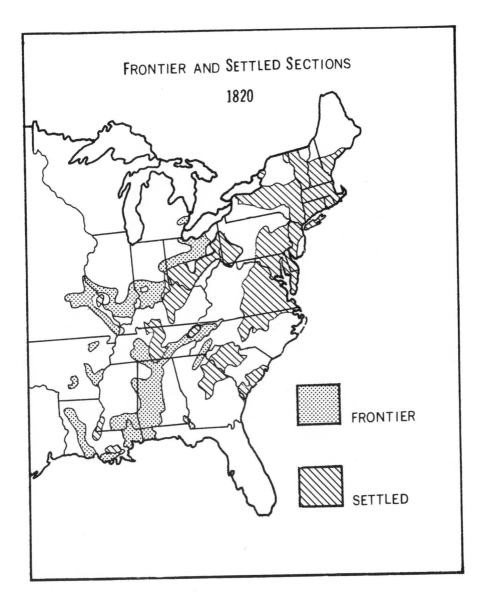

FRONTIER AND SETTLED SECTIONS

1820

FRONTIER

SETTLED

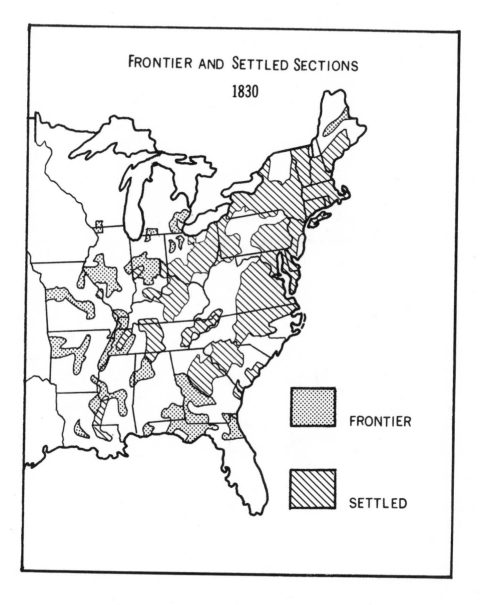

FRONTIER AND SETTLED SECTIONS

1830

FRONTIER

SETTLED

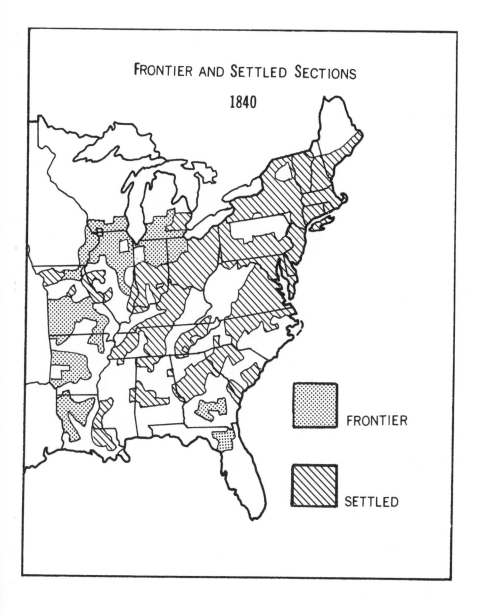

FRONTIER AND SETTLED SECTIONS

1840

FRONTIER

SETTLED

CHAPTER II

Household Size and Composition:
The North

William Gregory was an extraordinary participant in the westward migration. Born in Pittsylvania County, Virginia, in February 1776, he spent part of his youth in Tennessee and was married in North Carolina. He and his growing family moved to Kentucky in 1806 and then to Harrison County, Indiana, in 1811. Children were born to him in 1796, 1798, 1800, 1802, 1804, 1806, 1808, 1810, 1812, and 1814, the last just thirty minutes before the death of his wife. Within six months he married a widow with three children, and this marriage produced children in 1815, 1817, 1819, 1821, 1825, 1827, 1829, 1831, and stillborn twins in 1823. Keeping on the cutting edge of the frontier, the family pushed on to Morgan County, Indiana, in the 1820s. There he buried his second wife in the spring of 1835, and in the summer married a widow with eight children. But his marriage ended in divorce, his free grace Methodist beliefs not mixing well with his wife's unconditional election Calvinist doctrine. There were no children. The mother of two became his wife in 1840, and he promptly fathered a child in 1841, another in 1842, and a third in 1843. Beset by the economic troubles stemming from the late 1830s, William Gregory determined to push further west with his new and growing family. This he accomplished in 1843 at the age of sixty-seven, leading his household into the prairies of the Territory of Iowa and homesteading approximately twenty-two miles northwest of Burlington.

He spent the next fifteen years breaking the prairie with five yoke of oxen, farming, fathering children, and dispatching hundreds of rattlesnakes with deadly snaps of his ox-whip. Perhaps the snakes tried to get revenge. If they did, he survived their attempts; he also survived two wives, a number of his children, campaigning in the War of 1812, economic depression, six treks, and scores of years on or near the frontier. Death stilled this vigorous soul on September 25, 1858, sixty-two years after the birth of his first child and seven years after the birth of his last.[1]

---

[1]Logan Esarey, ed., "Pioneers of Morgan County: Memoirs of Noah J. Major," *Indiana Hist. Soc. Pubs.*, V, pp. 249-52. William Gregory had a great tendency to have children every two years, a tendency which may have been shared by many others on the frontier. If pioneer babies were breast-fed, and there is no indication to the contrary, then this process of lactation may have inhibited conception. It has been noted that "On a world-wide basis, prolonged breast-

William Gregory's overwhelming tendency to propagate wherever he went evokes feelings of both alarm and admiration. This tendency is viewed with general disfavor in the last quarter of the twentieth century, but in the opening decades of the nineteenth century conditions were different. The nation experienced astounding territorial growth from 1803 to 1848, creating an urgent need to populate the land, a need William Gregory met with utter abandon.

However, he was more than merely father of much of his country. He lived on or near the frontier most of his life. Since births, deaths, and migrations are the fundamental features of demography, Gregory's activities in the new lands raise essential questions concerning the nature of western settlement and western demography. Wherever he went, Gregory encountered demographic conditions; wherever he went he radically altered these conditions. The size of his households possibly never dipped below five and quite possibly reached eighteen or twenty on occasion. It appears likely that those in his home who were under the age of fourteen or fifteen—the age by which most youngsters then assumed full economic responsibility as family members—always topped those who produced more than they consumed.[2] On at least two occasions in Gregory's household there appears to have been no female old enough to assume economic responsibility. But it is also possible that the household always contained at least three or four adults. Of the four Gregory households, only one, the first one, during the mid-1790s, ever contained just one child or no children. Several questions spring from these facts: were these household traits more nearly typical of pioneer households or of households in settled areas? If some of these traits were quite common in 1800, were they still common in 1840? Which conditions tended to produce large households? Small households? Households in which the number of economic dependents exceeded the number of economic contributors?

Although the ax and the rifle were the technological means with which settlers like Gregory swept obstacles from their paths, the household was the basic social and economic institution by which this feat was accomplished.

---

feeding is one of the most important means by which a woman may temporarily reduce her fecundity." Perhaps the reduction is up to "13 months in a population which engages in prolonged lactation." David M. Heer, *Society and Population*, p. 57. Also, "In cultures where children are not weaned until they are 1 year or even older, the average fucundity of the population may be substantially lower than in a population where children are weaned at six months or even bottle-fed immediately." Donald J. Bogue, *Principles of Demography*, p. 721. For additional information on the effects of breast feeding on the birth rate, see William Peterson, *Population*, 2d ed.; p. 178, and John Demos, *A Little Commonwealth: Family Life in Plymouth Colony*, p. 133.

[2]In this study, the term "child" referred to those who were under age sixteen at the time of the federal census in 1800, 1810, or 1820 or under fifteen at the time of the census of either 1830 or 1840. The change in age reflects a change in the age classifications in the federal censuses. In any event, by the time a youth attained sixteen years he was expected to do the work of an adult. For example, see William M. Cockrum, *Pioneer History of Indiana*, p. 158.

Virtually everyone on the frontier over the four decades was a member of a household in which others lived, practically no one living alone. Since household size and composition sometimes reflect economic conditions, then a study of the characteristics of frontier households may shed some light on frontier economics. Similarly, since size and composition influence the personalities of householders, an examination of these traits may provide clues concerning the characters of frontiersmen. And inasmuch as the nature of the household unit helps to determine the cultures of societies, then aspects of frontier culture may be revealed by an analysis of frontier households.[3]

THE HYPOTHESES

Early in this study, research into primary and secondary literature of the frontier disclosed evidence concerning household characteristics. Most of the secondary literature suggests that the household was large: "Whatever other faults and failures the pioneers had ... failure to be fruitful and multiply could not be rekoned [sic] among them."[4] Other references were more specific, noting that "It was not unusual for fathers and mothers to have families of six or eight children before they were thirty years of age," and another reference claimed that "from six to ten children usually encircled the hearthstone, and it was no uncommon thing to find families numbering as high as fifteen."[5] In the wagons jolting their way westward sat "the mother of the family; and, peering over her head and shoulders, leaning out at her side, or gazing under the edge of the cotton-covering, are numerous flaxen heads, which you find it difficult to count."[6] Even the age, and possibly the spacing, of pioneer children was implicit in some accounts: "The young pioneer alights with his wife and small children from his ox-drawn and canvas-covered wagon."[7] Even poets have alluded to purportedly large households on the frontier.[8]

---

[3]James H. S. Bossard, *The Large Family System: An Ordinal Study in the Sociology of Family Behavior*, pp. 307-20. Also, perhaps "The number and size of families and households greatly affect the character of settlement." John I. Clarke, *Population Geography*, p. 83. The ordinal position of family members, evidence suggests, can also affect the character of members. See Robert R. Sears, "Ordinal Position in the Family as a Psychological Variable," *American Sociological Rev.*, xv, p. 401.

[4]Esarey, *op. cit.*, p. 248.

[5]Thomas D. Clark, *Frontier America: The Story of the Westward Movement*, p. 208; Esarey, *op. cit.*, p. 247.

[6]John C. McConnel, *Western Characters, or Types of Border Life in the Western States*, p. 140.

[7]John Anthony Caruso, *The Great Lakes Frontier: An Epic of the Old Northwest*, p. 315.

[8]From the close-covered depths of the big wagon-bed
Peeped out a lassie and tiny towhead—
Half a dozen at least, for the pioneer's wife
Thought to people the land was part of her life
James Ball Naylor in John T. Faris, *On the Trail of the Pioneers: Romance, Tragedy and Triumph on the Path of Empire*, p. 79.

It has been implied that certain household compositions were generally absent from the western lands. More specifically, households consisting of single women living alone and families headed by widows and other unmarried women were said to be rare: "Single women were at a premium on the frontier, and widows were not allowed to enjoy single bliss very long."[9] It was also claimed that widows "remarried for protection and to guard against starvation."[10]

This and similar evidence, although sometimes contradictory and rather impressionistic, led to the formulation of hypotheses concerning the pioneer household. Compared to households in the settled areas of the country, households in the western lands were hypothesized to have the following characteristics:

1. Larger average size, a difference which would increase somewhat over the forty years as eastern households diminished somewhat in size.
2. Larger modal size.
3. Relatively more households of at least eleven members.
4. Relatively more people living in these very large households.
5. Proportionately more individuals living alone.
6. Comparatively fewer adults who were obviously missing.[11]
7. Females constituting a majority of the missing adults on the frontier, and males forming a majority in the settled area.
8. Relatively fewer households containing from two to eight members.
9. Relatively fewer households containing from two to eight members in which no child was present.
10. Relatively fewer households containing from two to eight members in which just one child was present.
11. Relatively fewer children who were living in households containing two to eight members in which no other children were present.
12. Relatively more households containing from two to eight members in which children constituted at least one-half the membership.

---

[9]Everett Dick, *The Dixie Frontier: A Social History of the Frontier From the First Transmontane Beginnings to the Civil War*, p. 282.

[10]John Ernest Wright and Doris S. Corbett, *Pioneer Life in Western Pennsylvania*, p. 4.

[11]A "rule of reason" was used to determine whether or not adults were "missing" from households. For example, it was determined that there were no missing adults in a household in which a man in his sixties lived with a woman in her thirties and several small children. On the other hand, it was determined that there was a female missing from a household that contained a woman in her seventies, a man in his thirties, and several small children. In a few instances, however, it was not entirely clear whether or not a household was, in fact, missing an adult member. In such cases, caution prevailed and the households were said to be complete.

13. Relatively more people living in households containing two to eight members in which children formed at least one-half of the membership.
14. Relatively more children living in households containing from two to eight members in which children formed at least one-half the membership.
15. The three most prevalent household compositions on the frontier were generally larger than those of the East, but both declined in size over time.[12]
16. The three leading compositions on the frontier always contained just two adults; this was not always the case with those in the East.

Moreover, it was anticipated that most demographic distinctions between East and West would become sharper with time as the East, especially the Northeast, turned to non-agrarian pursuits. Because the Northeast acquired non-agrarian characteristics faster then the Southeast, it was expected that the resulting demographic differences between the northern frontier and the northern settled area would be increasingly more pronounced than those between the southern frontier and the southern settled area. One additional hypothesis: compared to the northern wilds, the southern wilds would display over the decades more salient frontier demographic features, the differences between the two frontiers possibly increasing with time.

HOUSEHOLD SIZE

The comparison of the northern frontier to the northern settled area, while generally confirming the hypotheses, produced some great surprises. One such surprise concerned household sizes. Flying in the face of expected results, over the years household size in the northern woods and prairies was not larger than that of the older, settled sections of the North. With the exception of 1830, every census year found the modal and average sizes of the pioneer household units to be either no larger or actually *smaller* than those in the settled sections (see Tables 1 and 2). The extent of the disparity in the average sizes ranged from two-tenths of a person in 1800 to one-tenth in 1840, and in 1810 and 1820 there was no difference. In terms of modal size, the disparity was two people in 1810 and one person in 1800, 1820, and 1840.

Many factors combined to produce in the lands of northern pioneer activity unexpectedly small household units. One possible factor has already received attention: the tendency for the process of lactation to

---

[12]The figure of *three* leading household compositions was chosen somewhat arbitrarily, but the selection of this figure was influenced by the fact that these household units usually composed from one-fourth to nearly one-third of all frontier households.

delay pregnancy. The frequency of birth on the frontier was possibly substantially reduced by the practice of breast feeding infants. It seems likely that both animal milk and wetnurses were more readily available in the more settled sections of the nation than on the frontier. As a result, perhaps fewer mothers breast-fed, thereby shortening the average interval between pregnancies to a point less than that of the interval on the frontier; the differences in size between pioneer households and eastern households may have been kept, as a consequence, surprisingly small.

The frequency of birth among wilderness dwellers was possibly further limited by the deliberate practice of birth control. The most common household compositions were those containing two adults and one child, and those with two adults and two children (see Table 15). There is evidence that pioneers, especially those from the middle class, practiced birth control since at least the early 1800s (see n. 116, this chapter).

Lactation and birth control, however, probably explain the presence of relatively few small households in the wilderness. Another factor encouraged unexpectedly small units: large units simply were not vital to success on the northern frontier, a fact known to contemporary observers. For example, on December 14, 1805, Robert Sutcliff visited the frontier near the New York-Pennsylvania state line. There he met "E. H." who, "with his wife and one fine child, had but lately come into this country, and he had cleared only a few acres, but which appeared to be well-organized, and very productive."[13]

Westerners were able to raise adequate amounts of food without the need for much labor, making large pools of farm labor unnecessary. Corn was the pioneers' first crop, ripening early and yielding abundantly and requiring comparatively little labor. It was eaten by man and beast, and it enabled many frontiersmen to become independent landowners. Wheat, requiring much more labor and many more skills, was generally grown only after the frontier had marshalled enough surplus labor and enough agricultural specialists to harvest it.[14] Such help was often absent from the western lands for at least twenty years after the initial settlement.

Deserving much credit for enabling the small households to persist in the northern backwoods were hogs. They accompanied settlers into the

---

[13]Robert Sutcliff, *Travels in Some Parts of North America, in the Years 1804, 1805, & 1806*, p. 167. Further references pertaining to the relative ease of supplying necessities of life in the West are found in Elias Pym Fordham, *Personal Narrative of Travels in Virginia, Maryland, Pennsylvania, Ohio, Indiana, Kentucky; and of a Residence in the Illinois Territory, 1817-1818*, ed. by Frederic A. Ogg, pp. 120-22; Isaac Holmes illustrated the point by noting "It has been calculated that two and a half acres are sufficient to support a human being." Holmes, *An Account of the United States of America*, p. 157; for additional evidence concerning the relative ease of supplying the basic necessities of life see Arthur W. Calhoun, *A Social History of the American Family*, II, pp. 14, 15, 52.

[14]Francis S. Philbrick, *The Rise of the West, 1754-1830*, p. 324.

wilderness and were "peculiarly adapted for the backwoods, where they are always able to procure plenty of grub for themselves, and after getting fat, they make very good grub for the settler and his family."[15] They ate mast from the forests and corn from the fields and supplied frontiersmen with food, soap, and other necessities. Perhaps the hog, not the dog, was man's best friend on the frontier. He contributed greatly to the success and comfort of small and moderate-sized pioneer households.

Other economic opportunities in the West, especially the opportunity to acquire good land with relative ease, further limited sizes in the northern backwoods. The promise of land was a giant magnet, drawing to it both previous landowner and non-owner alike. Those who had never owned land, many of whom had toiled as farm laborers, swarmed to the fresh, new lands with eager anticipation, creating in the rush countless situations similar to that which obtained in Indiana in 1817: "Men would not work for others when their work for themselves would pay for their farm."[16] If men did not *work* for others, they were surely less likely to *live* with others. Many hired laborers in the East lived with the farm families for which they worked; once they joined the westward trek, many managed to latch onto land of their own and live by themselves. Throughout the fresh lands in the West persistent wailing about the absence of hired labor demonstrates the fact that farmers were generally unable to add temporary members to their households. (This complaint is discussed in Chapter VII, "Occupations".) The inability to secure help had the effect of reducing household size in the northern frontier.

In a similar manner, maturing sons glanced around as they labored on the farms and in the shops, realized that their labor was valuable, learned of new lands in the West, and bid their parents farewell. For many young men and women, the stunning opportunity to farm and own sizeable parcels of land outweighed family loyalty and bonds of blood. Numerous households saw their youngsters drained away, often with an accompanying act of marriage, to new places to the west. This drain resulted in the creation of

[15]Thomas Yoseloff, ed., *Voyage to America: The Journal of Thomas Cather,* p. 132. Another visitor to the frontier recognized the services rendered by the hog: "Of domestic animals, the hog is decidedly the most useful and numerous." James Hall, *Notes on the Western States; containing descriptive sketches of their soil, climate, resources and scenery,* p. 145. For additional evidence concerning the importance of the hogs to the settler and the ability of the porkers to fend for themselves in the forests, consult Franklin D. Scott, ed. and trans., *Baron Klinkowstrom's America, 1818-1820,* p. 190; E. Douglas Branch, *Westward: The Romance of the American Frontier,* p. 286; and Walter Havighurst, *The Heartland: Ohio, Indiana, Illinois,* p. 165.

[16]John E. Inglehart, "The Coming of the English to Indiana in 1817 and their Hoosier Neighbors," *Indiana Mag. of His.,* XV, p. 110. James Hall advised "It would be recollected, that a very large majority of the western population, and of the emigrants to the new states, are farmers, and that very few of these are willing to be the tenants of other men." James Hall, *op. cit.,* p. 151.

many small, young households in the wilderness. The cumulative effect of these countless declarations of independence will, perhaps, never be known. But for scores of years before national independence and for scores of years afterwards, the American youngster—along with all Americans— was shaped and molded by the presence of plenty and the relative ease of getting it. One early demographer noted of the West

> facilities for making one's way by labor were abundant and thus children began early to produce for themselves. This economic self-sufficiency, uninvaded by any lure of artificial pastimes, matured and emancipated children from undue prolongment of parental control.[17]

Children became republican citizens *par excellence*, independent and boisterously self-assertive, and—to many foreign visitors, especially British Tories—brats. There is little reason to doubt that "The child is the quintessential American, and no other story better exemplifies the triumph of republicanism." And there is equally little reason to doubt that fresh land, relatively cheap and capable of promoting economic and psychological independence, was in some large measure responsible for the triumph.[18] It lured young sons westward, encouraged them to marry early, and left behind the old, the very young, and women. Land, above all, was sought; having been obtained, it tended to alter both western and eastern demography.

The manner in which the journey westward was accomplished often added to the likelihood that small households would migrate. Although the household was the unit in which the vast majority of settlers lived, the *group* very often eased entry into the beckoning lands. Given the hardships associated with the westward march and settlement, group efforts simply made good sense. Friends, cousins, employees, fellow church members, and others banded together into groups, sometimes makeshift in nature and sometimes highly structured, and thereby lent support to each other and encouraged a division of labor. Once in the fresh lands, the groups often dissolved amicably, leaving each household free to fend for itself and locate where it wished. This practice of group travel altered the demographic composition of the frontier. Because of group travel, some elderly couples and individuals, small families, families with a swarm of small children, and families that were largely female—types which often entertained doubts about their ability to weather the trip westward—were able to seize the opportunity to migrate with a group and then, upon arrival at the edge of civilization, scatter and live in relatively small households.

---

[17]Calhoun, *op. cit.,* II, p. 52.

[18]David J. Rothman, "Documents in Search of a Historian: Toward a History of Children and Youth in America," in *The Family in History: Interdisciplinary Essays,* ed. by Theodore K. Rabb and Robert I. Rotberg, p. 184.

Group travel was especially strong in the northern half of the nation, first in the form of wagon trains and then in the form of steamboats, canal boats, and trains.[19] That northerners were the ones who were especially prone to engage in group travel and group settlement was a fact which sometimes irked their southern co-settlers. Southern settlers in downstate Illinois, for example, "held it was preferable to arrive separately and quietly take on the coloration of the new neighborhood."[20] Southerners were reluctant to practice group settlement; they were even more reluctant to see Yankees practice it, suggesting that southern individualism—perhaps reinforced by a streak of Jacksonian Democracy and fear of organized efforts of special interest groups—stood in sharp contrast to the Yankee notions of community, mission, and cooperation. Habits and ideology, to some extent, influenced the migratory process and frontier demography.

Pre-arranged groups of wagons wound their way onto the northern prairies as late as the 1830s, and sometimes these trains had up to thirty wagons.[21] Trains of from fifty to sixty wagons were observed in Pennsylvania rumbling westward.[22] Households which had a marginal ability to journey westward on their own latched onto such trains and pushed west, aided by the group. Viewing the scene in 1817 in central Pennsylvania, Henry Fearon passed twenty westward-bound wagons, two of which were experiencing difficulties. He noted that "These emigrants preferred travelling in companies, forming a oneness of interest, and securing an interchange of

---

[19]Dan Elbert Clark, *The West in American History*, pp. 176-77. The tendency for group travel to occur to a greater extent in the North than in the South is indicated in the settlement of early Illinois. The state was settled first by southerners who poured into the southern sections of the state at an early date. They were followed by northerners, primarily New Englanders and New Yorkers, who flooded across the northern prairies of the state. "A special feature of the settlement of the north [of Illinois] was the coming of settlers in colonies or organized groups." Theodore Calvin Pease, *The Frontier State, 1818-1848*, Vol. II of *The Centennial History of Illinois*, ed. by Clarence Walworth Alvord, p. 178. For a detailed account of the organization and migration of a Yankee colony—the Union Colony, organized at East Poultney, Vermont—see Stewart H. Holbrook, *The Yankee Exodus: An Account of Migration from New England*, pp. 78-80. Other examples of Yankee group migration can be found in James Hall, *Letters from the West; containing Sketches of Scenery, Manners, and Customs; and Anecdotes connected with the First Settlements of the Western Sections of the United States*, p. 311 and Eliza W. Farnham, *Life in the Prairie Land*, pp. 154-55. Group migration from the North to Illinois occurred even after the 1840s. To cite one example, it was noted that in Illinois during the 1850s "The Yankees showed a strong tendency to migrate in parties or even well-organized colonies. Groups of from twenty to forty families being fairly common." Arthur Charles Cole, *The Era of the Civil War, 1848-1870*, Vol. III of Alvord, *op. cit.*, p. 13. Evidence suggests that migration, in general, before 1820 was accomplished more by individuals and families than by large groups. See Philbrick, *op. cit.*, p. 346.

[20]Robert P. Howard, *Illinois: A History of the Prairie State*, p. 128.

[21]Dan Clark, *op. cit.*, p. 187.

[22]John B. McMaster, *A History of the People of the United States from the Revolution to the Civil War*, IV, p. 387.

assistance when necessary."[23] William Howells, similarly, recalled that households in 1813 "usually traveled in groups for company and to assist one another by doubling teams on the steep hills, and to help in case of accidents."[24] Numerous other examples illustrate the fact that migrants often formed temporary associations in an attempt to facilitate travel.[25] Marginal households were able to reach the frontier and survive, for they had learned that in unity there was division of labor and overall security.

Frequently, those who traveled alone wished they had not: On June 15, 1836, Harriet Martineau, traveling from Detroit to Ypsilanti, Michigan, spotted a mother and eight children, including puny twins, struggling to get to the Michigan frontier. They had traveled over four hundred miles, had only one hundred to go before reaching her husband's new land, but had just been robbed of their baby items. The outcome of this particular act of migration is unknown. But the incident illustrates the rigors of traveling westward without a husband, and without a group.[26] In the same year, John M. Gordon happened upon a young couple west of Detroit who, traveling alone, had been stranded because of a broken wheel on their covered wagon.[27]

Group travel, lessening the likelihood that migrating individuals and households would be overwhelmed by troubles en route to the West, fostered migration and contributed to the relatively small household averages and modal sizes in the northern wilds. For reasons of security and comfort, marginal individuals and households coalesced into groups, acts which did much to promote relatively small pioneer households.

Innumerable groups negotiated the journey successfully and arrived on the frontier. There they provided instant community, further security for small households and other marginal units. Entire towns in the northern backwoods were populated by group migration. The examples are numerous and reflect attempts to create in the wilderness secure economic, political, religious, and ethnic enclaves, enclaves which were sometimes intended to be replicas of eastern communities.

Illustrative of group settlement was the English settlement to the west of Jacksonville, Illinois, which consisted of twenty-five families from Yorkshire

---

[23]Henry Bradshaw Fearon, *Sketches of America: A Narrative of a Journey of Five Thousand Miles through the Eastern and Western States of America*, pp. 190-91.

[24]William Cooper Howells, *Recollections of Life in Ohio, from 1813 to 1840*, p. 10.

[25]For example, George Flower noted that several English households from Liverpool and London met at Pittsburgh and formed one party before coming to Illinois. George Flower, *History of the English Settlement in Edwards County, Illinois, Founded in 1817 and 1818 by Morris Birkbeck and George Flower*, pp. 148-50. A fine interpretation of group travel is Daniel J. Boorstin, *The Americans: The National Experience*, pp. 49-57.

[26]Harriet Martineau, *Society in America*, I, p. 318.

[27]Douglas H. Gordon and George S. May, eds., "Michigan Journal, 1836, John M. Gordon," *Mich. Hist.*, XLIII, p. 259.

which arrived in 1829.[28] In a like manner, in 1831 a group of people from Northampton, Massachusetts, founded a religious colony at Princeton, Illinois. Several years later another group, motivated by a similar religious desire to enter the wilderness, migrated from Bergen, New York, to Geneseo, Illinois.[29] One historian has calculated that "Thirty-two New England colonies have been counted in Illinois. The Church was at the center of this movement; frequently a pastor and his congregation formed the nucleus of a migration."[30] The Puritan tendency to travel together in planned efforts motivated a group in Granville, Massachusetts, to move to Ohio in 1805 and found the settlement of Granville.[31] Whatever the motive for group migration and settlement, the practice lent assistance, encouragement, and companionship to those grappling with known and unknown challenges of the frontier: "It happens rather often that several families go together, buy land and colonize it. In such cases clearing and cultivating goes [sic] much faster."[32] Moreover, the sense of community generated during the westward trek sometimes remained fairly intact upon the successful completion of the journey, and newcomers were thereby assisted. Isaac Holmes, no advocate of the American West, admitted that if new arrivals had neighbors they "will come and assist them to erect a log house" and

> In addition to this assistance in building, it is not improbable that their friendly neighbors will furnish the new family with some part of their live stock. One will give poultry, another a hog, and a third a calf, for each of which the woods will furnish an ample supply of food.

He added that "there is no danger of actual want."[33]

Virtually every frontier county received at least one group of migrants sometime during its existence. As a result, if colored dots were placed on a map of the nation indicating specific instances of group migration, the map would appear to be covered by colored confetti. Possibly, however, even among New Englanders migration via formally organized groups tapered off by 1840.[34]

Occasionally group migration originating in the North assumed bizarre

[28]James Stuart, *Three Years in North America,* II, p. 381.

[29]Edward Channing, *A History of the United States,* V, pp. 60-61.

[30]Havighurst, *op. cit.,* p. 154. Illinois towns settled via group migration from New York or New England include Pittsfield, Weathersfield, Geneseo, Rockton, New Rutland, and Princeton. *Ibid.*

[31]Channing, *op. cit.,* V, pp. 59-60.

[32]Scott, *op. cit.,* p. 191.

[33]Holmes, *op. cit.,* pp. 132-33.

[34]Holbrook, *op. cit.,* p. 172. Additional instances of the practice of group travel are in the following: Havighurst, *op. cit.,* p. 153; Holbrook, *op. cit.,* p. 67; Solon Justice Buck, *Illinois in 1818,* introductory volume of Alvord, *op. cit.,* pp. 113-14.

forms. In 1818 a traveler passing through Tennessee came across a two-story
mobile home drawn by six horses, containing twenty-nine occupants,
lumbering its way from Maine to Alabama.[35] Strolling houses were far from
rare in early America, and their movements across the land illustrate the
lengths to which some settlers would go to travel in cozy groups. In
essence, for many marginal units—including small households—the
migrating group was a moving refuge, a source of security, and sometimes a
guarantee of instant community. Clearly, under the auspices of the group,
great numbers of households were shepherded into the new lands.

Group travel and the resulting propensity for rather small households to
locate in the northern wilderness were undoubtedly encouraged by the
development of relatively easy, universal, and cheap transportation.
Steamboat and canal transportation to much of the northern frontier was so
cheap and widespread by the late 1820s "that more than half the whole
number of immigrants now arrive in the West by water. This remark applies
to nine-tenths of those that come from Europe and the northern States."
Perhaps more than one-half of the migrants to the northern frontier
traveled west on the Erie Canal and Lake Erie.[36] By the 1820s travel by
steamboat in the West was ceasing to be an ordeal, terrible explosions and
other accidents notwithstanding. One English visitor wrote

> The American steam-boats are in point of elegance superior to those
> of other nations; and none but the English are able to compete with
> them. The funiture, carpets, beds, &c., are throughout elegant, and in
> good condition. Some of the new steam-boats are provided with small
> rooms, each containing two berths, which passengers may use for
> their accommodation in shaving, dressing, &c.[37]

Abner D. Jones, among many, noted that many westward-bound migrants
used the steamboat in their march west. In the 1830s he saw the western

---

[35]Dan Clark, *op. cit.*, p. 201.

[36]Timothy Flint, *op. cit.*, I, pp. 184-85. Tow-boats were popular because they were
inexpensive. See, for example, William Thomson, *A Tradesman's Travels in the United States
and Canada in the Years 1840, 41 & 42*, p. 48. For a fine description of canals, see *ibid.*, pp. 54-57.
Cheap transportation was also provided by lake barges. For an account of a passenger barge
being towed by a steamship, see Thomas L. McKenney, *Sketches of a Tour to the Lakes*, pp. 26-
27. If vessels that were towed were cheaper than steamboats, they must have been very
inexpensive, it costing as little as $5.00 to sail on a steamboat from Pittsburgh to the mouth of
the Ohio. This was the rate for deck passengers, who enjoyed a covered deck and berths. In
addition, there was often little concern about precisely where passengers boarded and
disembarked. Grund, *op. cit.*, II, pp. 207-08.

[37]Charles Sealsfield, *The Americans as They Are; Described in a Tour Through the Valley of
the Mississippi*, p.106. Many detailed glimpses of steamboat life are provided by McKenney,
op. cit. For a valuable account of the names of steamboats, where they were built, their
tonnage, date of destruction if lost, and manner of destruction see James Hall, *Notes on the
Western States*, pp. 252-63. Similar information is found in Grund, *op. cit.*, II, pp. 182-83.

waters clogged with "vast floating palaces vulgarly named steamboats, every one of which is freighted with men, women, and children seeking a new home in this new world."[38] Steamboats provided inexpensive, fast, and reasonably safe transportation for households entering the wilderness as part of a cohesive group or individually.

Turnpikes, steamboats, canals, Great Lake vessels, and finally railroads all pumped migrants toward the new lands of the North.[39] The migration of the Keyes household from Vermont to Jefferson County, Wisconsin, in May and June of 1837 serves to illustrate the variety of transportation available to settlers. The family moved across southern Michigan, northern Indiana and Illinois, and into Wisconsin by using a wagon for the first part of the journey, then a canal, a steamboat, and finally another wagon before reaching their destination.[40] In this instance, only one family used these means of transportation. In other instances, however, organized groups used a variety of locomotion. A small band that pushed from New England into the West illustrates the point and demonstrates some of the various forms of relatively efficient transportation in the late 1830s:

> [Ira] Hersey's band went from Portland [Maine] to Boston by ship; to Providence by rail; by water to Philadelphia; by rail to Pittsburgh, where they took passage down the Ohio to Cincinnati. Here they bought wagons, oxen, and provisions, then floated up the Mississippi and the Illinois as far as Ottawa, from which they rolled on wheels to their new home.[41]

Improved and varied transportation to and throughout the frontier helped mitigate some of the demographic differences between the northern settled area and the northern wilderness.

Many of those who witnessed the migratory surge westward after the War of 1812 apparently knew that the average westward-marching household was far from abnormally large. The *Niles Weekly Register* reported what appeared to be average pioneer households: it claimed that the new town of Mount Pleasant, Ohio, had "between 80 and 90 families, and about 500 souls besides journeymen and laborers [and] transient persons."[42] Nine years later, the *Register* noted that hundreds of wagons were passing through Vandalia, Illinois, bound for the Sangamon Country, and they contained an average of five people each.[43] At Haverhill,

---

[38]Abner D. Jones, *Illinois and the West*, pp. 30-31.

[39]Dan Clark, *op. cit.*, p. 185.

[40]Elisha W. Keyes, "Early Days in Jefferson County," *Colls. of the State Hist. Soc. of Wisc.*, XI, pp. 416-17.

[41]Holbrook, *op. cit.*, p. 75.

[42]*Niles Weekly Register*, X (June 8, 1816), p. 234.

[43]*Ibid.* XXIX (Nov. 26, 1825), p. 208.

Massachusetts, in the early part of the century 450 westward-bound migrants in seventy-three wagons passed through in thirteen days. And at Easton, Pennsylvania, a point through which funneled much of the early New England migration, one month witnessed 3066 migrants in 511 wagons rumbling toward the fresh western soil.[44]

In addition, the group approach to migration led to the development of two-stage migration. Often one or two adult males, possibly with a friend or relative, blazed the trail into the back country, selected a promising site for settlement, and spent months or even a year or two clearing the land, planting a crop, and building shelter. Often one member of these small trailblazing groups returned to the East and escorted the rest of the household or group to the West; in other instances, upon the receipt of favorable word, the rest of the household pushed westward alone. By way of example, the spring of 1819 found William Bush, James Willison, and Isreal Finch moving to a site just south of present-day Noblesville, Indiana. Not until mid-summer did their families arrive.[45] Sometimes a couple assaulted the wilderness with just one of their children, perhaps the strongest, and the others were temporarily farmed out to relatives and friends. If the assault proved to be successful, the family reunited on the frontier. And often those who had tended the children in the East during the assault migrated westward with their wards and lived with the reunited family briefly. The numerous examples of two-stage settlement sprinkled throughout this chapter illustrate the fact that this method of migration produced on the frontier small parties of adults who did battle with the elements; at the same time, the method created in the East rather large units which sometimes waited a year or two for the signal to advance westward. Demographic differences between East and West pertaining to household size and age were thereby somewhat negated.

One additional factor may have operated to limit the sizes of pioneer households. As will be seen, the typical frontiersman was a bit younger than the typical easterner. Furthermore, compared to the East, the frontier contained few elderly people. This age difference possibly operated to reduce the number of extended households on the frontier, households in which families had relatives living with them for some length of time, for extended family households tend today to be headed by older males.[46] The same may have been true in the early 1800s, a time in which few elderly males were on the frontier.

But did the West contain only small households? Did large households

---

[44]McMaster, op. cit., IV, p. 387.

[45]Charles N. Thompson, "Sons of the Wilderness: John and William Conner," Indiana Hist. Soc. Pubs., XII, p. 114.

[46]Barbara Laslett, "Household Structure on an American Frontier: Los Angeles, California, in 1850," Amer. Jour. of Soc., LXXXI, p. 123.

have practically no chance of exploiting the riches of the Garden? Clearly, a great number of large households entered the lands of new settlement and gave household size as their reason for migrating. Foremost among the reasons prompting the migration of large households to the wilderness was the fact that many couples started large families in the East or in Europe, realized that they could not adequately support them, and decided that the frontier afforded the best opportunity to attain economic security. Many large households in the East, perhaps reluctant to strike out into unfamiliar country, fought to stave off economic disaster until it became apparent that physical removal westward offered the best solution. Accordingly, these large households pushed west.

From numerous participatory accounts and related writings, it is clear that household size and concern over growing households prodded people into the forests and onto the prairies. In the introduction to his journal, Thomas Hulme wrote that he was doing well in England, but "along with my children had come and had gone on increasing to the number of *nine.*" He added that he feared for the economic security of his large family and noted that more than one-half of what he might earn "would be taken away to feed pensioned Lords and Ladies, Soldiers to shoot at us, Parsons to persecute us, and Fundholders, who had lent their money to be applied to purposes of enslaving us."[47] Thus worried, Hulme fled from economic hardships, hardships stemming from governmental oppression and numerical oppression. Hulme's sentiments were echoed by William Hall. He migrated to Wanborough, Illinois, in 1821, giving as his reasons difficulty in maintaining a large family and political oppression.[48] In 1802 David Hoover made the trek from Randolph County, North Carolina, to the area soon to become the state of Ohio. He wrote, "My father had a family of ten children, four sons and six daughters. In order to better our circumstances, he came to the conclusion of moving to a new country, and sold his possessions accordingly."[49] William Nowlin was the oldest of five children in the 1820s, and he recalled that then "it was impossible for a poor man to get along and support his family [in New York]," and the Nowlin family moved to present-day Dearborn, Michigan.[50] The example of

---

[47]Thomas Hulme, *A Journal Made During a Tour of the Western Countries of America: September 30, 1818-August 7, 1819,* Vol. x of *Early Western Travels, 1748-1846: A Series of Annotated Reprints of some of the best and rarest contemporary volumes of travel, descriptive of the Aborigines and Social and Economic Conditions in the Middle and Far West, during the Period of Early American Settlement,* ed. by Rueben Gold Thwaites, pp. 23-24: (Hereinafter referred to as *Early Western Travels.*) Italics in original.

[48]Jane Rodman, "The English Settlement in Southern Illinois, 1815-1825," *Indiana Mag. of Hist.,* XLIII, p. 331.

[49]Bernhard Knollenberg, "Pioneer Sketches of the Upper Whitewater Valley: Quaker Stronghold of the West," *Indiana Hist. Soc. Pubs.,* XV, p. 19.

[50]William Nowlin, *The Bark Covered House; Or, Back in the Woods Again,* ed. by Milo M. Quaife, p. 4.

Elkanah Brush is also typical of households joining the westward march in an effort to shake off numerical oppression. He moved to Green County, Illinois, from Massachusetts in 1821 with "a brood of young children" in order to "improve his economic status and to provide a more promising one for his children than the older East afforded."[51] Payton Wheeler, father of eight, came to Indiana in 1817 from Chelsea, England, after observing that he "had an increasing family and decreasing property."[52] The birth of five "children constituted the chief factor in the epochal decision of Edwin Bottomley's life," a decision to move from England to Racine County, Wisconsin, in 1842.[53] Size also convinced the Whitney household, consisting of two adults, ten children, and one black girl, to leave western New York in early July, 1822, and travel to Michigan by way of Canada. The Whitneys settled near Monroe, Michigan, for two years and then moved to the site of present-day Toledo, Ohio. Their neighbors there, the Coleman Keelers, had nine children and had moved to their home in 1818.[54] Intent on starting afresh in a new land, Rebecca Burlend, her husband, and a number of their children came from England to western Illinois in 1831. Numbering nine, they had been poor tenant farmers in Yorkshire, and Mrs. Burlend wrote that "the severe struggles we had to endure to meet our payments, the gradual diminution of our little property, and the entire absence of any prospects of being able to supply the wants of a large family" convinced her husband of the necessity of moving to the western world.[55] The advantages of raising a large family in the new lands quite likely led

---

[51]Daniel Harmon Brush, *Growing up with Southern Illinois, 1820 to 1861*, ed. by Milo M. Quaife, pp. xvii-xviii.

[52]William Faux, *Memorable Days in America: being a Journal of a Tour to the United States, principally undertaken to ascertain, by positive evidence, the condition and probable prospects of British emigrants; including accounts of Mr. Birkbeck's Settlement in the Illinois: and intended to show Men and Things as they are in America*. Vols. XI and XII of *Early Western Travels*, XI, p. 289.

[53]Milo M. Quaife, ed., "An English Settler in Pioneer Wisconsin: The Letters of Edwin Bottomley, 1842-1850," *Pub. of the State Hist. Soc. of Wisc.*, XXV, p. 14.

[54]Harriet Perry, "The Life History of Harriet Whitney Collins," *Northwest Ohio Qly.*, XXXI, pp. 147-48.

[55]Burlend, *op. cit.*, pp. 7-8. Sometimes large households in the East were so destitute that migration westward was accomplished only with incredible hardship. It was recorded, for example, that "A family of eight, on their way from Maine to Indiana, walked all the way to Easton, Pennsylvania, which they reached late in February, dragging the children and their wordly goods in a handcart. A blacksmith from Rhode Island made his way in the dead of winter across Massachusetts to Albany. In a little cart on four plank wheels a foot in diameter were some clothes, some food, and two children. Behind trudged the mother with an infant at breast and seven other children beside her. The father and a boy of twelve pulled the cart. A family of seven passed through Bridgeport, Connecticut, in March. They had come down from Three Rivers in Canada, the men drawing a small cart on four plank wheels, and the women and larger children following on foot." McMaster, *op. cit.*, IV, pp. 386-87.

James Duffield to remove his wife and their eight children to southeastern Iowa in 1837.[56]

Although sheer size and resulting poverty discouraged some large households from attempting to migrate westward, many who braved the uncertainties of the northern wilderness did so with the hope and expectation that the new environment would enable them to meet the expanding needs of their growing families. There is obviously some truth, however qualified, to the assertion that "It was the families with large numbers of children that moved west."[57] Very obviously economic pressure and the resulting crowded quarters—and perhaps other forms of pressure as well—were motivating factors in propelling large households into the uncrowded expanses of the Old Northwest.

Debt-ridden households also found the frontier attractive. Some large households in the East, having plunged into debt and entertaining no hope of ever getting out, found the western laws concerning usury and imprisonment for debt attractive. For example, if a large family in Connecticut found itself in debt in the early 1830s and, being a poor financial risk, could not borrow money, it might have found a move to Illinois advantageous. There, imprisonment for debt and laws against usury were abolished. At least poor risks could get loans, and if they failed to pay them back they would not go to jail. Of the two regions in the North, the frontier was decidedly the better place for big, destitute households.

Some huge pioneer households sprang up in their entirety on the frontier. Margaret Dwight Bell was born in Connecticut in 1790, migrated to Ohio, and married in 1811. During the remaining twenty-three years of her life, obviously hectic years, she bore thirteen children.[58] Countless individuals came to the wilderness, got married, and then flooded the sparsely-settled lands with offspring. In addition, childless couples and couples with only one or two children arrived on the frontier and then increased the size of their families enormously.

Three factors were among those encouraging the creation of big pioneer families: early marriage of frontier women; continuous marriage of these women; and the relative ease with which a large family could be raised in the new lands. Concerning early marriage, it was reported from Ohio in the

---

[56]George C. Duffield, "An Iowa Settler's Homestead," *Annals of Iowa*, VI, p. 206. The migrations of other large households can be found in James Flint, *Letters from America, containing Observations on the Climate and Agriculture of the western States, the Manners of the People, and the Prospects of Emigrants &c, &c.* p. 226, and John J. Daniels, "The Earliest Settlers of Linn County," *Annals of Iowa*, VI, pp. 585-86.

[57]Calhoun, *op. cit.*, II, p. 169.

[58]Margaret Dwight Bell, *A Journey to Ohio in 1810 as Recorded in the Journal of Margaret Van Horn Dwight Bell*, ed. by Max Farrand, pp. v-vi.

early 1820s that girls there generally married before they were seventeen.[59] Furthermore, nearly all western girls seem to have married, unmarried women being courted eargerly. In 1820, a young widower with two small children was on his way to the military lands in Illinois. Someone hinted to him that he should marry. He concurred, but then added "I have lately been in that country [the northern frontier] and I believe that the girls there are *all married up.*"[60] Among the frontier population, girls were generally "all married up," an observation which may have had some important demographic ramifications. Specifically, it has been noticed that

> In countries where young people growing up and approaching marriageable age enjoyed an abundance of available land, thus experiencing few impediments to early marriage, it seems likely that proportions of married women among all women aged sixteen to forty-four were further inflated as a result of new entry from outside. And so with states and territories.[61]

Simply stated, western conditions apparently produced early and continuous marriage for pioneer women; also of great importance, these conditions possibly produced similar marriage phenomena among women who were contemplating removal to the West.

Evidently, girls married young and were constantly in a state of matrimony, both conditions conducive to the creation of large families. One reason for early marriage and sizeable families was pre-nuptial pregnancy. In the nation today, between one-third and one-half of all young brides are pregnant before marriage.[62] This rate appears to be in rough accordance with rates in other eras of American history.[63] Regardless of the exact proportion, some brides got a headstart in the creation of a large household. That there appears to be a causal relationship between early and continuous marriage and a high birth rate has been noted by T. H. Hollingsworth.[64]

---

[59]George W. Ogden, *Letters from the West; comprising a Tour through the Western Country, and a residence of two Summers in the States of Ohio and Kentucky*, Vol. XIX of *Early Western Travels*, p. 81. Early marriages, it was noted, were caused "by the ease with which the necessities of life can be obtained." Fearon, *op. cit.*, p. 378.

[60]James Flint, *op. cit.*, p. 225. Italics in the original copy. Women, quite possibly, were more eager to marry than men. Calhoun, *op. cit.*, II, p. 11.

[61]Colin Forster and G. S. L. Tucker, *Economic Opportunity and White American Fertility Ratios, 1800-1860*, p. 50.

[62]Bogue, *op. cit.*, p. 640.

[63]Pre-marital conception was not new to American society. For example, between 1740 and 1760 in Bristol, Rhode Island, perhaps up to 49 per cent of the babies born were conceived before marriage. John Demos, "Families in Colonial Bristol, Rhode Island: An Exercize in Historical Demography," *The William and Mary Qtly.*, XXV, p. 56.

[64]T. H. Hollingsworth, *Historical Demography*, p. 331.

Also, westward migration lifted a number of economic shackles for those desiring large families, one observer noting that "Every log Cabin is swarming with half-naked children. Boys of 18 build huts, marry, and raise hogs and children at about the same expense."[65] Morris Birkbeck, after proclaiming, "This is a land of plenty, and we are proceeding [westward] to a land of abundance," observed, "In this land of plenty, young people first marry and then look out for the means of a livelihood, *without fear or cause for it.*"[66] Whatever the reason, many decided that the wilderness was a good place in which to raise a large family: some "pioneers found large families desirable; vast empty spaces kindled ambitions for dominion; the labor of growing children was valuable; and a sufficiency of stalwart sons increased security against the Indians."[67] Still, fragmentary evidence suggests that the percentage of large households that grew in their entirety on the frontier never equalled the percentage that had their origins elsewhere.

Another factor encouraged the creation of large households in the back country. Orphaned and abandoned children were often taken in by neighboring households, the additional household members being either active or potential economic assets.[68] In the East, the likelihood that such children were considered assets appears to be remote; the unfortunate children were probably shunted off to an orphanage, instead.

Frontier custom and law did nothing to discourage sizeable households. For those wishing to be married, civil officials and clergymen were often unavailable, but custom sometimes permitted pioneers to begin their families anyway. Couples paired off and lived together.[69] Marriage nearly always followed, and it was not extremely rare for children to attend their parents' wedding. Laws pertaining to the frontier also encouraged large families and, in particular, large household units with adults; the amount of land that could be obtained by one household was sometimes determined by the number of adults in the household: "Under the preemption law then in force [in territorial Wisconsin] a claimant of public lands could buy a quarter-section on which he had his house." However, each householder who could be classified as an independent cultivator, including such diverse people as "a son of full age, a father, the wife's brother or sister, or

---

[65]Fordham, *op. cit.*, p. 120. See also Lewis B. Ewbank, "A Real Pioneer," *Indiana Mag. of Hist.*, xxxviii, p. 154, and Henry Bamfield Parks, *The United States of America: A History*, p. 256.

[66]Morris Birkbeck, *Notes on a Journey in America, From the Coast of Virginia to the Territory of Illinois*, 2d ed., p. 86. Italics added.

[67]Calhoun, *op. cit.*, ii, p. 15. Family size may be somewhat dependent upon the amount of living space available. See, for instance, Willystine Goodsell, "Housing and the Birth Rate in Sweden," *Amer. Sociol. Rev.*, ii, pp. 857-59.

[68]Richard A. Bartlett, *The New Country: A Social History of the American Frontier, 1776-1890*, pp. 361-63.

[69]Calhoun, *op. cit.*, ii, pp. 34-36.

even more distant relatives," enjoyed "a floating right to half a quarter-section."[70] Elsewhere, a woman wanting to preempt land had to be either a widow or a head of a family. Women ineligible for land wasted no time circumventing the law and, temporarily at least, thereby increasing household size: "The young lady would borrow a child, sign the papers of adoption, swear she was head of a family, and pre-empt her claim. Afterwards she would annul the adoption papers, returning the child to its parents with an appropriate gift."[71] As will be seen, laws also encouraged the formation of large southern households, possibly with greater effect.

Large households in the northern wilds may have sprung from another condition: the frontier may have been a place in which neither neonates and infants nor their recently-delivered mothers were especially susceptible to death, popular histories and legends to the contrary. Perhaps the frontier, expecially the northern frontier, compared favorably with the older sections of the nation. Other demographic studies indicate that frontier conditions may have been surprisingly healthful for both newborn and mother.[72]

In short, physical, social, and political forces combined with custom and economic forces to influence frontier demography. But demography was more than a dependent variable upon which external forces operated; it was, while a dependent variable, also an independent variable, and certain aspects of frontier and national demography influenced other aspects of frontier demography.

There was one demographic condition which operated as an independent variable, influencing other aspects of demography: among settlers, as will be seen, there was a persistent, if surprisingly small, shortage of females, especially those over fifteen years of age. As a result of this shortage, women of nearly every description—even girls in their early teens—were hounded by enthusiastic suitors. Evidence from travel accounts and diaries reveals the actions of the suitors. Harriet Martineau witnessed "the early marriages of silly children in the south and west, where, *owing to the disproportion of numbers,* every woman is married before she knows how serious a matter human life is."[73] Charles Hoffman,

---

[70]Joseph Schafer, *Wisconsin Domesday Book, General Studies,* Vol. II: *Four Wisconsin Counties, Prairie and Forest,* p. 60.

[71]Boorstin, *op. cit.,* p. 77.

[72]In colonial Andover, Massachusetts, for example, "The chances of raising most of one's children to adulthood were far greater in [frontier] Andover than in many similar villages in the Old World and some of the older communities in the New." Philip Greven, Jr., *Four Generations: Population, Land, and Family in Colonial Andover, Massachusetts,* p. 26. Whether this was true in spite of frontier conditions or because of them seems debatable. Greven's findings of relatively great health may have been a function of the characteristics of the settlers, including education, social organization, and attitudes and customs. Perhaps the descendents of the Andover settlers and similar settlers carried with them these characteristics as they moved across New York and into the Old Northwest.

[73]Martineau, *op. cit.,* III, p. 120. Italics added.

visiting Galena, Illinois, in the winter of 1833-34, observed that "girls of fifteen (I might say twelve), or widows of fifty are alike snapped up with avidity by the disconsolate bachelors."[74] It was also noted that at this time the nation "was a farmer's country, productive land was plentiful, and it was easy to support a family. So from the early marriages came large numbers of children, often a dozen or more from one mariage."[75] And what was true of the entire country was especially true of the frontier. The sex ratio of the frontier enabled practically any woman to marry and this, in turn, increased the proportion of children in the general population.[76] In other words, "In new settlements the birth rate tends to increase most and to maintain itself best in the degree that the number of males is greater than that of females."[77] This is especially true if the difference between the number of males and females is greatest for the ages between twenty and fifty, a fact that surprises no one.[78] Beautiful or not, outnumbered western women apparently married earlier, had more children, and remained in matrimony longer than their eastern counterparts, resulting in more children per woman of childbearing age on the frontier than in the East. Young men from the East moved westward, married any and every available female, and left behind "those who should be their wives to marry widowers of double their age" or not at all.[79] Perhaps these eastern women not only married relatively old men, but very possibly their average age at marriage was quite high.[80] If these conditions were widespread, then the result may very well have been a lowered birth rate in the East and, therefore, a relatively higher rate in the West.

When pioneer women lost their husbands, they could usually marry any

---

[74]Charles F. Hoffman, *A Winter in the West*, p. 52. There may have been other reasons for early marriages. At least one individual implied that western women married earlier because they were more beautiful than their eastern sisters: "their figures were more perfect, and they were finer grown, not receiving the sudden checks [to beauty] to which the eastern women were exposed." (The nature of these "sudden checks" was not specified. Perhaps it was the "pox.") Frederick Marryat, *A Diary in America*, II, p. 4 Those travelers who noted the appearance of western women seem to have concurred in the belief that they were at least as good looking as women in the East, and in many instances a good deal better looking.

[75]Gaillard Hunt, *Life in America One Hundred Years Ago*, p. 77. The relationship between available land on the American frontier and high birth rates has been noted by Yasukichi Yasuba, *Birth Rates of the White Population in the United States 1800-1860*, pp. 158-59. The total agrarian way of life, including agrarian values and not just the availability of much land, may have caused the pioneer birth rate to be somewhat higher than the eastern birth rate. See, for example, John Modell, "Family and Fertility on the Indiana Frontier, 1820," *Amer. Quar.*, XXIII, pp. 626, 630-31.

[76]Joseph J. Spengler and Otis Dudley Duncan, eds., *Demographic Analysis: Selected Readings*, p. 54.

[77]George Parker, *Iowa Pioneer Foundations*, II, p. 387.

[78]*Ibid.*, 387.

[79]Martineau, *op. cit.*, III, p. 128. Consult also Thomas D. Clark, *Rampaging Frontier: Manners and Humors of Pioneer Days in the South and Middle West*, 2d ed, p. 286.

[80]Demos, "Families in Colonial Bristol," p. 55.

of a number of men who clamored at their doors. The sex ratio in the backwoods encouraged widows to marry, and those who avoided remarriage and those who had no children evidently returned to the settled sections of the nation. (The surprising tendency for women with children but without husbands to cling to the wilds will be discussed later.) In any event, compared to the East the new lands contained very few childless unmarried women to lower the average family size; they changed either their marital status or their location.

An additional factor tended to enlarge the size of some households in the northern wilds: some landowners, and others, did obtain hired help. In spite of the severe and chronic shortage of reasonably-priced, reliable, and competent hired help, some help was secured. Furthermore, very possibly such enlarged households were more closely associated with landowners than with non-landowners.[81] In other words, the greater the tendency for people to own land, the greater the tendency for an employee, apprentice, or some other working person to live with the family. The West was full of landowners, as will be seen.

In spite of the fact that an oppressive household size sent many households scurrying to the northern frontier and in spite of the fact that a set of conditions on the frontier permitted and encouraged the formation of large households, the average and modal sizes of frontier households were actually somewhat smaller than those in the northern settled area. The weight of evidence indicates that children in large households tend to be more involved with kin, more dependent upon others, more realistic, more conforming, more likely to be maladjusted to parents, more likely to do poorly in school, more antisocial in behavior, more likely to score low on IQ tests, and much more likely to be mentally deficient.[82] If so, there is no demographic reason to believe that frontiersmen displayed these characteristics to any appreciably greater degree than people in the East, at least insofar as the differences could be attributed to differences in household size.

Wilderness dwellers have long enjoyed the reputation of growing up in households swarming with family members and boarders. In reality, however, the percentages of household units on the northern frontier in which eleven or more lived exceeded those of the northern settled area only once, in 1820 (see Table 3). The relative number of such units on the

---

[81]Laslett, op. cit., p. 123.

[82]For a discussion of some of the characteristics associated with very large households and the members of such households, see Bossard, op. cit., pp. 310-320. Also, numerous related comments are found in Heer, op. cit. pp. 67-68; Catherine Chilman, "Some Psychological Aspects of Fertility, Family Planning, and Population Policy in the United States," in James T. Fawcett, ed., Psychological Perspectives on Population, pp. 163-182; and John A. Clausen and Suzanne R. Clausen, "The Effects of Family Size on Parents and Children," in Fawcett, ibid., pp. 185-208.

northern frontier spurted sharply after 1800, peaked in 1820, inched downward by 1830, and by 1840 slumped back to the 1810 level. (It is interesting to note that the figures for both the northern backwoods and the northern settled area for 1810 and 1840 were indentical, standing at 5%. This suggests that for these years the net results of all of the various forces operating on demography in both the northern wilds and the settled region were approximately equal.) Not unexpectedly, paralleling these trends were the relative numbers of settlers and northeasterners who lived in household units containing eleven or more people (see Table 4). On only two occasions, 1820 and 1840, did the percentages of population in the wilderness living in these units exceed those of the Northeast. In short, three facts are clear: the wilderness north of the Ohio River was not a place of relatively large households; therefore, the hypotheses concerning such units were largely refuted by the evidence; forces on the northern frontier operating to restrict household size were evidently stronger than forces operating to increase the size.

SINGLE PEOPLE

"A bachelor has no business in the Backwoods; for in a wild country, where it is impossible to hire assistance of any kind, either male or female, a man is thrown entirely upon himself," wrote William Blane, an observer of the frontier.[83] Apparently, many heeded his advice. In this study, individuals living alone were regarded as households. Compared to the northern settled section, the northern wilderness contained relatively more such units only in 1800 and 1840 (see Table 5). In 1830 there were comparatively fewer on the northern frontier than in the East, and in 1810 and 1820 there were no differences whatsoever. The wilderness, clearly, was not a place where individuals lived alone, and the hypothesis thus lacked strong support.

Several reasons help to account for the dearth of individuals in the wilds. Many individuals who trooped to the frontier in a single state did not remain single for long. The example of Margaret Dwight Bell has been cited. Similar patterns are found in the lives of Jacob Mann, Edward Crow, and Charles Haskin, single men when they became the first settlers of Linn County, Iowa; they remained single for just a few years.[84] James L. Scott arrived in Jefferson County, Iowa, in 1837 as a single man. Shortly, he became sheriff of the county, and married Mary A. Gilmer in 1839.[85] On the frontier, "The bachelor ever had one eye cocked for a worthwhile

---

[83]William Blane, *An Excursion Through the United States and Canada During the Years 1822-1823*, p. 163. Although it is clear that many in the United States heeded Blane's warning, it may have been true that in other places in the world "At one time migrants were mainly single." Clarke, *op. cit.*, p. 131.

[84]Daniels, *op. cit.*, p. 583.

[85]Ida M. Huntington, "Willson Alexander Scott," *Annals of Iowa*, XIII, p. 245.

helpmate, and the spinster preserved her single 'blessedness' only by insistent struggle."[86] The propensity of frontiersmen to marry was undoubtedly prompted by the realization that "Paradise without an Eve would be no Paradise at all," an opinion that was shared by many in the West.[87] It is perhaps true that "of all American myths, none is stronger than that of the loner moving across the land."[88] It is perhaps equally true that of all American myths none is more false.

The dearth of individuals can possibly be explained another way: some unmarried males escaped detection by ceasing to be true loners and living with others. When manuscript censuses were examined in the course of this study, such people were counted as members of small groups, not as individuals. Observers of the frontier knew that these groups existed. In 1820 James Flint encountered a Scotch settlement near Madison, Indiana: "it deserves notice that two of these [households] consist of two young men each, and one of them of three."[89] David Hoover, moving from North Carolina to present-day Ohio, finally settled with his four brothers north of Richmond, Indiana, in 1806.[90] The early settlement of Indianapolis included John McCormick and his brother, James.[91] Innumerable other bachelors and single women lived with other households. No serious attempt was made to determine the percentage of the population that lived in such households, but a survey of several hundred households in twelve randomly-selected frontier counties suggests that it was below 2 or 3%. Furthermore, those who banded together often had a style of life different from those who were true loners and lived completely alone. They had the advantage of physical security, possibly economic security, division of labor, companionship, and other benefits not shared by true loners.

One type of individual, often a true loner, consisted of men who had something to hide—themselves. James Hall called attention to the fact that "A frontier is often the retreat of loose individuals, who if not familiar with

---

[86]Keyes, op. cit., p. 196.

[87]Marryat, op. cit., II, pp. 50-51. In addition, while a bachelor in the East often had laundry, restaurant, sewing, and other services available in close proximity to where he lived, a bachelor pioneer enjoyed few of these services. Perhaps his tendency to marry reflected a desire to secure these services.

[88]Boorstin, op. cit., p. 51.

[89]James Flint, op. cit., p. 224.

[90]Chelsea L. Lawlis, "Settlement of the Whitewater Valley, 1790-1810." Indiana Mag. of Hist., XLIII, p. 31.

[91]Daniel Wait Howe, "Making a Capital in the Wilderness," Indiana Hist. Soc. Pubs., IV, p. 314. To illustrate the point further, the Crackles brothers—Joseph, Thomas, and Kelsey—came from Lincolnshire, England, and settled in Edwards County, Illinois, and lived together. Flower, op. cit., pp. 165-66. Some men hired others to accompany them to their place of settlement and help them to get established. Marryat, op. cit., pp. 50-51. These men often lived with the household for some time and were therefore not listed in the federal censuses as loners.

crime, have very blunt perceptions of virtue."[92] Such loose individuals often lurked around rivers and other lines of communication, avoiding the agrarian sections of the frontier. And, for reasons that are apparent, they were none too eager to be interviewed by the federal census taker. In any case, many of these "loose individuals" were not true loners; they were members of gangs.

Far more prevalent among loners was the trailblazer. Existing records show that most of these men were actually married men who entered the West to scout, file a claim, do preliminary work on the site, and then either return for their families or send for them. Perhaps some became trailblazers upon the advice of William Blane: If "four of five families from the same part of England wish to emigrate [to the frontier], they would do well to send first of all one of *their own* number, a poor man, but upon whom they could rely" to scour the countryside for a suitable place of settlement and make the needed preparations for the entire group.[93] The process by which trailblazers accomplished two-stage migration was described by one foreign observer: "The husband, the latter end of summer, repairs to the spot where the settlement is to be made." There he fells small trees, barks large ones, puts in some corn, constructs a small shelter, and then "returns to his former habitation; and at the beginning of spring, he brings his family and the best of his cattle to the new settlement."[94]

The process of trailblazing and two-stage migration is well-illustrated by several examples. Some of the trailblazers came in small groups, thereby avoiding classification as true loners; others entered the wilderness by themselves. Daniel Hahn wrote, "My brother-in-law, Charles Moberly, and I came to Linn County, Iowa, in the spring of 1837, made a claim and built a cabin on it." He added that they "did some breaking, and in the latter part of August, 1837 removed my wife and five children from Mercer County, Illinois, into this same cabin."[95] John Allen temporarily left his wife in Virginia in order to travel into the West and help found Ann Arbor, Michigan.[96] Richard Rue and George Holman were two members of a party that set out from Henry County, Kentucky, in early 1805 to explore the Whitewater country in Indiana. They were favorably impressed and returned to escort the rest of their families to Indiana, leaving Holman's

[92]James Hall, *Letters from the West*, p. 271. See also Charles A. Murray, *Travels in North America during the Years 1834, 1835 & 1836*, II, p. 105. Without doubt "the West attracted the lawless and dissolute as well as the sober and industrious." Robert E. Riegel and Robert G. Athearn, *America Moves West*, 5th ed., p. 130.

[93]Blane, *op. cit.*, p. 168. Italics in original.

[94]Duke de La Rochefoucault-Liancourt, *Travels through the United States of America, the Country of the Iroquois, and Upper Canada, in the Years 1795, 1796, and 1797*, I, pp. 293-94.

[95]Quoted in Daniels, *op. cit.*, p. 581.

[96]Orlando Stephenson, *Ann Arbor: The First Hundred Years*, p. 14.

two sons, a married couple, and another man to tend the site for more than two months.[97] John Woodhouse came from England and later his family joined him at Pottsville, Pennsylvania. In 1832 he again pushed westward alone, this time to the lead-mining region of southwestern Wisconsin, intending to accumulate enough capital there to embark upon farming.[98] Some loners on the northern frontier blazed trail for other people than their own families. Thomas Dean, for example, left a wife and five children in New York and did missionary work in the West for the Friends.[99]

Whatever the purpose and whatever the result, trailblazing was often the first stage of the two-stage act of migration, and it was widely practiced. Those who engaged in trailblazing appear to have heeded the advice of Henry Heald: "My advice to my friends who intend moving to the westward would be, by all means come and see the country without the incumbrance of a family."[100]

As was indicated, group migration affected the demographic characteristics of the western woods and grasslands by making it possible for many marginal migrants—women, young children, old folk, small or childladened households, and others—to reach the back country. This fact helped to preclude some potentially large demographic differences between the new lands and the settled area. Two-stage migration had somewhat the same effect. It thrust small units into the West, thereby reducing some of the differences in household size between East and West. On the other hand, since the first stage rarely involved young children or women, it almost certainly offset some of the effects of group migration, a process which encouraged the westward march of youngsters and women. The fact that males formed the majority of those who were blazing the trail in two-stage migration may largely explain the male majority, however small, on the frontier over the decades. (This majority will be examined in Chapter V, "Age and Sex."

[97]Knollenberg, op. cit., pp. 22-23.

[98]Peter J. Coleman, "The Woodhouse Family; Grant County Pioneers," Wisc. Mag. of Hist., XLII, p. 267. Other instances of trailblazing are found in Jesse Hart, et. al., "Pioneer History of the Settlement of Eaton County," Mich. Pioneer Colls., XXII, pp. 505-06; Nowlin, op. cit., pp. 6-7; John J. Horton, The Jonathon Hale Farm: A Chronicle of the Cuyahoga Valley, pp. 42-43; Riegel and Athearn, op. cit., p. 110; Farnham, op. cit., p. 83; and, Tilly Buttrick, Jr., Voyages, Travels and Discoveries, pp. 49-52. It is not unlikely that virtually every county and local history contains accounts of trailblazing.

[99]John C. Dean, ed., "Journal of Thomas Dean: A Voyage to Indiana in 1817," Ind. Hist. Soc. Pubs., VI, p. 275. Sometimes trails were blazed for people other than wife, children, or church members. Some single frontiersmen—perhaps those who dispaired of ever marrying a woman other than one with a litter of children—made special efforts to entice their parents into the backwoods. See, for example, Patrick Shirreff, A Tour Through North America, p. 232. Sometimes speculators hired young men as agents to go to western lands, locate prime sites, survey and mark the land, and record the land. An example of this practice is in Christiana Holmes Tillson, A Woman's Story of Pioneer Illinois, p. 6.

[100]Thomson, op. cit., p. 65.

Although some true loners were found in the wilderness, the notion that "a bachelor has no business in the Backwoods" is strongly supported by the demographic data. Unmarried men living alone were very rare on the frontier; single women living alone and once-married women without children living alone were practically non-existent, numbering just twenty over the four decades throughout the northern and southern frontiers in a sample that included nearly 50,000 settlers. Of the men who lived alone in the new lands, many did so with the expectation of either bringing their families out to the frontier or, if unmarried, of quickly getting married. The percentage of the frontier population living alone with the desire of remaining alone was extremely small, perhaps less than one-fifth of one per cent.

INCOMPLETE HOUSEHOLDS

Compared to the Northeast, the northern wilderness was hypothesized to contain relatively fewer households from which an adult member was missing. With the exception of 1830, this was always the case (see Table 6). Most of the missing adults, it was further hypothesized, would be female. This expectation rested upon several possible factors: high mortality at childbirth; the likelihood that widows had more difficulty than widowers maintaining themselves in the backwoods; and the evidence that widowed frontierswomen either took advantage of the favorable sex ratio and remarried or sought economic asylum in the East. The percentages of missing adults on the northern frontier who were male—exceeding 50% in 1810, 1820, and 1830—contradicted the expectation. (See Table 7.)

Conversely, it was hypothesized that males would constitute a majority of the adults missing from households in the Northeast. Several facts supported the hypothesis: some pioneer widows with children returned to the East from the frontier; eastern widows had a relatively smaller pool of men from which to select a new husband than their pioneer sisters; widows in the East were very possibly under less economic pressure to remarry quickly than pioneer widows. Certainly, women in towns and cities and other eastern places had more opportunity to sustain themselves outside of marriage than women on the largely agrarian frontier. Since at least 72% of the adults missing from northeastern households were male, the hypotheses receive strong support (see Table 7). In 1830 males constituted an astounding 98% of the missing adults in the settled area of the North, a figure that tumbled to 84% by 1840.

Some of the households in the West missing female adults either migrated without them or lost them along the way. For example, Smith Hunt, his three brothers, and his father settled in the Whitewater country of Indiana in 1806.[101] Thomas Bulla moved into Wayne County, Indiana, in the winter

---

[101]Lawlis, op. cit., p. 31.

of 1807-08, his wife having died on the way from North Carolina.[102] Similarly, William Wood of Wormswold, Leicestershire, England, migrated to Edwards County, Illinois, in 1819 with his son. His wife had died at the mouth of the Wabash River.[103] Other women accompanied their husbands almost to the place of settlement and then hesitated for a time while the site of the new home was improved.[104]

Instances in which recently widowed women brought their households westward are extremely rare. Mrs. Thomas Spring was an exception. In 1820 she, her husband, and four sons left Derbyshire, England, for the prairie country of Illinois. In Washington, Pennsylvania, Thomas Spring died and three sons—one son had remained in Baltimore—brought their mother on to Birk's prairie in Illinois.[105] The successful migration westward of female-headed households was highly unusual, especially if the children were female. At best, such units could expect a rough time as they pressed on to the new lands; by tagging along with some group, they could ease the ordeal somewhat. It seems likely that the vast majority of pioneer mothers without husbands had lost their husbands either on the frontier or rather close to it.

But the figures in Table 7 clearly indicate that mothers without husbands, once on the frontier, remained there, thereby generally refuting the hypothesized characteristics of missing adults on the frontier. Since unmarried pioneer women were generally hounded by hopeful suitors and remained single only with great effort and since it was usually no easy matter for a woman and her children to cling to the frontier without the presence of an adult male, some explanation, however speculative, is required:

1. Some of these women were, in fact, married to men who were not present. Some husbands made prolonged trips to other parts of the wilderness, perhaps taking animals to market (a task which sometimes took six months), or trips of equal duration to the East. In any case, some of these males were not recorded by the census taker as living with their families.
2. Some spouses deserted their families and lived elsewhere.
3. Inasmuch as western females often married at a young age, they were perhaps more prone to become widows at an early age. This idea is based upon the fact that today "A high proportion of young brides have an older husband; the difference in age is substantially greater than for adult marriages."[106] If this condition prevailed

---

[102]*Ibid.*, p. 30.

[103]Flower, *op. cit.*, p. 144. Another instance of a widowed father coming to the wilds to live with sons is found in Knollenberg, *op. cit.*, pp. 32, 36.

[104]Stephenson, *op. cit.*, p. 19.

[105]Flower, *op. cit.*, p. 155.

[106]Bogue, *op. cit.*, p. 640.

during the early national era and if marriages of young women were much more common in the West than in the East (both appear to be true), then it is likely that such women may have been widowed by the time they were thirty or forty, after having had several children, some of whom were economically self-supporting. Perhaps the husbands lived long enough to establish the household securely in the West, and perhaps the older offspring were able to assume many of the economic functions previously performed by the father. If these assumptions are correct, then such households could weather frontier conditions reasonably well, and there was no need for the mother to rush into marriage to stave off catastrophe.

4. Evidence suggests that widows, perhaps unlike William Gregory as noted earlier, usually waited a "respectable time" before remarrying.[107] Occasionally, the span of the "respectable time" was enforced by both custom and law:

> Proud husbands in some cases satisfied their vanities by making testimentary injunctions that kept their widows in mourning for a 'proper' length of time. Provisions were made in many regions for funeral services to be preached several months after a burial in order that a 'grieving' widow would not ride to the graveyard behind her husband's corpse, and ride back in the embrace of a prospective husband.[108]

Enforced mourning, alone, quite possibly accounts for a very sizeable proportion of incomplete households headed by females.

5. Some widows lacked the economic and physical means of returning eastward immediately. One woman on the Pennsylvania frontier of 1810 observed, "We have concluded the reason so few are willing to return from the Western country is not that the country is so good, but because the journey is so bad."[109]

6. Frontiersmen, eager to marry, were nevertheless a bit reluctant to acquire a pack of strange youngsters by marrying a widow with children, especially if the offspring were female.

---

[107]See Louis L. Ray, "Flatboat Letters from Samuel Gibson Brown," *Year Book of the Society of Indiana Pioneers, 1965,* and J. F. H. Claiborne, "A Trip Through the Piney Woods," *Pubs. of the Mississippi Hist. Soc.,* IX, pp. 532-33. Within a few months after arriving with his family at Bluffdale, Illinois, Elkanah Brush died. His wife, left with a "brood" of young children, waited an unusually long time before remarrying—eight years. Possibly no prospective husband wanted to take on the brood until some of them were economic assets. Brush, *op. cit.,* p. 48. Not every pioneer woman, however, waited a respectable length of time. One widow auctioned off her late husband's possessions and got "married the same evening to an adventurer from one of the eastern states." Gustaf Unonius, *A Pioneer in Northwest America, 1841-1848: The Memoirs of Gustaf Unonius,* ed. by Nils William Olsson, I, p. 246.

[108]Thomas D. Clark, *Rampaging Frontier,* p. 282.

[109]Reginald Horsman, *The Frontier in the Formative Years, 1783-1815,* p. 74.

7. Some female-headed households secured the assistance of nearby relatives, sympathetic neighbors, and even hired help.

8. Some women had children out of wedlock and kept them.

Regardless of the reason or combination of reasons, marriageable women who had children, perhaps especially female children, appear to have remained both marriageable and on the frontier for some time. Far from fleeing the wilderness, some embraced it.

The age of the female who headed a household may provide some clue concerning the tendency for such females to persist in the wilderness. Today "Female heads are found with greatest relative frequency at the very youngest (14-19) or at the oldest (65 and over) ages."[110] Perhaps this was true during the early national era. In both age groups, the female heads possibly lived with children, the likelihood perhaps being stronger among the younger female heads than among the older. As was seen, apparently suitors were none too eager to marry a female head if the marriage included the adoption of a litter of children, especially females. On the other hand, perhaps the elderly female head was in no great rush to marry. Today "Widowhood is by far the major cause of incomplete households where the head is 45 years or older."[111] This may have been equally true during the early 1800s. If so, then it seems reasonable to expect that the widows lived with or near grown children, people who were well enough established to provide for their mother and lift from her shoulders the pressing need of obtaining security via a new husband.[112]

A CLOSE LOOK AT COMMON HOUSEHOLDS

During the first four decades of the nineteenth century, between 75 and 86% of the households in both the northern frontier and the Northeast contained between two and eight people, inclusively (see Table 8). Since such a consistently high proportion of total units contained between two and eight members, these units were studied in detail to learn something of their composition. Once again, prior to 1830 adults were regarded as those people who had attained the age of sixteen; in 1830 and 1840 adults were regarded as those who had reached fifteen. In both instances, the age was the approximate time at which most youngsters in the nation assumed full economic responsibility as members of their households, some having started their own families.

The three hypotheses concerning households in which only one child or no child was present were strongly supported by the evidence (see Tables 9, 10, and 11). So were the three hypotheses concerning households in which

---

[110]Bogue, op. cit., p. 376.

[111]Ibid., p. 376.

[112]The surprising tendency for female-headed households to adhere to the frontier is noted in Modell, op. cit., p. 620.

children constituted at least 50% of the household membership (see Tables 12, 13, and 14). In all six hypotheses, the number of children was examined because "inasmuch as the head and wife represent relatively constant factors in family size, an important change in average size of a family usually reflects a change in the number of other family members."[113] Perhaps at least 5% of all couples in the world cannot have children due to physiological reasons. An additional 5% fail to have children due to separation, divorce, late marriage, psychological factors, and other reasons. If more than 10% of the couples are childless, "we may infer that it is either primarily voluntary childlessness resulting from the use of contraceptives or else a result of very irregular exposure to childbearing."[114] Some of these conditions possibly prevailed in the United States in the early part of the nineteenth century. Regardless of the exact conditions, an examination of the relative number of children in the most common household compositions can be revealing. (See Table 9.)

Over the four decades there were strong signs of convergence between the northern wilderness and the northern settled area. But nearly all of the convergence occurred during the 1830s. In fact, in terms of the household units in which only one or no child was present (see Tables 9, 10, and 11), through 1830 the real trend was one of divergence between the two regions in the North. Throughout the first three decades there was a slight relative divergence in the units in which children enjoyed at least numerical parity with adults (see Tables 12, 13, and 14). In all cases, as all six tables indicate, the dramatic convergence occurred during the 1830s. Perhaps the convergence was a response to the depression of the late 1830s, or an indication that birth control was increasingly effective; perhaps it signified that fewer hands were needed in the new lands in the West; or it may have reflected a belief that the good lands east of the Great Plains would soon be in short supply. It might have indicated that all of these, in varying degrees, were true, or it possibly indicated something else. Whatever the indication, the northern frontier by 1840 was acquiring some of the demographic characteristics of the northeastern states.

The first hypothesis concerning the three most prevalent household compositions was largely substantiated; the second received support only insofar as it pertained to the frontier. In every census year but 1840 the three leading units were, in fact, generally larger than those of the settled area. At no time, however, in either the new lands of the West or the settled area in the East did any of the three most common household compositions include other than two adults (see Table 15). The dominant nature of the two-adult household suggests that the "normal" household configuration was durable enough to withstand buffeting in the western wilds.

[113]Paul C. Glick, *American Families*, p. 21.
[114]Bogue, *op. cit.*, p. 725.

Among the three leading compositions on the northern frontier over the years, the composition found most often was a couple with only one or two children. Two compositions appeared every decade among the leading units in the back country: two adults and one child, and two adults and two children. Some couples were young—many migrated westward immediately after marrying—and they had little time in which to raise anything but a small family.[115] However, young adults were relatively no more numerous in the northern backwoods than in the settled regions to the east (see Table 16). Perhaps the answer, or part of it, lies in the possibility that birth control was practiced effectively throughout the nation before urbanization occurred in the eastern states, giving the inhabitants of the frontier the option of limiting their families.[116] Or the overwhelming impetus for family limitation was the belief that the economic environment of the frontier made large families possible, but not necessary. Some large households sought out the western lands as a means of relieving economic pressure, but there is little evidence that pioneer couples were under economic coercion, or any other form of coercion, to produce great numbers of offspring. Another part of the answer may lie in the possibility that children were undercounted in the federal censuses, the underenumeration varying from census to census.[117] There is also the possibility that the quality of medical care for pioneer youngsters, compared to the care for eastern youngsters, actually declined as the frontier moved further and further away from the professional institutions and organizations of the Northeast. The trend among the three most prevalent units on the northern frontier was clearly one of fewer children as the years passed, whatever the causes.

Among the northern settlers, childless couples entered the ranks of the three leading households only in 1840. Households with one child moved

---

[115]Three acts propelled young people into the wilderness: marriage, births, the deaths of one or more of their parents.

[116]Wilson Grabill, Clyde Kiser, and Pascal Whelpton, *The Fertility of American Women*, pp. 15-16. Additional evidence supports the contention that birth control, in one form or another, may have been practiced on the frontier: Hollingsworth, *op. cit.*, p. 327, and David M. Kennedy, *Birth Control in America: The Career of Margaret Sanger*, 42, 45. Some of the pioneers who came from Britain may have been imbued with birth control ideas early in life. See, for example, Angus McLaren, "Contraception and the Working Classes: The Social Ideology of the English Birth Control Movement in its Early Years," *Comp. Studies in Soc. and Hist.*, XVIII, pp. 236-51.

[117]A study of the 1950 census data indicated that the age of the mother influenced the likelihood of exclusion, the exclusion being greater for children whose mothers were under twenty-five than for those whose mothers were over twenty-five. John B. Sharpless and Ray M. Shortridge, "Biased Underenumeration in Census Manuscripts: Methodological Implications," *Jour. of Urban Hist.*, I, p. 413. A similar relationship between the ages of mothers and underenumeration may have existed during the early 1800s, the relatively youthful ages of many pioneer women resulting in some undercounting of children.

from third position in 1800 to first in 1840, a steep climb. (Approximately 10% of the household units in the northern back country in 1840 were composed of adult couples and just one child.) By 1840 units containing either three or four offspring faded completely from the ranks of the three most common household compositions. Rather surprisingly, units with three children were the most common unit by 1830. This is somewhat surprising because of the fact that the age groupings in the censuses, and therefore this study's definition of what constituted a child, changed between 1820 and 1830 (see Table 11). The three leading units of 1830 were those of 1800, although the order was somewhat scrambled.

The most popular trio of household units was two adults with one, two, or three children. This trio cropped up in 1800, 1820, and 1830. For all years, the most common three units formed approximately 31.3% of the total number of households in 1800, less than 28% in 1810, under 27% thereafter.[118] The passage of time ushered into the frontier an increasing variety of household size and composition. This may reflect the change in occupational characteristics, and accompanying changes in the structure and complexity of society, occuring in the northern wilds over the decades, a phenomenon which will be examined in detail in Chapter VII, "Occupations."

According to the hypotheses, dissimilarities in household sizes and compositions between the new lands and the northern settled section should have occurred over the years. The opposite was generally true. Most of the measurements pertaining to the seven tables of households consisting of from two to eight members showed pronounced signs of convergence by 1840, the greatest surge of which occurred in the 1830s. Concerning the three most prevalent household compositions in the northern wilderness and in the Northeast, there appears to be no definite sign of divergence and there are some signs of convergence. In short, this evidence failed to support the hypothesis that predicted divergence between pioneer households and households in the East.

SUMMARY AND CONCLUSION

An examination of the data for the northern frontier and the northern settled area yields several conclusions:

1. Most of the hypotheses were supported most of the time.
2. Some of the differences—such as some dealing with average household size, huge households, the people who lived in huge

---

[118]In late colonial Bristol, Rhode Island, "Households of four, five, and six persons were most common, comprising almost half of the total sample, though there were many units both smaller and larger." And "Nearly half of the families listed had one, two, or three children." Demos, "Families in Colonial Bristol, Rhode Island," pp. 44-45.

households, the percentage of total households containing two to eight people, and the three most common units—were negligible.

3. Some differences, including that of average household size, were the opposite of what was hypothesized.

4. Where hypothesized differences did exist, they tended to fade by 1840 as the northern frontier acquired, during the 1830s, some of the demographic traits possessed by the northern settled area.

Aside from some surprises, then, most of the hypotheses were given at least limited support, and some received substantial support. The various combinations of forces operating on the frontier and in the settled areas further to the east produced over the decades demographic conditions among the pioneer households which were in some aspects markedly different from conditions further to the east and in other aspects remarkably similar. Evidently, the demographic characteristics of households entering the frontier were not radically transformed by the settlement processes. Household size and composition remained fairly intact.[119]

---

[119]Of such recent publication that it cannot be included in this work in an organic manner is a highly pertinent work of considerable importance: Don R. Leet, "The Determinants of the Fertility Transition in Antebellum, Ohio," *Journal of Economic History*, xxxvi, pp. 359-378. This work demonstrates that economic conditions created by the availability of land and cultural conditions generated by the traits of settlers were paramount in determining fertility levels and changes in the levels. This work should be read in conjunction with Chapters II through V.

TABLE 1.—Average Sizes of Households, 1800-1840[a]

	1800	1810	1820	1830	1840
Northern Frontier	5.4	5.9	6.1	6.3	5.6
Northern Settled Section	5.6	5.9	6.1	5.9	5.7
Southern Frontier			5.7	6.0	6.3
Southern Settled Section	5.3	5.0	5.8	5.7	5.6

[a]The data for these tables were obtained from federal manuscript censuses. Unfortunately, few manuscript censuses for the counties comprising the early southern frontier are in existence, and the data for these counties were incomplete. Accordingly, reference to the size and composition of households on the southern frontiers of 1800 and 1810 was omitted.

TABLE 2.—Modal Sizes of Households, 1800-1840

	1800	1810	1820	1830	1840
Northern Frontier	4	4	4	5	4
Northern Settled Section	5	6	5	4	5
Southern Frontier			4	6	4
Southern Settled Section	4	4	4	6	5

TABLE 3.—Households of Eleven or More People as Percentages of All Households

	1800	1810	1820	1830	1840
Northern Frontier	2	5	8	7	5
Northern Settled Section	3	5	7	8	5
Southern Frontier			6	7	11
Southern Settled Section	4	3	6	6	5

TABLE 4.—Percentages of Total Population Living in Households Containing Eleven or More People

	1800	1810	1820	1830	1840
Northern Frontier	5	11	16	14	11
Northern Settled Section	7	11	13	17	10
Southern Frontier			13	14	22
Southern Settled Section	9	6	13	12	11

TABLE 5.—Percentages of Total Number of Households Consisting of Individuals Living Alone

	1800	1810	1820	1830	1840
Northern Frontier	3	1	2	2	3
Northern Settled Section	2	1	2	3	1
Southern Frontier			6	2	3
Southern Settled Section	6	9	4	4	5

TABLE 6.—Percentages of Households from which an Adult Is Missing[b]

	1800	1810	1820	1830	1840
Northern Frontier	3	2	4	5	3
Northern Settled Section	5	4	6	5	4
Southern Frontier			5	4	4
Southern Settled Section	11	8	9	14	9

bSee n. 11, Chapter II.

TABLE 7.—Males as Percentages of Missing Adults

	1800	1810	1820	1830	1840
Northern Frontier	34	67	53	62	47
Northern Settled Section	75	80	72	98	84
Southern Frontier			55	66	62
Southern Settled Section	55	68	72	76	84

TABLE 8.—Percentages of Total Households Containing Two To Eight Members

	1800	1810	1820	1830	1840
Northern Frontier	86	81	75	77	83
Northern Settled Section	83	82	76	76	84
Southern Frontier			76	79	75
Southern Settled Section	81	70	79	79	79

TABLE 9.—Percentages of Households in Which No Child Was Present

	1800	1810	1820	1830	1840
Northern Frontier	13	12	15	14	19
Northern Settled Section	16	19	21	18	18
Southern Frontier			15	15	16
Southern Settled Section	16	24	16	21	22

TABLE 10.—Percentages of Households with Just One Child

	1800	1810	1820	1830	1840
Northern Frontier	18	20	18	18	22
Northern Settled Section	22	21	22	26	24
Southern Frontier			19	18	20
Southern Settled Section	22	20	22	22	20

TABLE 11.—Percentages of Members under Fifteen or Sixteen Who Are Only Children Presently Living at Home[c]

	1800	1810	1820	1830	1840
Northern Frontier	7	8	7	7	10
Northern Settled Section	10	10	10	12	12
Southern Frontier			8	7	8
Southern Settled Section	10	10	9	10	10

[c]Through 1820 the breaking point in the federal censuses was at age sixteen. For 1830 and 1840 the breaking point was at age fifteen.

TABLE 12.—Percentages of Households in Which Children Constitute at Least One-Half of the Household

	1800	1810	1820	1830	1840
Northern Frontier	60	59	60	55	44
Northern Settled Section	51	46	45	43	45
Southern Frontier			57	57	53
Southern Settled Section	51	50	48	45	48

TABLE 13.—Percentages of Total Population Living in Households in Which Children Constitute at Least One-Half of the Household

	1800	1810	1820	1830	1840
Northern Frontier	69	67	69	62	51
Northern Settled Section	60	52	52	51	53
Southern Frontier			66	66	61
Southern Settled Section	58	57	55	54	58

TABLE 14.—Percentage of Total Children Living in Households in Which Children Constitute at Least One-Half of the Household

	1800	1810	1820	1830	1840
Northern Frontier	85	83	86	80	72
Northern Settled Section	79	74	77	74	78
Southern Frontier			83	83	83
Southern Settled Section	78	81	76	77	87

TABLE 15.—Adult-Child Compositions of the Three Most Prevalent
Households and the Percentages of Total Households
Represented by These Households

	Three Most Prevalent Household Compositions			Percentages of Total Households		
1800						
Northern Frontier	2-2,	2-3,	2-1	11.3,	10.2,	9.8
Northern Settled Section	2-1,	2-2,	2-3	10.0,	8.0,	7.5
Southern Frontier						
Southern Settled Section	2-2,	2-1,	2-3	7.8,	7.6,	7.1
1810						
Northern Frontier	2-2,	2-1,	2-4	10.0,	9.4,	8.3
Northern Settled Section	2-1,	2-3,	2-0	7.4,	7.3,	6.9
Southern Frontier						
Southern Settled Section	2-2,	2-0,	2-1	8.1,	8.0,	7.1
1820						
Northern Frontier	2-2,	2-3,	2-1	9.4,	9.2,	8.1
Northern Settled Section	2-0,	2-2,	2-3	7.6,	6.8,	6.2
Southern Frontier	2-2,	2-1,	2-0	9.5,	8.8,	7.6
Southern Settled Section	2-1,	2-2,	2-0	8.5,	7.1,	6.5
1830						
Northern Frontier	2-3,	2-1,	2-2	8.8,	8.4,	7.9
Northern Settled Section	2-1,	2-0,	2-2	8.9,	6.9,	6.8
Southern Frontier	2-1,	2-2,	2-0	8.4,	7.9,	7.8
Southern Settled Section	2-0,	2-1,	2-3/4 (tie)	8.4,	7.1,	5.4
1840						
Northern Frontier	2-1,	2-0,	2-2	10.0,	8.8,	7.7
Northern Settled Section	2-3,	2-1,	2-0	8.9,	8.7,	8.2
Southern Frontier	2-2,	2-1,	2-4	8.8,	7.8,	6.9
Southern Settled Section	2-0,	2-1,	2-3	8.6,	7.3,	6.6

TABLE 16.—Sex of White Age Groups as Percentages of Total White Population in Various Sections of the Nation[a]

Decade and Section	0-9 M	0-9 F	10-15 M	10-15 F	16-25 M	16-25 F	26-44 M	26-44 F	45+ M	45+ F
1800										
Northern Frontier	19	18	8	7	10	8	12	10	5	7
Northern Settled	16	16	8	8	9	9	10	10	7	7
Southern Frontier	21	20	8	8	9	8	10	8	5	4
Southern Settled	17	16	8	8	10	10	11	10	6	6
1810										
Northern Frontier	20	19	8	7	9	8	11	9	5	4
Northern Settled	16	15	8	8	10	10	10	10	7	7
Southern Frontier	21	20	8	7	9	9	10	8	4	3
Southern Settled	17	16	8	8	10	10	10	10	6	6
1820										
Northern Frontier	20	18	8	7	11	9	10	8	5	3
Northern Settled	17	16	8	8	10	10	10	10	6	6
Southern Frontier	20	18	8	8	11	10	10	8	5	4
Southern Settled	17	16	8	8	10	10	10	10	6	6
1830										
Northern Frontier	21	19	6	6	14	13	8	7	3	2
Northern Settled	15	15	6	6	15	15	9	9	5	5
Southern Frontier	20	19	6	6	14	13	9	7	3	2
Southern Settled	16	16	6	6	15	15	9	9	4	4
1840										
Northern Frontier	17	16	6	5	18	13	12	8	3	2
Northern Settled	15	14	6	6	15	15	10	10	5	5
Southern Frontier	21	19	7	6	14	13	9	7	3	2
Southern Settled	16	15	6	6	15	15	10	9	4	4

[a]From 1800 through 1820 the age categories were 0-9, 10-15, 16-25, 26-44, and 45 and above. In 1830 this changed to 0-9, 10-14, 15-29, 31-49, and 50 and over.

Due to the fact that the above percentages were rounded off, some of the totals do not equal 100 per cent.

TABLE 17.—Percentages of Whites Living in Various Sections of the Nation Who Are Male

Decade and Section	0-9	10-15	16-25	26-44	45+
1800					
Northern Frontier	51.8	55.2	54.2	55.4	55.8
Northern Settled	50.9	51.3	48.8	49.6	49.5
Southern Frontier	51.4	51.8	52.2	53.5	55.9
Southern Settled	51.4	50.6	47.9	51.6	50.7
1810					
Northern Frontier	51.4	53.2	51.9	54.9	57.1
Northern Settled	51.0	50.5	48.5	51.6	50.7
Southern Frontier	51.7	51.7	49.9	55.2	56.4
Southern Settled	51.4	50.5	48.5	51.6	50.7
1820					
Northern Frontier	52.2	51.8	53.8	56.4	58.8
Northern Settled	52.6	50.1	49.3	49.2	49.1
Southern Frontier	53.4	51.1	53.2	56.4	58.8
Southern Settled	51.5	49.7	49.0	50.6	51.6
1830					
Northern Frontier	51.7	52.3	50.9	54.7	57.1
Northern Settled	51.0	51.0	49.8	50.1	48.6
Southern Frontier	51.8	52.1	52.6	56.9	57.5
Southern Settled	51.2	50.9	50.2	51.5	50.1
1840					
Northern Frontier	52.4	52.0	57.5	60.2	58.0
Northern Settled	50.9	51.1	49.7	51.2	49.0
Southern Frontier	52.5	51.4	52.2	56.9	58.9
Southern Settled	51.4	50.8	50.2	52.5	49.8

An American Log-House
It did not take much land to enable a
large household to do rather well.
Courtesy, Illinois State Historical Library

CHAPTER III

Household Size and Composition: The South

In the beginning of the last chapter a number of reasons for studying the sizes and compositions of households on the northern frontier were given. These reasons are equally valid for the households on the southern frontier. Most of the conclusions, guesses, calculations, surmises, and conjectures made concerning the pioneer household on the northern frontier apply to the southern frontier as well. Accordingly, the hypotheses used in comparing the northern frontier to the northern settled area were used to compare the southern frontier to the southern settled area.

HOUSEHOLD SIZE

The demographic data pertaining to the southern wilderness and the settled regions of the South generally lent support to the hypotheses. Moreover, the support was usually quite strong and widespread, producing relatively few real surprises. With the exception of 1820, during which time the disparity was hardly noticeable, the average size of households in the southern back country was larger than the size of households in the Southeast (see Table 1).[1] Modal size was another matter (see Table 2). At no time was the hypothesis concerning modal size supported, and in 1840 the evidence yielded the opposite of what was expected.

Apparently, several basic factors conspired to produce in the fresh lands of the South substantially larger average household sizes than in the southern settled section. For one thing, as was the case on the northern frontier, large units often lived relatively easily in the Dixie frontier. It was possible to have large families without dire consequences. As was the case with northern settlers, southern settlers raised much of their own food supply and produced many of their household necessities from materials at

---

[1]Again, in this study blacks, free and slave, living with white households were not counted as members of the households. The decision not to count blacks as members rests heavily on the fact that the amount of freedom enjoyed by blacks was severely restricted, making their responses to the western experience necessarily and fundamentally different from those of the whites.

hand, accomplishments not always possible further east. Someone whose house overlooked Charleston harbor or was within walking distance of the state capitol in Richmond had little chance of being self-sufficient. A high degree of self-sufficiency was unlikely for people living in small towns and villages in the East. And even for those who lived in the eastern farming regions of Virginia and South Carolina, areas in which most of the land was privately owned and where timber and other natural resources were not free, a high degree of self-sufficiency was all but impossible. As a result, many easterners who either had a large household, were beginning one, or wanted one could remove themselves to the southern wilds and there solve many of the fundamental physical and economic problems associated with large households. There is evidence that it did not take much western land to enable a large household to do rather well. In 1807, for example, Fortescue Cuming passed down the Ohio River and landed in Kentucky just downstream from Portsmouth, Ohio. There he found a man by the name of Colgin, an Irishman, who had a wife and seven children, all born in the past "several years." Colgin had "only eight acres cleared, on which he maintains himself, his wife, and seven children, who are all and even becomingly drest [sic]."[2]

Not only did the fresh soil in the South support large units, it also attracted them. Between 1822 and 1824, to illustrate the fact, Silas Drake, his wife, and his seven children moved into Marion County, Mississippi, a frontier county in 1820.[3] The Philip Sublette family, to cite another example, numbered nine and came from Lincoln County, Kentucky. In 1818 it pushed to the frontier region north of St. Louis, Missouri.[4] In like manner, the Morse household, numbering eight or ten, migrated from Tennessee to near the Little Red River in Arkansas.[5] In early 1821 Benjamin Crowley of Kentucky was content, sixty-three, father of eight (three young girls and five unmarried sons under twenty-five), and a slaveowner. The family migrated westward, for some unknown reason, to a site just north of present-day Walcott, Arkansas. By Christmas Day, 1821, the family was comfortably situated in a new home.[6]

Another factor may explain why the southern wilderness attracted and produced relatively large households. The southern backwoods, as will be demonstrated in Chapter VII, "Occupations," was initially more agrarian then the northern backwoods, and it retained its agrarian nature longer

---

[2]Fortescue Cuming, *Sketches of a Tour to the Western Country, through the States of Ohio and Kentucky; A Voyage down the Ohio and Mississippi Rivers, and A Trip through the Mississippi Territory, and part of West Florida*, Vol. IV of *Early Western Travels*, p. 163.

[3]Louisa D. Enloe, "Silas Drake of Marion County, Mississippi, and His Descendants," *Jour. of Mississippi Hist.*, XXVII, p. 272.

[4]Doyce B. Nunis, Jr., "The Sublettes of Kentucky: Their Early Contribution to the Opening of the West," *Register of the Ky. Hist. Soc.*, LVII, p. 21.

[5]George W. Featherstonhaugh, *Excursion Through the Slave States*, II, p. 33.

[6]Vivian Hansbrough, "The Crowleys of Crowley's Ridge," *Ark. Hist. Qtly.*, XIII, pp. 52-53.

than the northern wilderness. Some large households were tempted to trek to a place where they could grow most of what they needed. The southern forests and fields encouraged the presence of sizeable households by supporting great numbers of hogs, and the rural features of the southern frontier lingered long after the northern frontier began to loose its rural nature.

By most standards of measurement, the southern wilderness was the most rural section of the nation during the first part of the nineteenth century. Due to this overwhelming rural nature, accompanying primitive characteristics, and associated isolation, sizeable households in the southern wilds may have been for some a necessity. This necessity was evidently absent from the northern frontier, which over the decades contained a large non-agrarian population and which was in constant contact with the East by the 1820s. Compared to his northern counterpart, the southern pioneer possibly needed more manual labor in order to do well.

By 1840 the northern woods and prairies began to feel the effects of labor-saving machinery.[7] Few pieces of such machinery, evidence suggests, made their way to the southern settler. Several reasons may account for this. By 1840, the southern frontier consisted of some rather rugged countryside, including southern Missouri and northwestern Arkansas. This reduced the potential for the effective use of machinery. Secondly, the distances from the factories producing the machinery to the southern frontier were greater than those from the factories to the new lands of the North, a fact which possibly discouraged the widespread use of machinery on the edge of southern settlement. Furthermore, the southern backwoodsmen evidently lagged behind his northern counterpart in income, education, and perhaps the desire to adopt agricultural improvements. In short, certain economic and social thresholds necessary for the successful introduction of machinery apparently were not met by 1840. As a consequence, the southern pioneer was probably in no position—physically, economically, or socially—to make use of the era's available machinery, however primitive the machinery or restricted its use. From all appearances, the southern settler valued manual labor, and the size of the pioneer household may be a partial reflection of this valuation.

Another factor probably contributed to relatively large households in the southern backwoods: white southerners, unlike white northerners, tended to migrate in households rather than in groups. In the South "people more generally moved westward as individuals or single families *without concerted action* either in moving or in choosing a place for settlement."[8] This stood in sharp contrast to the migratory habits of vast numbers of

---

[7]Milo M. Quaife, ed., *Fifty Years in Iowa: Being the Personal Reminiscences of J. M. D. Burrows,* p. 171.

[8]Dan Clark, *op. cit.,* pp. 176-77. For similar evidence, see the previous chapter. Italics added.

northerners. Group migration and the wholesale transplantation of communities from the Southeast to the southern backwoods were rare occurrences. Perhaps this merely reflected southern individualism, suspicion of the efforts of special-interest groups, or lack of cohesion and mission in southern society. Regardless of the reasons, southerners rarely banded together before shoving off into the western lands, a fact which probably mitigated against small households migrating.

Some westward-bound groups in the South were composed in part of slaves. It appears that slaves were ushered into the Southwest in two ways: either as part of gangs being driven to the site of a new plantation or some other enterprise, or as part of a group headed by a white household. In either case, migrating southerners seldom welcomed strangers into their groups or gangs. Perhaps those who were trying to herd slaves into the wilderness had enough difficulty without inviting more by including in their midst someone who was a crypto-abolitionist. Slave-owners wanted tranquility to prevail in the migratory parties. The northern willingness to include all types of people in migrating parties, even perfect strangers, was not duplicated among southern households moving west with slaves.

Perhaps somewhat typical of the large-scale slaveowners who trudged westward was the Lide family of Darlington County, South Carolina. In the fall of 1835 James Lide, age sixty-five, his wife, six of their twelve children, an overseer, and a number of slaves who were chiefly house servants moved from South Carolina to a point forty miles southwest of Birmingham, Alabama. Under the direction of an overseer, a large gang of field slaves had blazed the trail earlier, making needed preparations at the site. Three other white families tagged along behind the Lides, keeping within sight but not forming part of the group.[9]

Other slaveowning families made the journey into Alabama. In 1820, for example, the Taylor family, consisting of the mother and father and four children, left Georgia with their slaves and entered the Alabama frontier.[10] Leonard Covington moved from Maryland to Mississippi in 1809. Five or six of his slaves accompanied Covington on the trip, the main force having made the trip earlier under the supervision of several white men. All told, Covington transferred thirty-one slaves to Mississippi and, since he was unable to sell his plantation in Maryland, he had to leave twenty-five there under the direction of an overseer. (Those slaves entering the frontier were, interestingly enough, an average of five years younger than those who remained in Maryland.)[11] Another slave-owning household pushing into the rich lands of the Southwest was headed by the Rev. and Mrs. John

[9]Fletcher M. Green, ed., *The Lides Go South . . . and West: The Record of a Planter Migration in 1835*, pp. iv-vi.

[10]The Taylor migration to Alabama and several other acts of migration are found in Dick, *op. cit.*, pp. 59-60.

[11]Charles Sydnor, *Slavery in Mississippi*, p. 145.

Owen. They, their two children, and several slaves left their home in Norfolk County, Virginia, on October 24, 1818, and proceeded to Alabama. Had it not been for the presence of the slaves, the sundry mishaps sustained along the way by the family might have prevented their safe arrival in Alabama. They did make it, however, and he became a prominent planter at Tuscaloosa.[12]

The presence of able-bodied labor somewhat vitiated the need for slave-owning households to combine with other white households to facilitate travel. In effect, slave assistance served as surrogate groups, aiding the Lides, Taylors, Covingtons, Owens, and other households in the same manner as the presence of groups served northern migrants, providing security and encouragement to some household units which might otherwise have poked into the new lands only under great duress. Rather than combining into groups, many white southerners relied upon slave aid or struck into the wilderness in individual households, actions which probably screened some non-slaveowners from moving west: old people, female households, the weak, and households with a horde of dependent children. In addition, quite likely small households and individual migrants were screened, an action which possibly contributed to the relatively large average household size on the Dixie frontier. The modes of migration appear to have both reflected and influenced southern thinking concerning the nature of society, the future course of society, public responsibility, collective undertakings, the idea of community, and the idea of mission. The same was true with northern modes of migration. In short, the availability of large numbers of involuntary migrants altered both the demography and dynamics of southern migration and the totality of the southern frontier experience.

The establishment of a slave society in the fresh lands probably affected the southern pioneer household in yet another way. That social stratification was greater in the South than in the North is undeniable, especially with regard to the frontiers of each section.[13] The implications of this are impressive: "the greater the degree of social stratification in a society, the greater the degree for the extended, rather than the

---

[12]Dick, op. cit., pp. 61-62. Other instances of slave-owning households pushing west either with slaves or in the wake of an advanced party of slaves, or both, are numerous. See, for example, John Anthony Caruso, The Southern Frontier, p. 341, and Thomas Perkins Abernethy, The Formative Period in Alabama, 1815-1828, p. 36. Logic dictates that "The movement of large slave coffles, with the establishment of big western plantations, was not common until after the War of 1812." Riegel and Athearn, op. cit., p. 118. It was only with the conclusion of the war that the Indians of the Old Southwest, including the Creek, were negated as a real and perceived threat, making the rich earth of Mississippi and Alabama inviting.

[13]Stanley Elkins and Eric McKitrick, "A Meaning for Turner's Frontier, Part II: Democracy in the Old Northwest," Pol. Sci. Qly., LXIX, pp. 567-69, 577.

independent family system to be established." The extended family is designed to protect property.[14] Relatively great social stratification in the South, then, encouraged some southern settlers to live in large households, albeit neither the average size nor the modal size being more than slightly larger than northern household units.

Added to this is the fact that the northern frontier came to enjoy over the years better and more varied transportation systems than the southern frontier, a fact mentioned earlier and also stressed in Chapter VII, "Occupations." Migrants to places such as northern Illinois often used roads, trains, canals, and steamboats for all or part of their westward journeys. These systems sometimes overlapped each other, giving the traveler options. Such systems were available only in relatively few areas of the South. Unlike its northern counterpart, southern transportation did little to encourage couples with two or three small children, elderly couples without children, and other small households to seek a new home in the Southwest. This is probably all the more true if such marginal units were unable to join a group heading west or if the units had no slaves and were therefore typical of the majority of southern whites. By the 1820s it was considerably easier for a small household to travel alone from central New York to western Michigan than to travel from western North Carolina to Arkansas.

Custom and law on the southern frontier did nothing to impede the creation of large households. Couples, failing to find a clergymen or a magistrate, simply lived together and got around to formal marriage at their convenience. Others wanting to be married found unusual types to perform the ceremony. For example, in 1816 Jonathon York and Josiah Tilley, first settlers of Tuscaloosa, Alabama, were married to two daughters of Patrick Scott. There were no clerical or civil officials to be found, so a blacksmith, John Barton, forged the links between the couples, "a frontier style of marriage not uncommon in those heroic days" in the wilderness.[15] Those who wanted to be together managed to get together, one way or another. Undoubtedly, the product of such pairings was children who probably arrived rather quickly.

Large households were also encouraged by some of the regulations pertaining to the disposal of land. Illustrative of this is the headright system of land grants, a system which operated in parts of Georgia. Under this system the head of every household was granted two hundred acres of land, and each member of his household was granted fifty. Slaves were

---

[14]Meyer Nimkoff, ed., Comparative Family Systems, pp. 37-38.

[15]Thomas McCorvey, Alabama Historical Sketches, p. 97. Well before the War of 1812, settlers in the South complained that there were not enough ministers available to perform needed marriage ceremonies. As a result, people entered into marriage arrangements without the sanction of law or benefit of clergy. Otis K. Rice, The Allegheny Frontier, 1730-1830, p. 188.

actually counted as part of the household.[16] No imagination is required to realize that those coveting much land found it in their interests to pack their households with adults of all descriptions. (Yet paradoxically the northern frontier generally had a larger proportion of adults among its population than the southern frontier.) The extent to which laws and customs in the fresh lands of the South encouraged large households is unclear, but it is possible that the encouragement was far from negligible. Moreover, the headright system undoubtedly altered the racial composition of the frontier somewhat, persuading slaveowners to bring slaves to the edge of civilization and tempting non-slaveowners to purchase some.

Several factors which promoted the growth of large households in the northern wilderness also encouraged a similar growth in the southern wilderness. The phenomenon of early and continuous marriage was not confined to the northern wilderness. If anything, in fact, marriages in the South very likely occurred on the average earlier than in the North.[17] This may have helped to make the South, including the southern wilds, home to relatively more large household units than the North, including the northern frontier. Another factor common to both frontiers which tended to increase household size was the fact that even in the slaveowning part of the American frontier some white hired help was employed by pioneers, and such help very often lived with the frontier family. In addition, widows, with or without children, very often remarried, thereby effecting a merger which sometimes involved two sizeable sets of children.

Clearly, some of the economic, social, political, and physical factors working to increase the size of the household in the southern wilds were identical, or very nearly so, to forces in the northern wilds. Other factors, especially those pertaining to racial slavery and transportation, appear to be largely regional in nature. Whatever the origin of the factors and whatever their influence, it is clear that household demography in the southern backwoods was no mere extension of household demography in the southern settled area. The incomplete data for the southern frontiers of 1800 and 1810 notwithstanding, the southern wilderness generally contained more larger units than the northern frontier. (Surprisingly, however, the average size was a bit smaller.) For some reason, as the

---

[16]Ralph Flanders, *Plantation Slavery in Georgia*, p. 61. During 1827 the state of Georgia divided, by lottery, land between the Chatahoochie and Flint rivers recently secured from the Creek Indians. One eyewitness wrote, "Every citizen 21 years of age has one draw, as it is called, a married man two draws, a married man with a family three." Basil Hall, *Travels in North America in the Years 1827 and 1828*, III, p. 281. This system very possibly encouraged people to get married, or start a family, or borrow a child, or in some other way to augment household size.

[17]Martineau, *op. cit.*, III, p. 120. The custom of early marriage in the South, especially in the Old Southwest, may have led to today's state laws concerning marriage there, laws which permit boys and especially girls to marry at an earlier age than youngsters in the North.

southern household moved into and settled the new lands of the South, there was generally an increase in household size; the opposite was generally the case in the North. The reasons for these strange occurrences may have involved any one or any combination of a set of factors: the types of households making the trek, the nature of the journeys, industrialization and urbanization in the Northeast, racial slavery, social stratification in the South, the presence of plantation agriculture, laws and customs, the physical characteristics of the land, ideas concerning society and goals, and perceptions and fears and hopes. Some of the influencing factors may have been present on just one frontier; others may have been present on both. In addition, the relative strengths of each factor undoubtedly fluctuated over the decades.

Although household sizes in the southern backwoods were larger than those further to the east, several factors militated against very sizeable households in the backwoods. Dixie, too, had its share of trailblazers, people—usually men—who lived in small households on the frontier while they found and improved the site of the new homes: "like the children of Israel they sent their Calebs and Joshuas ahead to spy out the land and prepare the way."[18] Among those contemplating removal to the fresh soil of Missouri, "Some families, perhaps a little skeptical of this Canaan, sent a member ahead to spy out the land."[19]

Exceptions aside, trailblazing by just one person was probably rare. In 1804 or 1805 John Hunt scouted out the land in present-day Huntsville, Alabama, and later brought his family to the site.[20] In early 1817, James A. Tait, accompanied by his brother-in-law and father-in-law, came to Alabama from Georgia in order to select a likely place of settlement for Tait's father, Charles Tait. The next year James Tait returned to Alabama with some slaves—and possibly some neighbors from Georgia—and squatted on the public domain.[21] Two additional trailblazers, perhaps quite typical, were Joseph and Isaac Criner, brothers, who arrived at Huntsville, Alabama, in 1805 and built two cabins, one for Joseph and his family and one for Isaac.[22] Most trailblazing evidently lasted only a year, or even just several months, but for John C. Benedict it was something of an odyssey. In 1811 he left his family near Platton Creek in the Territory of Missouri and with William, David, and John Standlee, in-laws, pushed into Arkansas for

[18]Frank L. Owsley, *Plain Folk of the Old South*, p. 63.

[19]Marie George Windell, ed., "Westward Along the Boone's Lick Trail in 1826, the Diary of Colonel John Glover," *Missouri Hist. Rev.*, XXXIX, p. 185. Evidently, slaveowners, especially, were reluctant to plunge into the unknown of the southern wilds without first sending someone to reconnoiter the way. See, for example, Lewis Atherton, ed., "Life, Labor and Society in Boone County, Missouri, 1834-52, as Revealed in Correspondence of an Immigrant Slave Owning Family from North Carolina, Part 1," *Missouri Hist. Rev.*, XXXVIII, p. 282.

[20]Edward Chambers Betts, *Early History of Huntsville, Alabama, 1804 to 1870*, pp. 6-7.

[21]Owsley, *op. cit.*, pp. 64-66.

[22]Betts, *op. cit.*, p. 6.

two years of scouting and preparation before returning to his family. Several years later he, his wife, five children, and two Scotsmen left for Arkansas.[23]

Successful or not, trailblazing in the South usually placed a small party of strong men in the vanguard of the settlement process, men who selected a site, made some improvements, and returned for their families or sent for them. (The evidence is highly impressionistic, but it appears that trailblazers in the North more often *sent for* their families than did southern Trailblazers. If so, such differences possibly stemmed from better and more varied transportation leading into the northern wilderness compared to what was available in the South.) Prolonged trailblazing placed small groups of people on the frontier, groups which appeared in the censuses as small households; the net effect was to lower the average size of the backwoods household in the South.

Moreover, despite the fact that northerners practiced group migration more than southerners, some southern migrants did make use of the group to smooth the road leading west. In the more settled sections of the South, "friends and relatives in the same or neighboring communities formed one or more parties and moved out together."[24] For example, when John Murrell, his wife, and their six children left Horse Shoe bend on the Cumberland River in Tennessee in early 1818 for northwest Louisiana, they traveled with ten other households.[25] This act of group migration certainly lightened the loads of those involved, adding security and permitting some specialization of labor.

Group migration was practiced in the South as late as the 1830s. Sometime between 1833 and 1839 a large wagon train threaded its way from Alabama to Arkansas. It was led by Robert Black, the eldest son of Isabella Johnson Black, a widowed mother of many children. Isabella, her children, some of her grandchildren, other Blacks, and the Perrys, Wallaces, Rayfords, Connors, Mumfords, Davises, and Thomas Williams, William Carter, and Sanders Norris joined the train, such size and possible variety undoubtedly adding to its success.[26] Certainly some "early communities of the newer states and territories [in the South] were often transplanted

---

[23]Ted R. Worley, ed., "Story of an Early Settlement in Central Arkansas,"*Ark. Hist. Qtly.,* x, pp. 121-23. See also Francois A. Michaux, *Travels to the West of the Alleghany [sic] Mountains, in the States of Ohio, Kentucky, and Tennessee [sic] and back to Charleston, by the Upper Carolines ... undertaken in the Year 1802,* Vol. III of *Early Western Travels,* p. 215.

Sometimes trailblazing was counter-productive and ended in woe. In early 1816 Valentine Mayo left his family in Tennessee and explored part of Arkansas for a while in search of a new home. When he returned to Tennessee in 1817, he found that his family had vanished. All that he could learn was that "they had gone north." Walter H. Ryle, "A Study of Early Days in Randolph County, 1818-1860," *Missouri Historical Review,* xxiv, p. 218.

[24]Owsley, *op. cit.,* p. 62.

[25]Glenn Martel, "Early Days in Northwest Louisiana," *Ark. Hist. Qtly.,* xii, pp. 120-21.

[26]Annie L. Spencer, "The Blacks of Union County," *Ark. Hist. Qtly.,* xii, p. 233.

organisms rather than synthetic bodies" and "such transplantations were greatly facilitated by the institution of group travel."[27] Despite some evidence indicating that group migration in the South was relatively rare, some marginal households in the South (including small households) poked into the wilderness under the auspices and protection of groups. Whether southern groups, upon arrival in the Garden, remained as intact and functioned as long and as well as northern groups is highly debatable, however.

The very pronounced rural nature of the southern frontier also restricted the size of household units. The southern backwoods was overwhelmingly agrarian through 1840 and, while this made it possible for large households to achieve economic security, they were not prerequisite to success there. In fact, nearly everyone wanted to own land—Jefferson's philosophy was pervasive and potent on the frontier—and land was generally available in abundance to whites. As was the case in the northern wilderness, hired help and maturing sons were not overly eager to linger on someone else's farm when land was often available just across the next ridge. Consequently, households often broke into fragments in order to acquire as much land as could be cleared and farmed effectively.

Yet compared to the southern settled areas, the southern frontier contained relatively more very large households, the differences increasing over the years (see Table 3). From 1820 through 1840 the wilderness acquired proportionately more of these household units, the southern settled area proportionately fewer. Paralleling this trend were the trends in the percentages of people in the pioneer Southwest who lived in these large units as compared to the percentages found in the settled areas (see Table 4). On a comparative basis, the southern back country clearly contained more households of at least eleven people in size and more people living in such units than the settled regions lying eastward. This lent considerable support to the original hypothesis concerning household size.

The modal sizes of households in the southern wilds were no larger than those further to the east. Apparently, then, the westward transfer of comparatively few large household units helped create in the wilds average sizes larger than those in the settled sections. That the migration of a handful of huge households could have had an enormous impact on frontier demography is apparent in the census of 1820, for example, where households containing eleven or more people constituted only 6% of the total number of households, but 13% of all settlers lived in such household units (see Tables 3 and 4). Nearly all demographic measurements of the frontier were affected greatly by the addition of a few large households from the settled area. Not only did the frontier gain such units, but the

---

[27]Owsley, op. cit., p. 63. See also Frank L. Owsley, "The Pattern of Migration and Settlement on the Southern Frontier," Jour. of So. Hist., XI, p. 171.

settled area lost them, except in rare instances of immigration from Europe. The statistical effect of such movement of large households from settled to frontier regions is obvious.

SINGLE PEOPLE

According to the hypothesis, the new lands of the South would contain relatively more units consisting of individuals living alone than the southern settled area. This was the case only once, in 1820. The hypothesis was thereby refuted (see Table 5). Instances of true loners living on the southern frontier are plentiful compared to the northern frontier and rare compared to the southern settled section. One loner was S. E. Catterlin. Born in Ohio in 1810, he ventured at the age of eighteen to Marengo County, Alabama, and married in 1831.[28] As was the case in the northern wilds, some individuals concealed themselves, in a sense, by living with others of the same sex. The four Wyley brothers, living near Cadron Creek on the Arkansas River in Arkansas, illustrate the point. They lived as simply as the Indians, had no knowledge of books, "were as wonderfully ignorant and as full of superstition as their feeble minds were capeable [sic] of" but were also completely honest and friendly.[29]

There are numerous other instances of brothers and others living together on the southern frontier, possibly comprising several per cent of the population on the cutting edge of civilization,[30] some of whom irritated ordinary settlers. Along the Natchez Trace and elsewhere packs of thieves and cut-throats loitered, waiting for an opportunity to waylay the unsuspecting traveler. These men and others who lived with them were not true loners, however, and at no time did true loners ever constitute more than 6% of the total number of households on the southern frontier.

INCOMPLETE HOUSEHOLDS

The southern backwoods, it was expected, would contain proportionately fewer households from which an adult was missing than the more thoroughly settled areas eastward. This was always the case. (The relative number of such incomplete units in the wilds exceeded one-half that of the settled area only once, in 1820.) The striking differences throughout the years were due largely to the abnormally numerous incomplete units in the southern settled section. That particular region almost always contained at least twice the relative number of households from which an adult was missing than the southern back country or either section in the North. The hypothesized sex of the missing adults in the settled areas was supported by the evidence, males comprising more than 50% every year.

---

[28]Euba Du Bose, "A History of Mount Sterling," *Ala. Hist. Qtly.*, XXV, p. 303.
[29]Worley, *op, cit.*, p. 128.
[30]For example, see *Ibid.*, pp. 126-27.

On the other hand, the hypothesized sex of missing adults in the backwoods was not confirmed; at no time was the majority of the missing pioneer adults female.

Inasmuch as adults were missing from the homes of southern settlers at a rate almost identical with that of the northern frontier, it is not unreasonable to infer that the conditions operating to limit the number of households with missing adults on the southern frontier were either similar to conditions operating in the North or, at least, they were amazingly similar in results. In other words, perhaps some of the conditions described earlier were either present on the southern frontier or were similar in effect to conditions operating in the northern wilds. Remaining something of a mystery are the reasons why there was such a sharp difference between the southern frontier and the southern settled area.

A Close Look at Common Households

The three hypotheses pertaining to households containing from two to eight members were substantially validated by the data found in Tables 9, 10, and 11. The southern frontier did, in fact, boast of fewer households with either one or no child than the southern settled area. The hypotheses concerning households in which children constituted at least one-half the membership was also supported (see Tables 12, 13, 14). In 1840 in the southern settled area the percentage of children living in households where children comprised at least half the membership abruptly surpassed that of the southern wilderness. Over a period of time, the southern wilderness acquired some of the demographic characteristics present in the settled sections of the South. (Of the six tables from 9 through 14, only Table 9 fails to support this contention.) But, as was the case with the two regions in the North, much of this convergence occurred during the 1830s.

As was expected, the three most common pioneer household compositions were usually larger than those found further east, the year 1830 providing the only exception. The second hypothesis concerning such units was substantiated only insofar as the wilderness was concerned: in both the southern back country and the southern settled section, the number of adults included in the three leading units always numbered two (see Table 15). This suggests, once again, that despite the fact that the act of migration was somewhat selective, the journey westward often something of an ordeal, and the contest with the new environment sometimes brutal, the average household emerged from the tribulations in a remarkably "normal" fashion, at least with regard to household size and household composition.

The household composition found most often on the southern frontier was two adults—certainly a married couple in most cases—and two children (see Table 15). The next most prevalent unit was two adults and one child. Both were among the leading three compositions in all three decades, the former occupying first position in 1820 and 1840. The northern frontier contained among its most common units households with either one or two children; perhaps the reasons for such units being on both frontiers are somewhat similar. Regardless of the reasons, however, the piling up of so many small units on the frontier again clearly undrscores the fact that large units were not requisite to success in the wilderness. Also, the leading units in the southern backwoods were approximately the same size as those in the settled area, suggesting that certain influences on the formation of households—perhaps principally economic forces—were rather uniform throughout the South, the forces being not appreciably stronger in one section than in the other. In short, if the household unit adapted itself to changing economic forces by changing its size or composition and if such changes roughly reflected the power of these forces, then possibly such formative forces in the wilds of the South were not unlike those found elsewhere throughout the South.

Couples with no children appeared among the ranks of the leading trio in 1820 and 1830. Households with one child were present on all three occasions. The total size of the leading units remained constant from 1820 through 1830, and then spurted by 1840 with the introduction into the figures of a unit with two adults and four children. The three leading units comprised slightly less than 26% of the units in 1820, slumped to just over 24% in 1830, and slipped uner 24% by 1840. This decline was not paralleled by similar declines in the southern settled area.

There are problems in determining the degree of convergence between the southern frontier and the southern settled area. The fluctuation of the data is quite extreme at times, and few definite patterns are evident in some of the categories. Pronounced signs of divergence are apparent in data concerning average household size, modal size, the percentages of huge households, the percentages of the total population living in them, and the percentages of households consisting of loners. In these instances, the fresh lands became more "frontier" in its demographic traits, and sometimes the settled area became less like the frontier. Divergence was also apparent in the percentages of households in which no child was present. But here the settled area merely acquired, according to the hypotheses, more "settled" characteristics, the frontier moving only slightly in this direction over the years. Convergence, on the other hand, is evident in the trends of the percentages of households with just one child, the percentages of households in which children constituted at least one-half the membership, and the percentages of the total people and the total children who lived in such units. Perhaps time brought overall convergence, but wild gyrations in the trends of the data cast doubt upon firm conclusions concerning either divergence or convergence.

SUMMARY AND CONCLUSIONS

An analysis of the evidence for the southern wilderness and the southern settled area leads to several conclusions:

1. Most of the hypotheses concerning the household size in the South were supported most of the time.
2. Compared to the two regions in the North, the two southern regions had larger differences between them.
3. With the exception of the total number of households formed by individuals living alone, very few of the measurements indicated the opposite of what was hypothesized.
4. A number of the differences, such as those found in the households in which children enjoyed at least numerical parity with adults, faded with the passing of time.
5. Other differences grew more pronounced with time.

Briefly stated, then, the measurements of household size and composition often supported the hypotheses and, although some of the anticipated results failed to materialize, very few surprises emerged.

CHAPTER IV

Household Size and Composition: The North and South Compared

This chapter centers on one hypothesis: compared to northern pioneer households, those in the southern wilderness would display more demographic characteristics commonly thought to be typical of the frontier. According to the hypothesis, the southern woods and clearings should have been the home of relatively many large households, more people living in them, more adults living alone, and more households in which children enjoyed at least numerical parity. A comparison of the two frontiers, however, failed to clearly and persistently indicate that the demographic features of the southern pioneer household were, in fact, more frontier in nature than those of the northern pioneer household. Rather, the data suggest that in several respects the opposite was true, that the pioneer households north of the Mason-Dixon Line were in several important ways more typically frontier in their demographic composition than those south of the line.

Coming as a considerable surprise, the average household size for southern settlers generally failed to exceed that of northern frontiersmen. A bit more consistent with the hypothesis were the results produced by a comparison of the modal sizes, in which the northern frontier households never topped the southern. Even so, the southern modal size was larger only in 1830, the figures for 1820 and 1840 being equal at four members. Added is the fact that the relative number of huge households, those containing eleven, was greater in the southern backwoods only in 1840. (In 1820 the opposite was true, there being more huge households in the northern backwoods). With few exceptions, then, the southern frontier failed to either contain larger households or have a considerably larger proportion of population living in those households.

Several factors may have produced relatively larger households and larger modal sizes on the southern frontier, however slight the differences. Trailblazing by whites before 1840 was evidently somewhat more common in the North than in the South. Settlers from New England and New York, in particular, practiced trailblazing as part of their cooperative and conservative approach to settlement.[1] Since settlers from New York and New England formed a hefty bloc of the pioneers inhabiting the northern wilds, cautious settlement must have been widespread in the northern wilds. Such expeditions usually consisted of just several—perhaps three to five—men whose presence in the backwoods reduced the average size, and perhaps the modal size, of pioneer households. Trailblazing in the South may have been common chiefly among propertied households, especially those owning slaves. The sons and associates of slaveowners spied out the western lands in preparation for migration, masters being reluctant to wander with their bondsmen across the South in search of new land. Logically, this reluctance was not as great among the rank and file settlers in the South, and possibly many of these households pushed westward as a whole and often sizeable unit.[2] Trailblazing, in other words, may have helped to produce among northern settlers a slightly greater tendency to have smaller modal sizes and fewer very big households than was the case among southern settlers.

Group migration undoubtedly played much the same role. As has been seen, northerners were more prone than southerners to migrate in groups to pre-arranged sites selected by trailblazers. This fact, reinforced by the fact that some groups provided instant community in the wilderness, persuaded small households to affiliate with group efforts. Rapid strides in transportation throughout the North smoothed the way for groups wishing to travel and settle intact. After the War of 1812 steamboats began to ply the western waters, canals eased migrants into the wilderness, Great Lakes shipping poured great numbers of settlers into the upper Midwest, and railroads whisked many migrants from the eastern towns and cities to within striking distance of the fresh lands. Invention, innovation, and construction activities relating to transportation were generally more widespread in the North than in the South. The ingrained propensity of settlers from the Northeast to assault the West collectively was very possibily strengthened by transportation developments, the whole group being able to move swiftly and safely to the frontier. The demographic product of this propensity included numerous small households, perhaps enough to lower the modal size.

Added to trailblazing, group migration, and improved transportation, was the fact that the northern frontier was considerably less agrarian in nature than the southern frontier, at least insofar as can be determined by examining occupational compositions. As has been seen, the greater the agrarian aspects of the land, the greater the tendency for the extended household to exist. Relatively great non-agrarian activity among northern

---

[1]Dan Clark, op. cit., pp. 182-83.
[2]Ibid., pp. 176-77.

settlers may have militated against both huge households and high modal sizes.

And yet some powerful countervailing forces must have been at work. Compared to the northern frontier, the southern wilds was home to households of approximately equal average sizes. Only in 1840 did the average size for the southern frontier top that of the northern frontier. Evidently, something was working to negate the effects of trailblazing, group migration, and revolutions in technology.

One factor at work was very likely that of southern slavery. The southern wilds was home to a considerable number of slaves over the years. In the northern wilds slavery, never really strong, all but disappeared by 1840. Slaves were, for perhaps one-eighth of the southern pioneer households, "invisible" members of the household whose labors augmented those of the household, thereby adding to the household's chances for survival. These members were a ready source of labor, and their consumption rate for food, clothing, shelter, and general attention was usually below that of the average household member. This largely parasitic relationship benefitted not just the owning household; society in its aggregate saw slaves performing many tasks that were scorned by whites. Demographically, however, the basic product was that marginal white households were able to survive in the wilderness. Many small households, especially those with just two adults and a child or two, contemplated the wilderness venture with trepidation and gloom. This uneasiness was probably compounded by the relatively sad state of transportation across the South to the western lands. Small households low on white labor and aware of some of the difficulties that usually attended the westward trek wavered and then stayed put in the Southeast, the section of the nation with the smallest average household sizes. Similar households, owning slaves, were sometimes induced to move west, the presence of this involuntary labor tipping the scale in favor of migration. Such households, although perhaps not very numerous, were possibly numerous enough to lower the average household size.

In addition, the Southeast contained households with the smallest average sizes in the nation. Perhaps "invisible" members in the Southeast performed much the same function as their counterparts on the frontier, masking the true amount of labor available and aiding small households to survive. In any event, since the vast majority of migrants to the southern frontier originated in the Southeast, it comes as no surprise that the westward-bound households were not markedly larger than those streaming across the North to the fresh lands north of the Ohio River.

Data pertaining to average household size failed to support the hypotheses. Even more detrimental to the validity of the hypotheses were the data concerning the percentages of households missing adults and the percentages of households in which just one child or no children were present. The hypotheses received support only rarely from these data.

It was also anticipated that, compared to southern pioneer households, relatively more northern pioneer households would be lacking an adult and that more of these missing adults would be male. These expectations sprang largely from the belief that the southern frontier was more rugged than the northern frontier, making it more difficult for households missing an adult to function there than on the northern frontier. Only in 1830 was the hypothesis supported. Compared to the northern backwoods, the southern backwoods always contained more missing adults who were male. This, too, was unexpected. (Some female-headed households in the southern backwoods were aided by the presence of slaves in their tussle with the wilderness, thereby partially explaining the presence on the southern frontier of relatively many households from which an adult male was missing.) There was an additional surprise: among southern settlers, there were many households in which there were either no children or just one child. Only in 1840 did the northern backwoods contain more of such households than the southern backwoods. The overall validity of the hypotheses concerning the two frontiers received a further setback when the data pertaining to the three most prevalent households were examined. The leading trio among northern pioneers was, with the exception of 1840, larger than that among southern pioneers.

On the other hand, data supported some of the hypotheses, thereby lending some credence to the idea that of the two frontiers the southern was the more rugged. Conforming to expectations, the relative number of loners in the southern wilds was greater than the number in the northern wilds. But this was true only for 1820, the figures for 1830 and 1840 being equal. Perhaps the tendency, however slight, for more loners to reside in the southern wilderness than further to the north can be explained by just one factor: the practice of overseers living alone with slaves. Laws throughout the South required that at least one adult white male be present wherever slaves congregated. Although the laws were often flagrantly ignored, sometimes just one isolated white overseer directed the work of a number of slaves. If the overseer lived with no other white, and many did not, then his presence constituted a household of one. There is also the outside chance that the relative absence of loners throughout the North may reflect lingering New England anxiety over single males living alone. Some support, however feeble, was lent to the hypotheses by data from the households in which either no children or just one child lived. Only in 1830, for example, did the percentage of households which were childless on the southern frontier exceed the percentage for the northern frontier. Similarly, only in 1820 did the percentage of households on the southern frontier with just one child top that of the northern frontier. With the exception once again of 1820, abundant support was lent to the three hypotheses pertaining to households in which children composed at least one-half of the membership, and the degree of support given in 1840 was impressive.

Whatever the cause or set of causes, the hypotheses concerning the comparison of the two frontiers were often either refuted by the data or given only tentative support. Of the two frontiers, the northern often displayed demographic characteristics more in conformity with the hypothesized characteristics. Because the data neither strongly supported nor strongly refuted the hypotheses, few firm and unqualified conclusions can be drawn from the comparison of the two frontiers. It is difficult to assert any claim except possibly to note that the northern frontier was, unexpectedly, about as "frontier" in its household characteristics as the southern frontier.

According to evidence from traditional primary sources, a number of factors influenced the size and composition of pioneer households. Apparently either the affective forces were somewhat different for the two frontiers over time—i.e., the presence of large-scale slavery in the southern wilderness, selective migration, trailblazing, group migration, technological advances, aspirations and beliefs, and differences in occupation are several factors which make this likely—or the forces, perhaps basically similar, had somewhat different effects on the households residing within the two backwoods regions. However, since the households on the two frontiers were much more alike than was hypothesized, the differences between the various forces affecting pioneer households may have been surprisingly slight.

For example, the average household size on the northern frontier, largely an extension of migration from the northeastern states, was generally smaller than that of the Northeast. At the same time, however, the average household size in the southern backwoods, largely an extension of migration from southeastern states, generally exceeded that of the Southeast. In other words, something—occurring either en route to the western lands or after settlers arrived, or both—reduced the size of households pushing into the northern woods and prairies and inflated the size of the households settling in the southern wilds. Similar occurrences altered the percentages of households containing eleven or more people. (The northern settled area enjoyed, compared to the southern settled area, a decidedly larger average household size, modal size, and more households composed of at least eleven people.) Either fewer large households left the Northeast for the northern frontier or something happened to those that did leave to reduce their size; there were relatively fewer such units in the wilderness than back east. The opposite occured in the South, the southern wilds being home for relatively more such units than the Southeast. The same developments occurred for both frontiers for the proportions of people who lived in such households. Finally, similar patterns are found for the percentages of total households on each frontier and in each settled area consisting of loners.

The exact nature of the conflicting forces affecting household size and composition is debatable. Clearly, however, some set of factors worked to prevent households, northern and southern, from migrating undisturbed to the fresh lands of the West and there remaining wholly intact. Because households migrating from the Southeast were affected differently from those migrating from the Northeast, it seems likely that the contributing factors varied from North to South and their effects varied over time.

One fact is central to pioneer households in the North: the journey westward and its hardships or conditions in the northern wilderness, or both, diminished the size of the household units as they left the East and Europe, pushed west, and settled in the West. The opposite was true for units leaving the Southeast and trooping into the fresh lands of the Southwest. Perhaps much of the difference hinges on the fact that in the North there was more trailblazing, group migration, good transportation, and non-agrarian pioneer activity, while in the South there were more agrarian pioneer efforts and more racial slavery. These factors, partly the products of beliefs and attitudes, had the effect of influencing beliefs and attitudes, including those affecting migration.

Demographic differences between the frontiers and their respective settled areas, sometimes surprisingly slight, often narrowed with the passing of time, a fact which was especially true in the North and which contradicted hypothesized results. Unlike some of the differences between the frontiers and the settled areas, however, those between the northern and southern frontiers failed to diminish greatly with time. Perhaps this was partially true because some differences between the two wildernesses were the opposite of what was expected, this being especially true for the northern frontier. Overall, then, the differences between the frontiers and their respective settled areas were quite moderate, and there is some indication that the differences faded with time. Differences between the two frontiers were for the most part far from gross, but there is little evidence that the passing of time brought convergence.

Evidence indicates that the desire for a higher standard of living is possibly the most important inducement for the restriction of births, and in virtually every society cultural norms and kinship institutions foster restriction.[3] The resulting size and composition of the household, whatever their nature, affect several vital aspects of household life: values held by its members, the nature of the problems faced by its members, and the dynamics of relationships between its members. In addition, size and

---

[3]Dennis H. Wrong, *Population and Society*, 3d ed., pp. 43, 55.

composition configurations create patterns of life which affect the personality development of each member.[4] In short, values, aspirations, and institutions often influence the size and composition of households, which in turn influence personality traits and the totality of human character and behavior.

Based upon these relationships, there is little reason to believe that frontier personality and society were remarkably different, at least insofar as the differences were products of differences in household size and composition. If differences in personality and culture were sharp, perhaps the causes were due more to the act of migration, opportunities present in the West, or some other facet of the western experience than to the size and composition of the pioneer household. Similarly, there is little reason to believe that differences in household demography were responsible for possible differences in personality and culture between the northern and southern frontier.

Of the several comparisons between the frontiers and their respective settled areas, the most striking finding was the similarity between pioneer households and eastern households.[5] The relatively few large differences between East and West were also striking. Certainly of equal importance, but perhaps far less conspicuous, was the fundamental fact that it was, after all, the *household* that formed the basic economic and social unit in the wilderness. The frontier household, however it differed in size and composition from the eastern household, signified that conditions in the wilds roughly approximated conditions further east, and therefore no new and exotic social and economic unit had to be devised to facilitate thorough settlement. The household was able to subdue physical obstacles in the West, compete effectively in western economics, and transplant to the wilderness many of the values, customs, institutions, and power arrangements present in the East. The household, not the work brigade, commune, or large-scale corporation, successfully advanced the frontier. This fact suggests that the problems confronted by the settler were such that he and those further to the east who had a stake in the settlement process were convinced that the household unit was successfully transporting and transplanting the most desirable and most needed features of eastern culture.

---

[4]Bossard, *op. cit.*, pp. 16-17. Consult also Chapter II, *passim.*

[5]The normal nature of households on the frontier was evident the wilds of Indiana in 1820: "'Normal' families in Indiana in 1820, therefore, were like 'normal' American families now: nuclear families with both spouses present, and their minor children. Deviance from this pattern [in Indiana] was unrelated to how close the family was to the frontier." Modell, *op. cit.*, p. 620.

CHAPTER V

Age and Sex

"Go West! Young man."[1] Secondary works suggest that it was precisely the young and the male who journeyed westward: "the largest single element [of all settlers] was young men," wrote one historian. He likewise noted that "The greatest single group of migrants was composed of young, unmarried farm boys. The usual age was twenty-one."[2] Another writer claimed, simply, that "Males outnumbered females," and still another concluded that "Girls were scarce on the frontier."[3]

The youthful nature of the settler, whether male or female, was stressed in many sources. One writer observed that "a population that is receiving foreign additions in any considerable numbers will have a high proportion of young people," and another claimed that "In most cases the first settlers were young men, just married, who, with their young wives . . . came boldly into the then dense wilderness."[4] "The youth of important officials" in frontier government impressed another observer of the West.[5] "The women," another noted, "were the pioneer mothers who came to the frontier young, healthy, and stronghearted."[6] One historian was fairly specific, writing that "A very large majority of the early settlers in Ann Arbor [Michigan] was made up of men and women in their twenties."[7] Another was even more specific when she wrote of early nineteenth-century Dearborn County, Indiana: "Seventy-four and four-tenths per cent of the white people were twenty-five years of age or less and ninety-one and seven-tenths per cent were under forty-five."[8] The age composition has been attributed to some extent to differences in the sex ratio on the frontier.[9] Finally, the consensus concerning the youthful nature of the

---

[1]This admonition by Ralph A. Gabriel was made popular by Horace Greeley.
[2]Riegel and Athearn, op. cit., 81, 110.
[3]Thomas D. Clark, Frontier America, p. 201. Thomas D. Clark, Rampaging Frontier, p. 284.
[4]Charles S. Sydnor, "Life Span of Mississippi Slaves," Amer. Hist. Rev., xxxv, p. 568; William M. Cockrum, Pioneer History of Indiana, p. 160.
[5]Philbrick, op. cit., p. 249.
[6]Wright and Corbett, op. cit., p. 3.
[7]Stephenson, op. cit., p. 7.
[8]Lawlis, op. cit., p. 39.
[9]Thomas D. Clark, Frontier America, p. 201.

pioneers included the sentiments of no less a poet than Walt Whitman.[10]

Accordingly, it was anticipated that this study would indicate strongly that a disproportionately large number of young men did go west. More specifically, it was hypothesized that the differences in age and sex between the northern backwoods and the Northeast would be quite pronounced, the differences in sex composition being greater among the elderly. The differences in sex, it was expected, would be much greater for adults than for children, for adults presumably had the option of migrating or staying put; small children, whatever their sex, usually obediently accompanied their parents. Less pronounced, it was hypothesized, would be the differences in age and sex between the southern wilds and the Southeast.

The expectation that the differences would be greater in the North than in the South resulted from certain revolutionary developments that were underway in the northeastern part of the nation by 1840. Heavy commercialization, invention and innovation in transportation, the beginnings of northern industrialization, heavy farm-to-city migration, startling urbanization, and other changes, it was hypothesized, exacerbated differences between the still largely agrarian northern wilderness and the swiftly changing Northeast. Compared to the Northeast, the Southeast experienced relatively few sweeping changes. As a result, it was expected that the differences in age and sex between the two northern regions would exceed those between the southern regions. Furthermore, because the rush toward modernity in the Northeast impacted upon the

---

[10]In "Pioneers! O Pioneers!" he wrote the following:

Come my tan-faced children
Follow well in order, get your weapons ready,
Have you your pistols? have you your sharp-edged axes?
    Pioneers! O Pioneers!

For we cannot tarry here,
We must my darlings, we must bear the brunt of danger,
We the youthful sinewy races, all the rest on us depend,
    Pioneers! O Pioneers!

O you youths, Western youths,
So impatient, full of action, full of manly pride and friendship
Plain I see you Western youths, see you trampling with the foremost,
    Pioneers! O Pioneers!

Over twenty years before Whitman wrote "Pioneers! O Pioneers!" the following lines were found in *The Forget-Me-Not Songster*, a collection of old ballads:

Come, all you young men, who have a mind to range
Into the Western country, your station for to change;
For seeking some new pleasure we'll altogether go,
Come along, lively lads, and we'll altogether go
And we'll settle on the banks of the pleasant Ohio.

in Nelson Beecher Keyes, *The American Frontier: Our Unique Heritage*, p. 195.

northern wilderness to a greater extent than upon the Southwest, it was hypothesized that relatively more pioneers in Dixie would be both young and male.

Some of the hypotheses were substantiated: the frontier did contain relatively more youth and males than in the East. In terms of sex composition, the differences between the northern settlers and those living in the Northeast were greater than those found in the South. In terms of age, the opposite was true to some degree; the gap between southern frontiersmen and inhabitants of the Southeast exceeded that of the North. Southern pioneers, evidence indicates, were somewhat younger than their northern counterparts, but relatively fewer were males.

AGE

In the three chapters on household size and composition, large households were seen to gravitate toward the fresh lands of the West. Large households usually meant large numbers of youngsters, a fact oppressively apparent to many of those considering migration. The presence of young, hungry mouths and their subsequent removal to the new lands naturally reduced the average age of settlers. Likewise, large households, fretting about yet another impending birth, found the wilderness attractive, and expectant mothers jolted their way westward.[11] Often the threatening arrival of the fifth or the seventh or the twelfth child was the final incentive needed to send easterners packing. The arrival of recently prolific households in the backwoods increased, inevitably and obviously, the percentage of the population under fifteen. Recent births and expected births made the frontier seem reasonably attractive and gave to the frontier a somewhat youthful feature, at the same time draining from the East a goodly proportion of its youth.

Similarly, death promoted youthful traits among settlers. Sometimes death snapped the bonds of affection and economic cohesion present in most households, often resulting in dislocation and relocation. Death set into motion a series of actions—the division, loss, or sale of property—within the bereaved family that often sent the members, including the surviving adult, hiking westward. Instances cited in the three preceding chapters illustrate the fact that some recently-bereaved households migrated westward with an adult, either the mother or father, missing. The arrival in the fresh lands of a household in which there was only one older person, along with perhaps several youngsters from six to eighteen,

---

[11]Accounts of the westward movement have many instances of pregnant women making the trip in covered wagons and boats, the impending birth frequently being the stated reason for the trip. A number of examples have been cited. Others are in Stephenson, op. cit., p. 32; Emma S. Vonnegut, ed., "The Schramm Letters: Written by Jacob Schramm and Members of his Family from Indiana to Germany in the Year 1836," Indiana Hist. Soc. Pubs., XI, p. 265; and McConnel, op. cit., p. 141.

injected many youths into the wilds and heightened age differences between East and West.

A third factor giving the settler a comparatively youthful cast was pioneer women who, spurred by the favorable sex ratio and perhaps reassured by the fact that families rarely went hungry in the West, married at an early age. These early marriages produced fifteen-year-old mothers and thirty-year-old grandmothers. Children sometimes arrived early and often, a fact not always reflected in household size because some of the older offspring left to begin their own households before the census taker had a chance to count them as teen-age members of their parents' household. Children in the western forests and fields were always relatively more numerous than in the eastern settled areas (see Table 16).[12]

Other forces generated a youthful population on the frontier. Fear and, worse, anxiety conspired to keep some elderly people out of the western Garden. Many gray-beards agreed that "As a general rule . . . those who had emigrated [to the frontier], after arriving at middle life, regretted they had come out."[13] Since many elderly folk were comfortably situated in familiar surroundings and since great distances and possibly primitive conditions awaited those undertaking the westward trek, few risked the venture.

Moreover, group travel also ushered young folk into the West. Included, for example, in a small group that ventured to frontier Ann Arbor, Michigan, was the Goodrich family, a family consisting of parents, two girls, and six boys. The oldest child was a boy of fifteen.[14] Group travel thus sometimes accentuated age differences between the frontier and the settled area by encouraging parents to embark on the westward trip with a slew of children, thereby pumping more youth into the frontier and siphoning youth from the East's supply.

Adding to the relatively youthful nature of the frontier was foreign immigration. Although pre-1840 immigration was nowhere as great as immigration soon became, those entering the nation before 1850 contained relatively few youngsters in their ranks.[15] Immigrants (especially

---

[12]Although the children of frontiersmen often left home at an early age and were therefore not recorded as being members of their parents' households, this in no way suggests that the process of taking the census was less accurate on the frontier than in the settled area. On the contrary, "Errors of enumeration normally increase inversely with the area and directly with the size of the population." Jack Eblen, "An Analysis of Nineteenth-Century Frontier Populations," *Demography,* II, 1965, p. 400. In thinly settled areas, the presence of virtually everyone was known by others; this was not true in the teeming cities.

[13]Thomson, *op. cit.,* p. 92. Although Thomson's comments referred to the Canadian frontier, there is little reason to believe they are not equally applicable to the frontier in the U.S.

[14]Stephenson, *op. cit.,* p. 47.

[15]J. Potter, "The growth of Population in America, 1700-1860," in *Population in History: Essays in Historical Demography,* D. V. Glass and D. E. C. Eversley, eds., p. 668. One modern demographer notes, "Between two-thirds and four-fifths of the immigrants to the United States in the nineteenth century were aged between fifteen and forty years." Peterson, *op. cit.,* p. 262.

the Irish) tended to pile up on the seaboard, probably contributing to the age differences between East and West. On the other hand, immigrants—although on the average older than natives—were most numerous in the 15-45 age group.[16] This fact almost certainly led to large numbers of offspring within a few years, thereby partly or perhaps even completely offsetting the statistical impact of the older immigrant. The effect of the infusion of older immigrants into the East is thus difficult to gauge.

The exact reasons for the youthful nature of the frontier, whatever they were, perhaps hinged upon two basic factors: youths tend to adapt to new conditions better than adults; youths change jobs more often than older people, a fact which frequently encourages migration.[17] America's westward thrust appears to conform to one important aspect of migration elsewhere: "At most times and in most places voluntary migration is largely a phenomenon of youth."[18]

Yet, for all this, there were countervailing forces at work in the nation which blurred some of the age differences between East and West. One of the most powerful forces, as seen earlier, was the practice of trailblazing. Small parties of trailblazers, as demonstrated in the chapters on household size and composition, reduced the distinction between frontier and settled area in terms of household size. They also helped to diminish age differences. Nearly everyone who grappled with the wilderness for months or years to prepare the way for others was an adult, trailblazing children being virtually non-existent. The percentage of frontier population consisting of trailblazers is unknown, but it possibly reached 5 or 6% at times, a ratio sizeable enough to sharply alter the age composition of the pioneer population. Over the decades virtually every frontier county witnessed probing exploratory parties, usually small, and almost always composed entirely of adults. Back east the young offspring and younger brothers and sisters of trailblazers waited with their mothers or relatives, anticipating either the safe return of those probing the West or favorable word from them. The presence of exploring adults on the frontier and waiting children in the settled areas—both products of the trailblazing process—obviously militated against the creation of vast age differences between East and West.

Age differences between frontier and settled area may have been reduced by another influence. As mentioned earlier, pioneer mothers may have been more prone to breast-feed than their eastern sisters. Such regional differences, as was suggested, possibly caused births in the backwoods to be biologically limited to roughly regular intervals of approximately two years. The breast-feeding western mother, rendered

---

[16]See, Holmes, op. cit., p. 158.
[17]Peterson, op. cit., p. 262.
[18]T. Lynn Smith and Paul E. Zopf, Jr., Demography: Principles and Methods, p. 521.

less capable of having as many children as the eastern woman, probably helped to reduce the age gap between backwoods and settled area.

Possibly group travel constituted another countervailing force. Although such travel was responsible for admitting to the wilds households ladened with children, it also enabled the elderly to make their way west. Sometimes those in the closing years of life fastened themselves to wagon trains wending westward and, perhaps by providing baby-sitting services or helping in some other way, convinced others to lead them to the frontier. Few couples in their sixties negotiated trips into the new lands on their own; rather, they bound themselves to group efforts and thus received protection and assistance.

Other forms of group travel also eased older folk into the backwoods. For example, James Hall floated down the Ohio River and "passed two large rafts lashed together, by which simple conveyance several families from New England were transporting themselves and their property to the land of promise in the western woods." He noted that on one of the rafts "A respectable looking old woman . . . was seated on a chair at the door of one of the cabins, employed in knitting; another female was at the washtub; the men were chewing their tobacco." Hall added "In this manner these people travel at a slight expense."[19] Abner Jones tops Hall's raft story: he describes a two hundred by sixty foot raft on the Ohio containing at least forty people, several shacks, wagons, hogs, dogs, etc., and drifting placidly downstream.[20] There is no indication that any elderly people were aboard, but on such vessels many older folk drifted into the new world of the West, helping to equalize age differences between the wilderness and the East.

Natural ignorance, enhanced by fast promotional talk, enticed some older people into the West.[21] Tales of flourishing towns, smooth roads, fabulous soil, and fantastic crops—whether true or false—persuaded some elderly folk to head west. Perhaps some were coaxed westward by Daniel Blowe's anticipatory description of economic activity in Wayne County, Ohio: "Its surplus is consumed by the numerous emigrants, who are crowding into the country. Ultimately its commerce will find its way to the

---

[19]Hall, Letters from the West, p. 87. Hall also witnessed a relatively rare sight for the era, an elderly couple traveling alone to new lands in the West. The gray-headed couple was observed on the Ohio River tugging at the oars of a crude skiff and they "looked as if they might have been pulling together down the stream of life for half a century." Of even greater surprise to Hall was the fact that this particular act of migration was entirely voluntary. The couple's children having married and left, the old couple simply wanted to venture westward "to try their luck at something new." Hall, ibid., pp. 138-40.

[20]Jones, op. cit., pp. 36-37.

[21]That some settlers were blissfully ignorant of actual conditions is apparent. One example is found in Flower, op. cit., p. 189. Perhaps ignorance, in some instances, was advantageous. Had all English settlers, for example, known of the vast distances involved in the western trek some might have had reservations about leaving cozy England.

shores of Lake Erie, distant only forty-six miles."[22] One wilderness commentator, expounding on the booster talk directed at the prospective settler, noted "An *El Dorado* had been described to them, or they have created it."[23] It made little difference over the short run if optimistic booster talk conquered fear only, in turn, to be overwhelmed by some of the harsh realities of the West. Eastern dreams sometimes produced a western product of bitterness and grief, but dreams tempted both the unsuspecting and the eager-to-believe into the West. And, once there, many settlers of all ages shouldered the unexpected burden and survived, gaining new feelings of self-esteem. The bubbly promoter of western schemes often lured the gullible, including some gray-beards, to the frontier, group travel easing the journey to the New Canaan.

Perhaps of great importance in narrowing the age gap was the fact that a great many married pioneers were either recently wed or otherwise quite young. As was the case with births and deaths, marriages often triggered migration into the fresh lands. Furthermore, marriage, youth, and migration were somewhat causally associated: "it may well have been that the average age at first marriage of many of those who migrated soon afterward was affected by the prospect of moving to a new area where it would be easy to establish a new agricultural household."[24] Frequently, couples came to the frontier directly after getting married or directly after the birth of their first child, their migration narrowing the age differences between the western lands and the East. This stemmed from the fact that newlyweds usually brought no offspring with them, and young couples who had been married a year or two probably brought no more than one or two. The average age on the frontier was thereby raised, most married pioneers being over fifteen or sixteen. Had the frontier couples been five or

---

[22]Daniel Blowe, *A Geographical, Historical, Commercial, and Agricultural View of the United States of America; forming a Complete Emigrant's Directory Through Every Part of the Republic*, p. 541. The role that boosterism played in developing the frontier is interpreted brilliantly in several places in Boorstin, *op. cit.* Another instance of anticipatory description was provided by Chandler R. Gilman, a physician from New York, who toured the northern Great Lakes region in 1835. He predicted that Alton, Illinois, would someday be a very crucial link in the nation's transportation system. He then claimed that "the trip from New-York to Alton will be but a pleasure jaunt of a few days; and the rich products of the Mississippi valley be as easily, rapidly, and almost as cheaply conveyed to New-York as now to New Orleans." Paul M. Angle, ed., *Prairie State: Impressions of Illinois, 1673-1967, by Travelers and Other Observers*, pp. 155-59.

[23]Hall, *Letters from the West*, p. 316.

[24]Forster and Tucker, *op. cit.*, p. 52, and Tillson, *op. cit.*, pp. 11-12. For more on the youthful, just-married traits of the migrants see Lawlis, *op. cit.*, p. 39; Riegle and Athearn, *op. cit.*, pp. 79, 110. "The call of the new lands has usually sounded loudest to youth." Sydnor, "Life Span of Mississippi Slaves," p. 568; Gordon and May, eds., *op. cit.*, p. 259; Cockrum, *op. cit.*, p. 160; Keyes, *op. cit.*, p. 196; Charles Dickens, *American Notes*, p. 66; Timothy Flint, *op. cit.*, I, p. 181; Philbrick, *op. cit.*, p. 349; Stephenson, *op. cit.*, p. 7; Thomas Clark, *Rampaging Frontier*, p. 286; See also numerous references in Chapters II-IV on household size and composition.

ten years older, then ironically the average age might have been lowered by the presence of many children.

Added to this is the fact that for some restless souls the pioneer experience was addictive. Always beset by the urge to stay slightly ahead of the prongs of settlement, these folk—including some over fifty—made every effort to keep on the leading edge of the frontier. A story recounted by Basil Hall is a case in point. A prosperous man of sixty had entered the wilderness as a youth and met with success. But others were now lighting nearby and the man "missed the ardent excitement of his past life, and sighed to be once again in the heart of the thicket." The brave soul "made over his farm to his children, and carrying with him only his axe and his wife, a few dollars, a team of oxen, and a wagon and horses, set off for the territory of Michigan." Hall added that "he is now chopping down wood, and labouring in a sort of wild happiness from morning til night."[25] Some, hunters and trappers and Indian traders, kept on the cutting edge of settlement for economic reasons; others, having run afoul of the law, did so for legal reasons; still others, having insatiable appetites for new places, did so for adventure. Whatever the reason, the result was a further closing of the age gap between East and West.

Some elderly people joined the westward procession simply because they could not afford to stay behind. In the era in which children assumed the responsibility for the care of their aged parents, some gray-haired individuals were totally dependent upon their offspring. If the supporting offspring decided to settle on the frontier, the parents often went along, more out of necessity than adventure. No social security lifted from the shoulders of sons and daughters the economic responsibility for the parents' physical well-being, and no change in thought removed the social and moral duties to care for parents. John C. Brown, the enumerator of the federal census in 1840 for Clinton County, Iowa, observed that "some elderly people were taken west because there was no place to leave them in the East."[26] As a result, some senior citizens found themselves on the frontier, their presence there obviously negating some of the demographic distinctions between East and West.

Finally, differences in age were possibly reduced by parental aspirations for children. Among educated people in the West, perhaps especially among recent arrivals, "Their grand ambition for their children is to send them to school in some Eastern City."[27] Given the state of education in most frontier localities, these ambitions are perfectly understandable. School-

---

[25]Basil Hall, *Travels in North America*, I, pp. 147-48.

[26]Eblen, *op. cit.*, p. 413n. In addition, consult Howard Johnson, "A Home in the Woods: Oliver Johnson's Reminiscences of Early Marion County," *Ind. Hist. Soc. Pub.*, XVI, p. 143, and Shirreff, *op. cit.*, pp. 232, 427.

[27]Mason Wade, ed., *The Writings of Margaret Fuller*, p. 45.

age children from the West boarding in the East with aunts and uncles or friends of the family further diminished the age gap. If just one per cent of the pioneer children spent all or some of their school days near the coast, the resulting effect on age was quite appreciable, for not only did the western lands lose children but the settled areas gained them.

During the first three decades of the nineteenth century, the net effect of all the factors operating for and against the presence of both elderly and young settlers caused the percentage of frontier inhabitants in the North who were under sixteen to never slump under 52% (see Table 16). During the same time, the comparable figure for the northern settled area never topped 49%. Almost certainly reflecting this fact was John Woods' observation in September 1819, that "The first thing that strikes a traveller on the Ohio [River] is the immense number of children, many of them almost naked." He added "They do not appear healthy; but they look happy, rolling in the water and dirt."[28] Even after the census of 1830 changed age categories, the percentage of the population in the northern woods under sixteen remained stable at 52%. By 1840, however, the percentage had plunged to 44%. During the first two decades the percentage in the settled area slipped only slightly, from 48% to 47%, then peaked at 49% in 1820 before tumbling to 42% in 1830 and 41% a decade later. (Perhaps this decline was due to increased life expectancy, and increased tendency for children to accompany their parents on the westward trek rather than remain behind for months, or, more likely, diminished birth rates—or some combination of all three and some other possible factors.) The differences in age between the northern frontiersmen and northeasterners remained fairly constant for several decades, increased by 1830, and then abruptly narrowed. Even in 1830, however, the relative number of children in the northern wilderness, as a percentage of the total population, exceeded the relative number in the northern settled section by less than 25%. Overall then, the forty years under study created neither marked convergence nor pronounced divergence in age characteristics between frontier and settled regions in the north.

A comparison of the age characteristics of the southern frontier to those of the southern settled section yielded many of the same results as those found in the North. Both regions lost some of their youthful nature over time, neither loss, however, being as precipitous as that in both sections of the North. Initially, relatively more people in the southern settled section and in the southern backwoods were children—49% and 57%, respectively—than in the two comparable northern regions; by 1840 the relative gaps between the southern regions and the northern regions had

---

[28]John Woods, *Two Years' Residence in the Settlement on the English Prairie, in the Illinois Country, United States.* Vol. x of *Early Western Travels*, p. 247.

widened. Compared to the previous decade, 1840 found proportionately more children on the southern frontier.

A comparison of the northern and southern frontiers demonstrates the youthful nature of southern settlers. Specifically, the southern wilderness contained relatively more children. An exception to this rule occurred in 1830, and in 1820 the difference between the two frontiers was quite moderate. Of the two frontiers, the southern in 1830 contained comparatively fewer children only because there were fewer girls between the ages of 10 and 15. The 1830s swiftly normalized this anomalous situation, and by 1840 the gap between the two frontiers had widened greatly. North and South, over the decades proportionately fewer pioneers were children, a trend which was particularly pronounced among the northern settlers.[29]

Compared to other age groups, the elderly showed the greatest differences between the frontiers and their respective settled areas. In several instances, particularly after the age category for older people was raised from forty-five to fifty in 1830, the percentage of the population in the northern settled area composed of elderly folk was at least twice that of the northern wilderness. In every instance, the settled areas had comparatively more older people than the backwoods, this being especially true in the North. With the exceptions of 1800 and 1810, the relative differences between the new lands of the North and the northeastern states were greater than those between the comparable regions of the South, a fact which lends support to the hypothesis.

Three hypotheses were supported: the West had comparatively fewer older folk than the East; the southern wilderness had fewer than the northern wilderness; and the differences between the northern regions were generally greater than those between the two southern regions.[30] Taking into account the change in age categories in 1830, in neither the North nor the South was there a strong tendency from 1800 to 1840 for the two frontiers to either converge or diverge with regard to their respective settled areas, though it does appear the northern wilderness was home to comparatively fewer older people in 1840 than in 1800. On balance, the gray-haired population was a fairly stable element of the people in both the frontier and the settled area.

---

[29]The fact that by 1840 only 44% of the people on the northern frontier were children may have been due, at least in part, to a decline in the birthrate. The birthrate, falling throughout the nineteenth century, dropped rapidly during the 1830s, precipitously during the 1840s, and then leveled off until almost 1860. Bogue, op. cit., 133. Perhaps part of the decrease was caused by the dismal economic scene of the late 1830s and early 1840s. Evidence indicates that, at least in modern times, "Births and marriages conform positively to the business cycle." Morris Silver, "Births, Marriages, and Business Cycles in the United States," The Jour. of Pol. Econ., LXXIII, pp. 251-52. For whatever reason, births were being limited.

[30]It is possible that northerners, in general, enjoyed a longer life span than southerners. At least one contemporary observer thought so: Holmes, op. cit., p. 160.

Sex

As previously mentioned, there were comparatively more males on the frontier than in the settled area. One reason is evident: some women simply refused to risk tomahawk, panther, toil, loneliness, and other known and unknown terrors of the wilderness.[31] This attitude is well-illustrated by the dilemma that confronted John Logan Black. He came from Blacksburg, South Carolina, to visit Union County, Arkansas, and then asked his girl-friend in South Carolina to marry him and move there. She agreed to marry—and they did—but she adamantly refused to budge from South Carolina out of fear of the unknown, and poor John Black "spent the remainder of his life talking about the wonderful country on the Ouachita River."[32] In this instance, both a man and a woman were prevented from roughing it in the backwoods by the woman's intransigence; in other instances, the man went west anyway, leaving the girl behind. Modern demographers have noted that the greater the obstacles in the paths of migrants, the greater the tendency for the migrants to be male.[33] Migration in the early national era was no exception.

The nature of the migration into the fresh lands and of the potential opportunities and tribulations served as filters, screening some females from the western lands. Trailblazing, part of the migration process for many settlers, certainly helped to tip the demographic scales in the West in favor of males. With men surveying and probing the new lands and women staying in the East, differences in the sexual compositions were created. Men trailblazed, not women. The early settlement of Eaton County, Michigan, is a case in point. After the Union Colony was formed at East Poultney, Vermont, the members, wanting "to spy out the land of Canaan," sent Simon S. Church, Wait S. Squier, and William G. Henry—all men—into the unsettled region to locate a good site for the colony. This the spies did, buying land and attaching the name Vermontville, now a town in Eaton County, Michigan. The trailblazers felled trees, built cabins, and then signalled those still waiting in Vermont to proceed westward.[34] This act of

---

[31]Numerous accounts of maulings and even deaths by wildcats indicate that these animals, now virtually extinct in the Old Northwest, were both feared and fearsome. In any event, it is clear that to some degree migrations were sex-selective. The *degree* of the selection and the forces operating to determine the degree are the questions here. In addition, the length of the migration possibly influenced the sex of the migrants: "For long-distance moves, males predominate; for short-distance, females." Ralph Thomlinson, *Population Dynamics: Causes and Consequences of World Demographic Change*, p. 227. Similar comments are found in Smith and Zopf, *op. cit.*, p. 195. Some of the migrants made very long trips to the new lands, arriving from the east coast or even Europe after a journey of weeks; others, living just behind the frontier, found themselves on the frontier after a hike of just two or three days. The proportions of migrants making each type of journey is unknown.

[32]Spencer, *op. cit.*, p. 235.

[33]Bogue, *op. cit.*, p. 765.

[34]Holbrook, *op. cit.*, pp. 78-80.

trailblazing illustrates, once again, the male aspect of the practice. And, even if trailblazers composed just 1 or 2% of the total frontier population, the fact that this small bloc was almost exclusively male certainly accounts in large measure for the persistent (if slight) tendency of the frontiers to be predominantly male. Given the practice of trailblazing, the male majority comes as no surprise.

For households not practicing trailblazing, other aspects of migration nevertheless screened some females. The sad tale of Mrs. Thomas Spring, whose husband died in western Pennsylvania as the household was traveling to the frontier, has been cited and further illustrates the point.[35] Her three sons escorted her to Illinois, completing the planned journey. Had the Spring children consisted of girls at the time of Mr. Spring's death, the all-female unit might have flagged and faltered. The mother and daughters probably would have either settled in western Pennsylvania or retreated to the East, a difficult undertaking in itself. Had the females unexpectedly made it to the frontier and had the mother not remarried, the nature of the available work there and the generally crude conditions there would have buffeted them severely.[36]

In addition, the mere availability of good land in the West may have contributed to the male majority. Patrick Shirreff observed that

> The youth of Britain do not engage in the bustle of the world so easily as the Americans, and family intercourse is consequently more enduring. But it is the difficulty of earning a subsistence and not affection which binds the young men of Britain to the roof of their parents, and in all probability the emotions of the heart are the same in both countries.[37]

Fresh land very definitely enabled young Americans to escape being bound "to the roof of their parents," a fact which altered demographic traits and perhaps household dynamics and individual personalities.

A related factor possibly contributed to the creation of numerical male superiority on the frontier, at least on certain portions of the frontier. Federal laws sometimes encouraged males to occupy new lands in the West. Veterans of the War of 1812, for example, were given at the conclusion of the war, congressional rewards in the form of six million acres of land for settlement, two million of which were located in Michigan.[38] Some who qualified for this land never got it, and some who did receive it

---

[35]Flower, op. cit., p. 155.

[36]The West was considerably more agrarian than the settled areas in the East, a fact that precluded many women from successfully heading households. The fact that women were not expected to head pioneer households undoubtedly led to relatively few female-headed households. For the degree to which the frontier was agrarian, see Tables 19 and 20.

[37]Shirreff, op. cit., p. 428.

[38]Henry O. Severance, Michigan Trailmakers, p.1.

never came west to live on it. Others came west with women. But some single men, curious about the nature of the land and possibly spurred westward by that desire to wander that seems to follow wars, went forth to the wilderness to satisfy their curiosity. Furthermore, speculators often bought up the land from the soldiers and then sent *men* out to the new lands to prepare the land for quick sale. Whether these people were curious veterans or agents of speculators, they were *men*, and their presence added to the male majority.

Finally, some women lingered in the East, caring for those for whom the journey westward was too arduous. Arthur Calhoun wrote, "To the settlement of the Great West went the young and vigorous leaving the elderly, the invalids, the orphans to the care of some widowed or unmarried *sister* or *daughter.* Throughout the older states *there were countless such broken families.''*[39] Social custom foisted onto women the tasks of caring for those needing special attention, thereby preventing some women who wanted to try their hand in the West from ever leaving home. The result, again, was relatively more females in the East, fewer in the West.

Although some females were screened out of the western opportunities, at no time did males ever experience overwhelming numerical superiority. Only once did males ever reach 55% of the total pioneer population. This occurred on the northern frontier in 1840. Usually only 5 to 8 percentage points separated the sexes on both frontiers, a surprisingly small difference made smaller by the fact that in *both* settled areas males enjoyed a slight numerical advantage over females.

Several factors help account for the surprisingly small difference. Just as anticipatory talk convinced some aging men that conditions in the wilds were superb—or at least completely tolerable—so, too, some women were similarly convinced. Those women in the East who relished the thought of a cottage by a gurgling brook were eager to accept good news from the West.[40] Spreading good news were those who stood to gain by western development.

---

[39]Calhoun, *op. cit.,* II, p. 169.

[40]Letters and other forms of communication did flow from the new lands in the West to the more settled areas in the East, the crushing postal rates notwithstanding. Postal rates were so high that to send a one-sheet letter 250-350 miles in 1797 cost 20 cents, a sum that then represented one-fourth of a day's wage for many. Jedidiah Morse, *The American Gazetteer,* unpaginated. The high postal rates encouraged three practices: writing on the envelope; writing not only on both sides of the sheet but also in a different color at 90^0 to the first lines on the letter; and fraud. Fraud was encouraged by the fact that the person *receiving* the letter often paid the postage, retaining the option to reject the letter. Capitalizing on this fact, individuals concocted codes of dots and other marks and placed these symbols on the outside of the letter. The receiver, in looking over the envelope to determine whether or not he wanted to receive the letter, would read the symbols and then reject the letter. Whatever the means, news concerning the West got through to easterners, convincing many to risk the trek.

And for those women who became convinced of the opportunities in the West, group travel and improving transportation eased the move by providing security and companionship. Had all of the wagons traveled individually through the forests, many women (and some men) would have found the attractions of the West overshadowed by the fear of extreme toil and privation and the dread of the unknown. But many—perhaps most— pioneer wagons rattled westward in trains, and small households, the aged, and women thereby received encouragement to migrate. The development of steamboats, canals, and later railroads provided further encouragement.

Added to this was another fact concerning group travel: it was almost always one-way. Small households, single people, incomplete households, child-laden households, the elderly, and females were sometimes lured into *entering* the West by group travel, but very few groups were formed to ease the burden of those wishing to return to the East.[41] In other words, group travel facilitated the westward trek of some fairly marginal people, but once on the frontier such people had to succeed either as they were or combine with others via marriage or the *ad hoc* creation of larger units. Those who dragged themselves back East after experiencing defeat did so largely on their own.

Another basic frontier condition tended to vitiate the differences in sex composition: very nearly all the dwellers in the back country lived in relatively complete households, an important fact noted in the preceding chapters. Those who observed the wagons as they wound their way across the forests and onto the prairies were well aware of the fact that *households* were making the trips, and women and children were part of the households. The *Niles Weekly Register* merely related an oft-told story when, in reporting about New York, it wrote that during the winter of 1814-15 the "roads have been thronged with families [households] moving westerly." It was noted that the wagons were "ladened" with women, children, and furniture.[42] Loners were rare—extremely rare—and households missing an adult member were also rare. (There is no way of knowing what percentage of the trailblazers were loners, but the percentage probably was not great since the vast majority of trailblazers scouted the West in small groups.) Virtually all loners were male. But since they were so few in number, they added little to the male majority. The husband-wife household, not the solitary individual, was the dominant demographic feature on the western landscape. It is hard to overemphasize the importance of the household in the demographic development of the West. It was the unit by which the frontier was settled, and its size and composition frequently differed comparatively little from the size and

---

[41]See item 5 on p. xx
[42]*Niles Weekly Register*, VIII (Apr. 15, 1815).

composition of eastern households. This fact helped to normalize conditions in the wilderness and facilitate the reconstruction of older demographic patterns, including sex ratios.

Another condition helped to reduce differences between the sex compositions to less than 8%: immigration. If figures from the 1840s and 1850s are accurate, and they may not be, males entering the nation outnumbered females by at least 40%.[43] The vast majority of all arrivals poured into the settled sections of the nation, not the frontier. In doing so, they diminished differences in sex composition.

Affection, perhaps coupled with a strong sense of duty, propelled some unattached women into the forests and prairies of the West. The life of Mrs. Jotham Cushman of Halifax, Nova Scotia, illustrates the fact. Her son, Joshua, went to Ohio, married, had a daughter, and then lost his wife. Mrs. Cushman, having lost her husband, determined to join her son: "Her desire to be with her son and to take charge of his little daughter made her prefer the uncertainty of a new western home to the comfortable provision her brother had extended to her in his own family."[44] Possibly the loss of her husband broke her ties with Halifax, but duty and affection probably played a decisive role in her decision to abandon the comforts of Halifax and enter the wilderness. She was not alone in yielding to these forces.

Whatever the conflicting forces operating to affect the sex composition on the frontier and whatever their relative strengths, the net result produced over the years doggedly persistent but unexpectedly small male majorities on both frontiers. No prevailing trend appears in the degree to which the northern frontier was male; its low point occurred in 1830 when fewer than 52.5% of the northern newcomers were male, its high point a decade later when over 55% were male. Over the four decades, each settled area experienced an almost imperceptible but consistent male majority. This sliver of a majority inched from 50.1% in 1800 to 50.7% in 1840, a gain of just six-tenths of one per cent. Compared to the northern settled area, the northern frontier always contained, over the four decades, relatively more males. But this majority was surprisingly slim, ranging from approximately 2% in 1830 to over 4.5% in 1840.

When the sex compositions of the two southern regions are compared, a weak and highly irregular increase in male majorities in both areas is detected. Less than 52.5% of the southern pioneers in 1800 and 1810 were male; this peaked at almost 54% in 1820, and then skidded to less than 53.5% for the next two decades. The male majority in the southern settled region remained virtually unchanged through 1820, hovering at slightly over 50.5%, but in 1830 it approached 51% and in 1840 it topped that percentage. The differences in the majorities in the two regions of habitation in the

[43]Seventh Census of the United States, 1850: Population, xc.
[44]Tillson, op. cit., p. 39.

South usually wavered around 2%, a remarkably small difference, except for 1820 when the difference spurted to nearly 3.5%. When the two regions are compared, it is difficult to state conclusively whether the trends of the sex composition converged, diverged, or remained unchanged. Insofar as the fragile differences increased slightly over the years, perhaps it can be said there was some divergence.

As was demonstrated earlier, the presence of a female minority, however small the gap separating it from the male majority, resulted in early marriage among women. The continuous shortage of women, a demographic condition, excited the imaginations of some men concerning the best way to court those women who were available. When a group of forty-one women arrived by steamboat to offer themselves as brides to frontiersmen, the men devised a system that was as romantic as it was subtle: having never met any of the women, they lined the shore next to the boatload of women and blared their proposals through speaking trumpets.[45]

Evidence strongly refutes the hypothesis that anticipated relatively more males in the southern wilderness compared to the northern wilderness. Of the two frontiers, the northern boasted the larger male majorities in 1800, 1810, and 1840. However thin the margins, the northern frontier usually contained relatively more males than the southern frontier. The majority of males among settlers in the South may have increased slightly over the years; no trend whatsoever is readily apparent among northern pioneers.

Differences in the sex compositions, it is important to note, varied according to the age group being examined, and variations were considerably larger on the frontier than in the settled area, a fact which was hypothesized. Males always predominated among children on both frontiers and in both settled areas. But the sex differences for children in the backwoods were relatively slight when compared to other age groups. For example, the largest difference between the sexes for children was just 10.4%. This occurred for children between ten to sixteen years on the northern frontier of 1800. Usually the differences were much less than that. Very obviously, children had no control over where they were born—whether on the frontier or in the settled area—and only slight control over where their parents toted them. An examination of the sex composition of children is thus hardly the most fruitful line of inquiry.

A more fruitful line pertains to adults. Differences in sex increased with

---

[45]Thomas Clark, *Rampaging Frontier,* p. 284. The great demand for women in the wilderness was produced by a surprisingly slim difference in the pioneer sex composition. Moreover, the total percentage of people on the frontier who were women may have been higher than indicated by the censuses. Possibly, men "often sent from three to five wives to the cemetary" due to numerous pregnancies, a possibility which, if true, implies that the total number of females who reached the frontier was greater than indicated by the censuses. *Ibid.,* p. 281. Also, consult Wright and Corbett, *op. cit.,* p. 4.

age. The greatest difference in people in their teens and twenties occurred in 1840 on the northern frontier; it reached 15%. The same year also found the northern frontier boasting of the largest difference for those in their thirties and forties, a difference of 20%, a figure unsurpassed by the differences in any other age group over the forty years. The differences were *consistently* greater, however, for the older portion of the population: three times between 1810 and 1840 the percentages of the population in both frontiers consisting of older folk who were male topped 58.8% and on four other occasions the figures were between 57.1 and 58.0%. During the four decades, the percentages of all groups in the northern settled area who were male ranged from 48.5% to 52.6%, the latter figure reflecting males under ten in 1820. The southern settled section showed a slight tendency to have larger differences in sex composition, the percentage of age groups composed of males once falling to 47.9% and six times rising to at least 51.5%. The hypothesized results were generally obtained: the differences in sex composition on the frontier did become more pronounced with age.

Summary and Conclusion

The evidence indicates that claims made by most literature on the West concerning age and sex were fairly correct. The frontier, compared to the settled area, did contain over the years more young people and males. However encouraging the prospects of obtaining land and a home, even more persuasive for some of the elderly and some of the female prospective migrants were the difficulties attending migration and settlement. The elderly, especially, were frequently loath to budge. Clearly, too, the differences in sex composition between those living in the northern wilderness and those living in the northern settled area topped those found between the two southern regions. On the other hand, the opposite was true for age: differences between the southern frontier and the Southeast generally exceeded those between the northern frontier and the Northeast. Furthermore, compared to northern settlers, southern settlers tended to be younger. But the expectation that the southern wilderness would house relatively more males than the northern wilderness was contradicted by the data. (Aside from 1830, the other census years never found relatively more males on the southern frontier than on the northern.) Because of the conflicting evidence, it is unclear which frontier contained more demographic traits in comformity with the hypotheses.

Births, knowledge of impending births, deaths among adults in the East, early and continuous marriage in the West, and possibly other influences operated to varying degrees to overcome countervailing elements that included trailblazing, group travel, and breast-feeding. The product of the interplay of forces was a settler who was younger than the resident of the East and who lived in an environment in which children were relatively more numerous. Trailblazing, the nature of perceived opportunities and hardships inherent in the westward trek and settlement, and custom and law combined to mitigate the effects of anticipatory talk, group travel, migration by household units, immigration, and ideas of duty, and produced on the frontier proportionately more males than in the settled area.

Frank McWhorter Surveys His Land
A painting by Anna McCullough
commissioned by the Illinois Emancipation Centennial
By 1840 practically no blacks were reported in chains on the northern frontier.
Courtesy, Illinois State Historical Library

CHAPTER VI

Racial Characteristics of the Frontier and the Condition of Blacks

Few scholarly efforts have examined closely the racial characteristics of the frontier. In nearly every frontier county between 1800 and 1840, some blacks were found to be present, most of whom languished in chains. Nevertheless, the term "frontiersman" generally connotes *white* settlers.[1] The extension of slavery into the new lands of the South, the attempts to either preserve or implant the "peculiar institution" north of the Ohio River, and the precarious situations in which free blacks in the northern wilds often found themselves, have been subjects of numerous studies in recent years. But little effort has been directed toward studying and analyzing the racial characteristics of the pioneers and the condition—free or slave—of blacks.

The Northern Frontier and Northern Settled Area

An obvious, and very profound, conclusion springs from a comparison of the northern and southern frontiers to their respective settled areas: the relative dearth of black pioneers (see Table 18). This dearth was especially notable in the North. North of the Ohio River, blacks—free and enslaved—comprised more than 1% of the total pioneer population only once, in 1820, and sagged to just three-tenths of one per cent by 1840. In the northern settled area, blacks formed 3.7% of the population in 1800 and then slumped steadily thereafter, bottoming at 2% by 1840. Obviously, from 1800 through 1820 the racial compositions of the northern wilds and the northern settled area were converging. The 1820s reversed the movement toward convergence, however, with the northern wilderness after 1820

---

[1]Of the 252 counties identified as forming part of the frontier sometime between 1800 and 1840, only fifteen of them (all in the North) contained neither free blacks nor slaves. Ninety-four counties (all in the North) contained free blacks but no slaves. The same four decades found eighteen counties (all but one in the South) housing slaves but no free blacks. For a decade-by-decade development of these phenomena, see App. E.

displaying an increasingly white nature to a degree even greater than the northern settled area.

In 1800 approximately 70% of the blacks in the new lands of the North were free, a figure that slipped only slightly by 1810. The following decade it plunged to just 53%, and then in 1830 rocketed abruptly to 90%.[2] Only a handful of slaves were held in the northern wilderness by 1840.[3] Although proportionately fewer settlers were black by 1840, fewer faced severe restrictions on their freedom inasmuch as they were not slaves. In the Northeast, free blacks formed over 59% of the black population in 1800, approximately 75% in 1810, over 85% in 1820, more than 97% in 1830, and by 1840 practically no blacks were reported in chains. On balance, the tendency toward freedom for blacks was stronger in the settled sections of the North than in the new lands. Stated another way, of the two northern regions the frontier generally contained relatively more—if sometimes only slightly more—slaves among its black population.

Over the decades free blacks continuously, and usually overwhelmingly, outnumbered slaves in both the northern wilderness and the Northeast. Accordingly, the percentages of total populations in these two areas composed of free blacks somewhat approximated the percentages composed of total blacks. Obviously, this approximation became increasingly true as the black population throughout the North gradually achieved freedom; the two percentages were almost identical in 1840, the year by which virtually all blacks throughout both northern regions were free.

In the North over the decades, the relative numbers of total pioneer population consisting of free blacks exhibited tendencies similar to those of

---

[2]The census figures failed to reveal the whole story, however. Various forms of subterfuge were employed to place or keep blacks in de facto slavery, even in violation of explicit legal sanctions against slavery. A case in point is the census taken in Vincennes, Indiana, in 1830, a census ordered by the Board of Trustees of the town. It showed that thirty-two slaves lived in the town; the federal census for the same year yielded just three slaves. Long-term indentured servitudes, some up to ninety-nine years, were used to create for blacks a condition tantamount to slavery. Emma Lou Thornbrough, "The Negro in Indiana before 1900," *Ind. Hist. Colls.*, xxxvii, p. 30. It was also claimed "This baleful practice promises a perpetuation of practical slavery throughout America," Fearon, *op. cit.*, p. 264. For more on this practice, see Flower, *op. cit.*, pp. 198-99.

[3]The laws against slavery in the territories and states carved out of the Old Northwest, passed or generally enforced during the 1820s, seem to have taken effect by the 1830s. Supportive of this argument are Thornbrough, *op. cit.*, pp. 27-30, and Arthur Clinton Boggess, *The Settlement of Illinois, 1718-1830*, p. 187. (Boggess provides a detailed account of the struggle over slavery in the territory and state of Illinois.) For additional evidence on laws pertaining to blacks see Elliott Anthony, *The Constitutional History of Illinois;* Eugene Berwanger, *The Frontier Against Slavery: Western Anti-Negro Prejudice and Slavery Extension Controversy;* Leon F. Litwak, *North of Slavery: The Negro in the Free States, 1790-1860.*

the percentages for the total black population: an increase from 1800, a high point occuring in 1820, and a vigorous decline thereafter. A different trend prevailed in the settled sections of the North, however. There the percentages of the total population composed of blacks, free and slave, sagged steadily from 1800. In the same settled sections, the percentage of the population consisting of free blacks rose briskly from 2.2% in 1800 to 2.7% in 1810, remained steady through 1820, slipped during the 1820s, and sank to 2% by 1840. In short, from 1800 through 1820 the overall trend in both northern regions was one of relatively more free blacks. After 1820 in both regions the overall trend was one of fewer free blacks. By 1840 in both regions the relative number of people who were both black and free plummeted to a level somewhat below the depressed level of 1800.

Such trends did not occur independently of other phenomena in the North. Forces at work in the North and throughout the nation altered the racial composition and the status of blacks in the fresh lands as well as the settled lands. The degree to which whites encountered blacks, both free and fettered, or thought they might encounter them in the future affected many facets of society throughout the North. For these reasons, racial composition and the condition of blacks were regarded as both dependent and independent variables, variables that operated over time in some instances in conjunction with each other and on other occasions possibly free from one another.

Whatever the exact interaction of forces in the two northern regions *on* the racial composition and resulting *from* the racial composition, certain conditions and actions prompted trends in race; the racial trends, in turn, triggered other trends. As a result, it becomes difficult to determine at any one point in time whether a specific phenomenon is the cause of the racial characteristic present somewhere in the North, a product of the characteristic, or both.

Regardless, the attitudes and actions of whites concerning the blacks greatly influenced the number of blacks and their status, free or slave, in the fresh lands of the North. (The attitudes may themselves be partially products of the relative number of blacks in the West. For example, the greater the number of free blacks, possibly the greater the white hostility.) Slaves generally went where they were told and performed what was demanded of them, some effective instances of slave resistance notwithstanding. Free blacks, too, were usually under the dictates of whites; they lived, worked, spoke, and exercised options within limits carefully prescribed—if not always codified—by whites. Some slaveowners, prospective slaveowners, and abolitionists aside, most settlers were thrown into various forms of consternation by the presence, or even the threat of the presence, of either slaves or free blacks.[4] When whites responded, their response was usually vigorous.[5] Often through pressure and threats, whites sought to dissuade the blacks from gaining admission to the Garden.

The relative influences of the diverse forces operating to prevent blacks from entering the West can be disputed. What cannot be disputed are the results of the restraining forces. For example, by 1840 the percentage of people on the northern frontier who were free blacks, three-tenths of one per cent, was proportionately hardly one-seventh the number of people in the Northeast who were free blacks (see Table 18). Officially, by 1840 virtually no slaves existed in the new lands of the North. (At this time free blacks constituted approximately 5% of the population in the Southeast, slaves over 38%.) Clearly, the lands of opportunity in the North offered little opportunity to blacks.

The propensity for free blacks to gravitate to the frontier was small, and many who were on the frontier were there largely because manumitting

---

[4] Apparently typical of northern sentiment—or at least of articulated northern sentiment—concerning blacks was a petition sent from Harrison County, Indiana, to Congress in 1813: "We are opposed to the introduction of slaves or free Negroes in any shape . . . Our corn Houses, kitchens, Smoke Houses . . . may no doubt be robbed and our wives, children and daughters may and no doubt will be insulted and abused by those Africans." (The priority of concern is interesting.) Thornbrough, op. cit., p. 20. On May 27, 1835, the Detroit Journal reported that one of delegates to the constitutional convention of the Territory of Michigan, John Norvell of Wayne, addressed the convention by saying "Sir, we are free from the evils of a black population now. Let us remain so. We are called upon by no constitutional duty to open our doors to them." Harold M. Dorr, ed., The Michigan Constitutional Conventions of 1835-36, Debates and Proceedings, p. 168. To investigate the "negro problem," the Ohio Legislature appointed a special committee, and its chairman concluded that "The negroes are in many parts of the State a serious political and moral evil. Although they are nominally free, that freedom confers only the privilege of being more idle and vicious than slaves." Frank V. Quillin, The Color Line in Ohio, pp. 26, 55.

[5] The success in restricting free blacks from the northern wilds is apparent in Table 18 when the percentage of population there that was free black is compared to that of the northern settled area. The differences are given additional meaning when it is realized that many of the free blacks in the northern wilds were from the South. The means by which blacks were excluded from the pioneer experience varied greatly, but they included political, economic, and social pressures, and the threat of kidnapping into slavery. For example, often free blacks had to register with county authorities upon entering western lands, pay a heavy bond for good behavior, and obtain passes in order to travel. In addition, it was usually impossible for them to vote, serve in the militia, or testify in court in cases involving whites. See Thornbrough, op. cit., pp. 31-36, passim; Boggess, op. cit., pp. 178-79; David B. Warden, A Statistical, Political, and Historical Account of the United States of North America, II, p. 364; Isaac Patterson, ed., The Constitutions of Ohio, Amendments and Proposed Amendments, pp. 84-85; Flower, op. cit., p. 340; and Helen M. Thurston, "The 1802 Constitutional Convention and the Status of the Negro," Ohio Hist., LXXXI. However, in spite of some vicious statutes in the states and territories comprising the northern frontier, the manner and degree to which they were actually enforced varied from place to place and time to time, depending upon local white sentiment.

TABLE 18.—Percentages of People Living in Various Sections of the Nation by Race, Condition of Blacks, and Sex of Whites

Decade and Section	Sex of Whites		Condition of Blacks	
	White Males	White Females	Slaves	Free Blacks
1800				
Northern Frontier	53.7	46.0	.1	.3
Northern Settled	48.2	48.0	1.5	2.2
Southern Frontier	46.9	42.7	9.9	.5
Southern Settled	26.9	26.4	42.3	4.4
1810				
Northern Frontier	52.6	47.0	.2	.5
Northern Settled	48.4	48.0	.9	2.7
Southern Frontier	41.4	37.7	20.7	.2
Southern Settled	26.5	25.8	41.6	6.0
1820				
Northern Frontier	54.2	44.7	.5	.6
Northern Settled	48.8	48.0	.4	2.7
Southern Frontier	40.0	33.0	26.8	.3
Southern Settled	27.3	26.7	41.2	4.9
1830				
Northern Frontier	52.4	47.5	.0	.4
Northern Settled	49.1	48.6	.0	2.3
Southern Frontier	37.2	32.8	29.7	.4
Southern Settled	27.7	26.7	40.3	5.2
1840				
Northern Frontier	55.0	44.7	.0	.3
Northern Settled	49.5	48.6	.0	2.0
Southern Frontier	46.1	40.5	13.1	.3
Southern Settled	29.0	27.8	38.2	5.0

masters or Quakers brought them into the northern wilderness.[6] The willingness of some whites to persecute blacks, black awareness of this willingness, and the lack of effective means of resisting persecution—certainly reinforced by crushing poverty—severely deterred the flow of blacks into the lands of opportunity. Unlike other people, blacks simply lacked the economic clout necessary to make the trek, the protection of law during the settlement process, and overall positive reinforcements and encouragement. As a result, the wave of pioneers surging westward was a white wave.

Be that as it may, some blacks did appear in the new lands of the North, motivated by several reasons and arriving from several directions. Some blacks were indigenous to the northern woods and were on hand to greet the first American pioneers when they trickled into the backwoods. Other blacks, belonging to northern masters who realized that slavery was dying in the Northeast, were hurried westward.[7] Some masters in the South, becoming convinced either of the evils of slavery or the impracticality of it, or both, slipped their bondsmen into the Northwest and freed them, it becoming increasingly difficult to do so in the South. Such acts of manumission accounted for a sizeable proportion of the black pioneer population. Other shackled blacks were granted their freedom by anti-slavery northerners, especially Quakers, who sent teams into the South to purchase slaves out of captivity and then release the ransomed blacks in the northern wilderness.[8] Added to these were those southern slaves who, not being fortunate enough to have a master with manumitting sentiments or to be selected by the Quakers, bolted from bondage and darted to pioneer lands in the North. Finally, some newly-arrived black settlers had never known slavery. These blacks *chose* to come to the frontier, settling there in the face of severe and mounting legal, economic, and social obstacles

---

[6]Blacks could gain entrance to the Garden if they had skills needed by white settlers, were "sponsored" by whites (the Quakers were foremost in sponsoring free blacks), or in some other manner convinced their neighbors they were harmless and should be permitted to stay. However, even blacks who found favor with nearby whites were subject to kidnappings, sometimes to the dismay of their white neighbors. See Thompson, op. cit., p. 130; Faux, op. cit., p. 260; Boggess, op. cit., pp. 186-87; Simon A. Ferrall, A Ramble of Six Thousand Miles Through the United States, p. 60; Flower, op. cit., pp. 260-65, who claimed that "The kidnapping of whole families of free blacks in the South of Indiana was no uncommon thing." Ibid., p. 263; and N. Dwight Harris, The History of Negro Servitude in Illinois and of the Slavery Agitation in that State, 1719-1864, p. 53.

[7]Illustrating the point is Perry, op. cit., pp. 144-45 and A. W. Harlan, "Slavery in Iowa Territory," Annals of Iowa, II, p. 631.

[8]Thornbrough, op. cit., pp. 34-35. Additional evidence is found in John D. Barnhart, "Sources of Southern Migration into the Old Northwest," Miss. Val. Hist. Rev., XXII, p. 61. The Shakers also aided black settlers. See Flower, op. cit., p. 260.

nths from
at which
leases are

to take
tion that
of these
er a vast
the time
eveloped.
ger from
sided and
to all an
ipating in
of the
cannot be

egister,
ceiver.
. 4.—tf.

oncern :
the next
llatin, for
f *Marvil*
rson hav-
estate are
forward
enticated,
old their

, *admr.*
8—8t.

shortly become a place of business.
LEGNARD WHITE,
LOWRY HAY,

Proprietors.

June 12, 1816. 8 tds.

---

25 *DOLLARS REWARD.*

RANAWAY from the subscri-
ber on the 13th ult. a negro fellow
NAMED RANDAL,
five feet six or seven inches high,
about twenty eight years of age, good
features, smiles when spoken to or in
speaking, stutters in talking, knock-
ed kneed, turns his toes out very
much when he walks, crippled in his
right hand, two or three of the fin-
gers growing to the inside of the
hand, took with him a couple of linen
shirts, a pair of overalls of the same,
and a shirt and overalls of deer skin,
and an old wool hat.

The above negro crossed into the
Illinois territory, at Smelser's Ferry,
on the night of the 1st inst. Any
person securing said negro in any
jail so that I get him in possession
again, shall receive the above reward,
or the reward and all reasonable char-
ges if delivered to me in St. Charles.
ROBERT SPENCER.

St. Charles county, M. Territory,
June 5, 1816. 9— 5t

tate, I shal
After that
of any der
trator, as
tate togetl
thereon, I
court at th

June 7, 18

SALI

TOWN

WILL
on the 15t
Town of I
said Town
chase mon
epual inst
twelve and
date of th
the plan of
the Saline.
office of tl
Upon the
security be
be immed
by Conro
wife.

Saline, on

Runaway Slave Advertisement
From the "Western Intelligencer," June 25, 1816.

placed in their paths by hostile whites.[9] They were, in every sense, the epitome of the frontiersman. Whatever the modes of their arrival and whatever the sources of their migration, a few blacks did become pioneers in the northern woods and prairies.

With the exception of these few, however, the most salient racial feature of the northern frontier is the almost total absence of blacks, free blacks in particular. The numbers of blacks in the northern backwoods, whether relatively large or small at any given time, were both a cause and a result of white reaction to blacks. Whites had a number of fears and anxieties concerning blacks: the number of slaves on the frontier would enable slavery to take root and thrive; the number would not enable it to succeed; blacks were not human enough to allow them to mingle in society on any basis approaching equality; blacks were too human to be treated inhumanely. Blacks, too, had fears and anxieties concerning their place in the lands of opportunity, and these concerns centered on the type of treatment they would receive at the hands of whites. All of these worries evoked responses that helped to produce on the northern frontier a society remarkable for its racial homogeneity.

THE SOUTHERN FRONTIER AND SOUTHERN SETTLED AREA

Over the years the percentage of southern pioneers who were black fluctuated wildly. In 1800 they constituted 10.4% of the total pioneer population. This figure more than doubled in the next decade, surged to 27.1% during the following decade, and by 1830 over 30% of all frontiersmen in the South were black. By 1840 the percentage had collapsed to just 13.4.[10] In the southern settled areas, blacks formed 46.7% of the total population in 1800, well over 47% a decade later, just over 46% by 1820, and the figure sagged to just 45.5% by 1830. Within another decade, only 43.2% of the southeastern population were black. (The fluctuation over the whole period was just 4.4% of the total population.) Through 1830 the racial characteristics of the southern frontier and the southern settled area

---

[9]For a very detailed and useful discussion of many of the legal and other restrictions gradually placed on free blacks over the years throughout the nation and the ways in which blacks managed to surmount some of them, see Carter G. Woodson, *Free Negro Heads of Families in the United States in 1830 . . . with a Brief Treatment of the Free Negro*, pp. v-lvii.

[10]The location of the southern frontier of 1840 certainly helped to reverse the trend. The frontier was found almost exclusively in Missouri and Arkansas and, in numerous instances, the frontier counties were located in rugged terrain that was in no way conducive to large-scale plantation operations. Slavery, in general, appears to have fared rather poorly on the southern frontier of 1840, at least insofar as well-being is associated with numerical size. The fact that the topography of the frontier affected the racial composition was made even more apparent when a survey of the southern frontier counties of 1850, located almost exclusively in Texas, indicated that slightly more than one-third of the settlers were black, nearly all slaves.

were converging; the wilderness became increasingly black and the Southeast increasingly white until 1830, a time when the frontier contained proportionately nearly two-thirds as many blacks as the East. This trend toward covergence snapped abruptly during the 1830s. And by 1840 the southern wilderness contained, proportionately, less than one-third the number of blacks present in the southern settled section.

Free blacks never constituted 5% of the black population on the southern frontier, and in 1810 and 1820 accounted for hardly 1%. Slipping from nearly 5% in 1800 to barely 1% during the next two decades, the percentage of black pioneers who were without fetters rebounded slightly by 1830 and then spurted more, topping 2% by 1840. No pattern emerges other than the tendency for slaves to consistently outnumber free blacks in the fresh lands of the South. In the southern settled area the percentages of blacks who were free hovered around 10% every decade. In 1800 less than 10% were free, but this figure crept to above 12% a decade later, slipped a bit by 1820, and then remained fairly constant at over 11%. Obviously, the southern backwoods offered little hope of freedom to blacks. Compared to the settled area, the Dixie frontier contained very few free blacks among its black inhabitants, and there were few signs that this discrepancy was fading with time. Simply put, the southern wilderness always found a higher proportion of its blacks in chains than did the settled region, the difference being quite slight only in 1800.

Throughout the forty years, slaves constituted a consistent and sizeable majority among blacks in both regions in the South. Logically, then, the percentages of total populations in these regions consisting of slaves differed only slightly from the percentages consisting of blacks. As a percentage of the total southern frontier population, slaves displayed tendencies nearly identical to those for the total black population: a sharp spurt from 1800 to 1810, a further increase by 1820, a gentle rise to a peak in 1830, and a brisk decline by 1840.

Thus, from 1800 to 1830 the southern frontier became increasingly unfree. In the settled section the percentage of the total population composed of slaves declined moderately but steadily from 1800 to 1840, the sharpest decline—only a trifle more than 2%—occuring during the last decade. Given several more decades, the two regions could have been identical. But the census figures of 1840 destroyed the slide toward convergence, sharply reversing the trend toward an enslaved black frontier.

In terms of numbers, slavery on the northern frontier was feeble in 1800, became stronger numerically in 1810, peaked in 1820. By 1830 black settlers there legally enjoyed freedom, however precarious and however subject to a mounting barrage of legal, social, political, economic, and sometimes physical restrictions. The southern frontier experienced no corresponding tendency toward freedom over the years—approximately 98% of the black settlers were slaves in 1840—and even those few who clung to legal freedom were closely regulated by the customs, whims, and laws of whites.

Although a very high percentage of black pioneers was in chains, whites dictated that slaves could not be present in the southern wilderness in numbers roughly proportionate to their numbers in the southern settled section. Free blacks who wanted to venture to the southern frontier were even more severely restricted; only in 1800 did free blacks in the southern back country exceed in relative terms ten per cent of those in the southern settled region. Essentially, the southern frontier contained few free blacks compared to the Southeast.

Because slaves labored directly for whites, they were welcomed by at least some frontiersmen. Free blacks, on the other hand, were never welcomed in the southern backwoods, however securely fettered by custom and law. The institution of racial slavery—encountering difficulties in adapting to primitive frontier conditions, receiving heavy flak from abolitionists, smarting under world-wide condemnation, pummelled numerically in the North and languishing in the border states, occasionally rocked by startling slave revolts, and responding increasingly inappropriately and dysfunctionately to these and other perceived threats—was in no condition to tolerate throngs of free blacks mingling more or less at will with enslaved blacks. The absence of free blacks from the southern wilderness suggests that the Upper South and urban centers of the South were more attractive, offering as they did greater latitude; the absence also indicates the degree to which free blacks were anathema to most white pioneers. The fact that free blacks never became southern settlers in numbers even remotely approximating their number throughout the South strongly suggests an inability to enter the frontier, an inability which resulted from an act of deliberate exclusion. The ambitious unfettered black was denied the opportunities of the West.

A COMPARISON OF THE NORTHERN AND SOUTHERN FRONTIERS

Not surprisingly, the population of the southern wilderness contained a much higher percentage of black pioneers than the population of the northern wilderness. Each frontier's population over the years was derived, in large measure, from its respective settled area. As a consequence, massive and chronic racial differences between the two frontiers were forecast. In 1800 approximately one-half of one per cent of the northern settlers were black as compared to over 10% of the settlers in the South, a ratio of less than one to twenty-three. In 1810 almost exactly three-fourths of one per cent of those of the northern frontier were black as compared to nearly 21% on the southern frontier, a ratio of less than one to twenty-seven. A decade later blacks composed slightly more than 1 per cent of the settlers in the northern wilderness and more than 27% of those in the southern wilds, the ratio being less than one to twenty-four, a slight decline from the previous decade. By 1830 the percentage of settlers on the northern frontier who were black slipped to less than one-half of one per cent as compared to over 30% for those on the southern frontier, a ratio of less than one to sixty-two. The percentage of blacks on the northern frontier in 1840 stood at just three-tenths of one per cent and over 13% in the southern backwoods, a ratio of less than one to forty-four. In general, therefore, the two frontiers over the decades were vastly different in terms of racial composition and experienced divergent racial trends from 1800 through 1830, followed by a partial reversal of this trend by 1840.

The comparison of the two frontiers also yields some interesting facts concerning the condition of free black pioneers. At no time from 1800 to 1840 did free blacks compose less than a majority of the black population in the northern wilds. The forty years, in fact, witnessed the virtual extinction of legal slavery in the northern frontier. During the same time span, however, no similar fate befell slavery in the new lands of the South. Slavery there thrived and, with the exception of 1800, free blacks never climbed much above 2% of the total black population. Clearly, the trend among the northern states and territories was one of *de jure*—if not always *de facto*—freedom for the black man. Equally clear, no such trend existed on the southern frontier or throughout the South. The two frontiers thus experienced over the years divergent trends in the condition of their black settlers.

As was expected, the northern and southern frontiers reflected the racial compositions of their respective areas. Equally expected, the two frontiers reflected the fact that each had received some settlers and ideas from each other and from each other's corresponding settled area. Some people, for example, had migrated from Virginia to Illinois while others had moved from Pennsylvania to Missouri. And so, the northern wilderness—largely a product of settlers from the Northeast by 1840 but also containing some elements, usually non-slaveholding elements, from the South—contained relatively few blacks compared to the southern wilds. (Most of the blacks, including slaves, in the northern wilderness were usually located in areas fairly close to the Ohio River, areas in which pioneers from the South lived.) Nevertheless, perhaps as a result of migratory masters, the fresh lands in the North generally housed proportionately more fettered blacks among its black population than the northern settled region. Some enthusiastic owners ushered their bondsmen into the Old Northwest, hopeful and even confident that such states as Illinois would condone and protect slavery and suppress free blacks. Such hope and confidence lingered until the 1820s. The southern backwoods, largely a product of migrants from the southeastern section of the nation, contained both absolutely and relatively many more blacks than the northern frontier, and a far greater percentage of these blacks were slaves.

Compared to the two settled regions, the respective frontiers had fewer blacks but a greater proportion of these were enslaved, a fact which indicates a great deal about opportunity for blacks over the years in the West. It also indicates that whites simply did not want free blacks in the West. Some slaveowners in the North, under mounting pressures from abolitionist forces and possibly economic forces, tried to place distance between their slaves and elements hostile to slavery. Also, southern masters attempted to stray a bit north in their generally westward treks, and regions adjacent to the Ohio River heard the crack of the slaver's whip. Moreover, slaveowners in the older sections of the South, in economic difficulty or anxious about the high concentration of blacks in the older sections, lashed their slaves into becoming pioneers in the fresh lands of the West. The soil was fresh, the economic and social foundations were highly agrarian, and few free blacks were there to pester the slaves. As a result, hefty numbers of bonded blacks were rushed into the newly-settled lands of the South. Stated another way, each frontier contained racial traits somewhat similar to those of its respective settled area and also somewhat similar to those of the other settled area.

Summary and Conclusions

This chapter yields three conclusions. First, compared to their respective settled areas, the two frontiers contained few blacks. This was especially true for the northen frontier. Of those who did manage to reach the northern back country, most were free and proportionately more became free from 1800 through 1830, and by 1840 the northern frontier was all but free from overt slavery. Of blacks in the southern backwoods, almost all were in chains and there occurred little, if any, discernible movement toward emancipation. On both frontiers, the percentages of blacks who were slaves were greater than in the two settled areas, an important finding.

Second, although it is impossible to determine the exact number of blacks, free and slave, who were excluded from the frontier by overt actions of whites, the number is certainly large compared to the number who actually managed to live in the West. With or without leg irons, some blacks did enter the northern backwoods with the explicit or tacit approval of whites, or at the command of whites. Some free blacks were shepherded into the woods north of the Ohio River by whites who wished them well, some were marched into the region by whites who wished profit and power, some arrived there after a dash to freedom, and some venturous blacks left the East and braved the difficulties of the West in an effort to build a new life. These blacks met other blacks who had lived all of their lives in the

Northwest. Free or in chains, blacks were hardly made to feel welcome by most whites. Most of the settlers in the Northwest were simply none too eager to share the riches and opportunities of the West with blacks of any condition. Given the blatant anti-black sentiment existing among white settlers, it is no wonder that few blacks were willing to expose themselves and their families to the risks and uncertainties. Although some managed to muster a little money and equipment in an effort to join in the scramble for western opportunities, the pervasive and virtually unchecked prejudice against blacks effectively filtered many of them out of the migration process.

Third, white motives in restricting blacks are varied and somewhat shrouded in mystery. Some whites were appalled by the slave system and all it entailed, some were appalled by blacks, and some were appalled by both. Some masters surmised that the embattled institution of slavery was too fragile to be transplanted intact in western soil, a fact which kept some blacks out of the western lands.

Regardless of the exact motives for or modes of restriction, the wilderness was home to comparatively few blacks, especially free blacks. The consequences of this monumental act of exclusion are impossible to determine precisely and fully, but the undeniable fact that relatively few blacks settled on the frontier (and few of these did so of their own volition) vigorously suggests that fresh western soil—for hundreds of thousands of eager whites the instrument by which astounding economic success and social advancement were obtained—was of little direct consequence in the lives in the vast majority of black people. The skills and determination possessed by blacks made little difference; most whites either wanted blacks excluded from the Garden or did nothing to prevent exclusion, and very few blacks enjoyed success in the West. The repercussions of this act of denial reverberate even now across the land.

The Half-faced Camp

The rustic nature of the frontier had the effect of
emphasizing agrarian and other self-sustaining occupations.

Courtesy, Illinois State Historical Library

CHAPTER VII

Occupations

As demographic traits of the frontier, age and sex were immutable, and race, although often blurred by gradation, was strictly defined by custom and law. The condition of blacks, whether enslaved or comparatively free, also was generally determined before birth, the condition remaining pemanent throughout life for nearly all blacks. (In spite of a substantial rise in the number of free blacks in the Upper South in the decades preceding the Civil War, only comparatively few slaves were fortunate enough to bolt to freedom, purchase freedom, or have it granted to them; even fewer free blacks were unfortunate enough to have been kidnapped into slavery.) Whatever else age, sex, race, and the condition of blacks had in common as they pertained to the individual, they were all essentially incapable of being changed by the individuals upon whom they had been conferred. Not so with occupation, and it is to this demographic variable that we now turn.

Compared to the analysis of other demographic variables, the analysis of occupation is difficult.[1] In few instances is there great confusion about whether or not the census deemed a person to be black or white, free or slave, or young or old. However, there were sometimes nagging and bothersome questions about whether a person was primarily engaged in agriculture or commerce, navigation or commerce, agriculture or manufacturing, mining or manufacturing. Contemporary sources demonstrate conclusively that a great many individuals held jobs that did not fit neatly into any single specific category; other individuals held two or more jobs of apparent equal importance, although they were grouped in the census according to *one* job or the other. The jobs thus excluded from the census were often of basic importance in the struggle to master frontier conditions. The difficulty of categorizing was compounded by the fact that the census of 1820 contained three occupational classifications, that of 1840, seven.[2]

---

[1]Much of the difficulty stems from the fact that federal census data prior to 1850 pertaining to occupations are present only in the census of 1820 and 1840.

[2]For purposes of comparison in this study, the seven classifications of 1840 were condensed to three —the three used in 1820—in order to obtain occupational classifications nearly similar to those of 1820 (see Table 19).

Difficulties aside, this chapter uses census data to make three occupational comparisons: one between the northern frontier and the northern settled area; another between the southern frontier and the southern settled area; the third between the northern and southern frontiers. In the course of these comparisons, some of the relationships between pioneer occupations and the rustic nature of the back country are investigated.

Explicit references to the occupational composition of the frontier are relatively rare. Implicit in the references made concerning the livelihood of the typical pioneer, however, is the assumption that the pioneer derived his wealth from the land. Probably most historians of the West would concur with one who claimed, "At least six-sevenths of the settlers were farmers, raising corn and wheat, owning cattle."[3] (Actually, this figure is not far from accurate, as will be seen.)

Risk accompanies any claim of persistent trends in the development of various occupations on the frontiers. And yet, incontrovertibly, the vast majority of people streaming west in the opening decades of the nineteenth century eventually tilled the soil. Census data in the following pages strongly indicate it and contemporary evidence supports it. One observer, perhaps unusually perceptive, noted

> The possession of land is the aim of all action, generally speaking, and the cure for all social evils, among men in the United States. If a man is dissappointed in politics or love, he goes and buys land. If he disgraces himself, he betakes himself to a lot in the west. If the demand for any article of manufacturing slakens [sic], the operatives drop into the unsettled lands. If a citizen's neighbors rise above him in towns, he betakes himself where he can be monarch of all he surveys.[4]

This sentiment was echoed by Francis Grund in advice he gave to prospective immigrants to the United States:

---

[3]E. Douglas Branch, *Westward: The Romance of the American Frontier*, p. 296

[4]Martineau, *op. cit.*, II, pp. 30-31. Perhaps the reasons for settling on the frontier were not as negative as these, but that land was the objective of the majority of those streaming westward appears beyond doubt. Not only did most willfully engage in agriculture, but there was also a Cincinnatus quality associated with it by republican Americans: "The tailor or the shoemaker who works house to house in his particular calling; the blacksmith, the miller, the store and tavern keeper—all employ their leisure time in clearing their land or cultivating it. Nor are agriculture pursuits in Ohio esteemed at all derogatory to any office or profession whatever, civil or ecclesiastic. The doctor returns from his rounds . . . takes off the empty saddle bags . . . feeds his pigs; and yet his skill as a physician is not doubted on that account. Nor is the sentence of the magistrate or 'Squire,' as they call him, esteemed less wise or impartial, even by the losing party of his wrangling disputants, because Cincinnatus-like, he is called from the plough tail to the bench of justice. The good people of Ohio never dream either that the word of God is less worthy of credit, because it is dispensed on the Sabbath-day by a clergyman whom they have seen milking his cows, or driving his corn to mill during the week." Griffiths, *op. cit.*, pp. 79-80.

Let them bear in mind, that in the cities, though individuals may prosper, they will hardly be able to raise themselves to an equality with the native inhabitants; whereas in the country, and especially on new land, they must, by persevering industry, become as respectable and powerful as the rest of their fellow-citizens.[5]

The advice may not have been an accurate assessment of the facts, but thousands *believed* it was accurate and often acted upon this belief. Without doubt, the mode of production for which the typical pioneer yearned and strove was not commercial or industrial, but agricultural.

So, the first people into the fresh lands of the West usually sought land: "More than nine tenths of all people who emigrate to the west are *farmers or planters* ... Commerce and manufactures, it is true, *follow* the path of the new settlers; but they never lead the way to those regions, and are rather accesseries [*sic*] than originators of civilization."[6] The term "never" overstates the case—commercial and manufacturing interests were, in fact, sometimes in the vanguard of settlement—but unmistakably most backwoodsmen engaged primarily in agriculture.[7]

Agrarian or non-agrarian, the nature of frontier occupations was recorded in the federal censuses of 1820 and 1840. The evidence forces three conclusions:

1. In 1820 the northern frontier was more agrarian than the northern settled area, but the differences greatly decreased by 1840.
2. The southern frontier was more agrarian than the southern settled area in 1820, the differences increasing slightly by 1840.
3. The southern frontier was more agrarian than the northern frontier in 1820, and the relative gap increased considerably by 1840.

In short, the northern frontier became more like the rest of the nation in terms of occupational composition, but the opposite was true for the southern frontier.

AGRICULTURE ON THE NORTHERN FRONTIER AND IN THE NORTHEAST

In 1820 approximately 90% of the newcomers to the northern wilderness told the federal census takers they were agriculturalists (see Table 19). In the settled area, this figure stood at 69%. Only 1% of the pioneers claimed commerce as their primary livelihood compared to 5% in the Northeast. Nine per cent of those northerners making a living in the lands of new settlement worked in manufacturing, 26% in the northern settled area.

---

[5]Grund, *op. cit.*, II, p. 59.

[6]*Ibid.*, II, p. 45.

[7]Preceding even the farmer was the hunter. See, for example, Flower, *op. cit.*, p. 184 and Owsley, "The Pattern of Migration," p. 147. For a detailed account of the sequence of settlement of new lands see John Mason Peck, *A New Guide for Emigrants to the West, containing sketches of Ohio, Indiana, Illinois, Missouri, Michigan, with the Territories of Wisconsin and Arkansas, and the adjacent parts*, pp. 114-16.

By 1840 the percentage of working settlers who described themselves as agriculturalists had sagged to 84%, a loss of 6%. There was no comparable decline in the northern settled area, the percentage in 1840 standing at 68%, a loss of just 1% since 1820. In other words, the two northern regions became more alike over the decades in terms of employment in agriculture. Additional convergence is evident in commerce and manufacturing. By 1840 commercial activities provided work to 4% of those employed in the northern backwoods, a figure over one-half that of the northern settled section. In 1820, roughly five times as many persons engaged in commerce in the northeastern states than in the northern wilderness. Convergence was also present in the trends of those employed in manufacturing. The percentage of the frontier work force active in manufacturing reached 13% in 1840, a hefty increase from the figure of 9% in 1820. During this same period in the Northeast, the proportion of the work force engaged in manufacturing slipped from 26% to 25%. Unmistakably, during the twenty years occupational convergence occurred between the two northern regions, and nearly all of this convergence occurred because the frontier acquired some of the occupational traits possessed by the Northeast.[8]

One of the factors contributing to the general absence of non-agrarian occupations from the northern frontier was the fact that many individuals needed little more than land to survive economically. A sizeable portion of the frontier population engaged in essentially subsistence or, more commonly, near-subsistence farming. They entered into interdependent relationships with non-farmers only when they sold their meager surplus crops or purchased goods and services. Stated another way, a goodly number of frontiersmen scratched a living from the soil in near isolation, consumed most or all of what they produced, and only rarely transacted business with others.

Not so with businessmen, manufacturers, and professionals. These individuals thrived only by securing and maintaining interdependent relationships with others. It required a minimum number of farmers and others—people with specific economic traits—living in a prescribed area to support one non-farmer. This minimum number, or threshold, varied with the occupation and other factors. Possibly an average of 200 frontiersmen was needed to support a blacksmith, 400 for a gristmill, 600 for a newspaper, and perhaps 800 for a lawyer. The thresholds were lower among settlers

---

[8]Much of this convergence was undoubtedly due to the lead-mining activities of northwestern Illinois and southwestern Wisconsin. The thousands of men employed in the mines and associated efforts gave to the northern frontier in 1840 a sizeable non-agrarian minority. For an interesting account of the mining activities, see James O. Andrew, *Miscellanies: Comprising Letters, Essays, and Addresses; to which is Added a Biographical Sketch of Mrs. Ann Amelia Andrew,* pp. 41-43.

TABLE 19.—Per Cent of the Work Force Engaged in Various Occupations

	Northern Frontier	Northern Settled Section	Southern Frontier	Southern Settled Section
1820				
Agriculture	90	69	96	88
Commerce	1	5	1	2
Manufacturing	9	26	3	10
1840				
Agriculture	84	68	95	84
Commerce	2	3	1	3
Manufacturing	11	25	3	11
Mining	2	0	0	0
Navigation of Ocean	0	1	0	0
Navigation of Inland Waters	0	1	0	1
Learned Professions	2	2	1	1

TABLE 20.—The Extent to Which Occupations in Frontier Counties Were Non-Agricultural

Counties in Which Non-Agricultural Occupations Exceeded Five Per Cent of the Agricultural Occupations

	North	South
1820	13 out of 22	8 out of 23
1840	62 out of 70	5 out of 14

Counties in Which Non-Agricultural Occupations Exceeded Ten Per Cent of the Agricultural Occupations

	North	South
1820	9 out of 22	3 out of 23
1840	51 out of 70	2 out of 14

Counties in Which Non-Agricultural Occupations Exceeded Twenty Per Cent of the Agricultural Occupations

	North	South
1820	3 out of 22	0 out of 23
1840	32 out of 70	0 out of 14

who were relatively prosperous, interdependent, and prone to rely on others for some of their needs.

Compared to northeasterners, settlers in the Northwest engaging in non-agrarian activity were scarce, and this scarcity suggests at least four possibilities:

1. Many areas of the northern frontier failed to meet the thresholds for non-agrarian activities.
2. The thresholds were, in fact, met, but the settlers thought it was more economical to purchase their goods and services elsewhere.
3. The settlers had little inclination to want many goods and services normally proffered by non-agrarian types.
4. The goods and services were sought and were rendered, but those providing the services and goods were essentially farmers who were engaged in a little moonlighting.

Whatever the reason—whether due to lack of population density, lack of a needed propensity, inadequate transportation, or some other cause—the northern backwoods in 1840 was obviously still largely agricultural.

Non-Agrarian Activities in the North

Be that as it may, several non-agricultural vocations either accompanied or immediately followed the march of the farmers into the northern wilderness. Some of these, such as those dealing with travel, often established themselves in frontier areas before the farmers arrived, especially in areas of wilderness situated between two parallel forks of human habitation.[9] Once those who provided refreshment and repair for man and beast—the innkeepers and blacksmiths—located themselves on the developing arteries of transportation, their presence encouraged others to settle nearby. Those serving the needs of travelers frequently

---

[9]The size, services, and importance of early inns varied greatly. Some were similar to the two-room log huts described by Chandler R. Gilman, a New York physician, on a tour of the Great Lakes region in 1835. Angle, ed., *op. cit.*, pp. 155-56. Others were like the tavern and stable in Albion, Illinois, where "Any man could now get his horse shod and get drunk . . . privileges which were soon enjoyed, the latter especially." It was these two germs of civilization that made the village "no longer a myth, but a reality." Flower, *op. cit.*, p. 129. The entertainment varied from inn to inn, but that offered to William Richardson at Morristown, Ohio, on November 13, 1815 was possibly as extraordinary as it was despicable: the innkeeper showed him the room he kept for the accomodation of travelers and added that in case ten or twelve wanted to lodge he could "stow two or three in bed with my daughters." Richardson peered into the room and saw a girl of about twenty years old who was quite good looking, and then asked the innkeeper if this was "the arrangement he had made for our lodging, to which he replied, turning to the one in the room, 'that you must settle with them.'" Richardson gives no clue concerning the nature of the final arrangements. William Richardson, *Journal from Boston to the Western Country and down the Ohio and Mississippi Rivers to New Orleans, 1815-1816*, p. 8. For an account of a log tavern that stuffed great numbers of guests into limited quarters, see John A. Clark, *Gleaning By the Way*, p. 121.

Merrymaking at a Wayside Inn
Courtesy, Illinois State Historical Library

established themselves before agrarian settlers flocked in. Still, very few places of business poked into the wilds far in advance of those who tilled the soil.

Saw mills turned out some of the lumber used in pioneer houses and cabins—not everyone on the frontier was raised in a log cabin—and grist mills promoted the profitable accumulation, storage, and transportation of grain. (Saw mills and grist mills often occupied the same building and received power from the same source.) Mills sprang into operation within a short time after the first farmers settled in an area.[10] Poor transportation added to the ubiquitous nature of mills by generating a demand for mills every dozen miles or so, and the hum of mills was heard everywhere.[11] Mills, furthermore, were often the economic foundations for the creation of a hamlet or village.[12] One student of mills made the following astute observation concerning the economic power of mills in generating other economic functions:

> Besides stimulating the local economy and extending the geographical boundaries of the community's trade patterns, the presence of a gristmill encouraged subsequent establishment of associated industries. A blacksmith shop nearby, for example, assured the repair of metal gears and machinery parts and the forging of pecking tools to sharpen or dress the buhrstones. Such a shop was located in or near 39 of the mills [out of a total of 52 in Missouri], and in six of them the millers also worked as the blacksmiths. Gristmills promoted the establishment of distilleries and breweries, sawmills, woolen and carding mills and cotton gins.[13]

Another non-agrarian activity focused on governance. Although settlements sometimes out-stripped the effective reach of territorial, state, and federal government, some form of governance usually occurred quickly at the local level.[14] It therefore devolved upon local government,

---

[10]Nearly every county history and other accounts of pioneer life indicate that mills were early products of settlement and were ubiquitous. The unanimity with which these sources point to the fact that mills dotted the wilderness is impressive. Examples are found in Green, op. cit., p. vi and Stephenson, op. cit., pp. 44, 46. It is possible that in many counties "there were more millers and mill-wrights than all other tradesmen combined." George C. Duffield, "Frontier Mills," *Annals of Iowa*, VI, pp. 425-28, 431. Consult also, John, M. Swisher, *Iowa: Land of Many Mills.*

[11]Priscilla Ann Evans, "Merchant Gristmills and Communities, 1820-1880: An Economic Relationship," *Mo. Hist. Rev.*, LXVIII, pp. 320-21.

[12]Howard, op. cit., p. 111 and Pease, op. cit., p. 85.

[13]Evans, op. cit., p. 321.

[14]The pioneer, for all his reputation of being a raucous hell-raiser, was in reality greatly interested in bringing order to areas without order and law to lawless regions. Only then could he obtain what he wanted: a secure title to land. Accordingly, institutions were created, and positions were filled with energetic men. These positions, while often of a part-time and low-paying nature, did require that a certain number of individuals in each county devote

especially county government, to perform many of the mundane but vital tasks necessary to newly-settled areas. Two tasks of paramount importance, stability and physical movement, demanded much attention from county officials.[15] Violators of the law—at least violators of those laws the settlers wanted enforced—had to be awed into submission if the northern forests and prairies hoped to attract settlers. Also, those who tried to gouge the public at land sales, places of accommodation, and ferries and bridges had to be regulated. While stability was being created, the need for physical movement had to be met, and local government poured much time and expense into improving local transportation and encouraging state and federal governments to do the same. In addition to the numerous county offices, territorial or state and federal political positions had to be filled. For example, virtually every frontier county contained at least one post office and many sported several. These offices provided at least part-time work to hundreds of pioneers. (Frequently, the post office was located in a general store, and one person manned both.) The state and national legislatures, executive and judicial positions created by state and federal action, land offices, military installations, and other public institutions attracted the services of eager settlers.[16] Here and there, military posts greatly stimulated both agrarian activity and non-agrarian activity:

> For thirty years the army posts were a stimulus to the economic life of the Northwest. They were a constant market for provisions and forage, for building materials and skilled labor, for fresh beef and

themselves to the duties of government. And every time new counties were formed, a pack of ambitious individuals stampeded after the newly-created positions. It was noted in Indiana shortly after statehood that "In all directions candidates were perpetually scouring the country . . . defending and accusing, defaming and clearing up, making licentious speeches, treating to corn whiskey, violating the Sabbath, and cursing the existing administration or the administration's wife and wife's father! And every body expected at some time to be a candidate for something . . . till the state of nasty, pitiful intrigues and licentious slanders and fierce hostility, was like a rotten carcass where maggots are, each for himself and against his neighbor, wriggling and worming about." Baynard Rush Hall, *The New Purchase: or, Seven and A Half Years in the Far West*, ed. by James Albert Woodburn, pp. 177-78. The fine opportunities for migrants to enter into local politics soon after appearing in the back country are apparent in Holbrook, *op. cit.*, p. 92.

[15]Within weeks after Morgan County, Indiana, was established, to cite but one example, William W. Wick became judge of the first court, and he was assisted by two associate judges, Jacob Cutler and John Gray. George Beeler was the first clerk of the circuit court and Benjamin Cutler became the first sheriff. Larkin Reynolds, Samuel Reed, James Burris, and Hiram Mathews occupied the four offices of justice of the peace. Esarey, *op. cit.*, p. 245. Supportive evidence is found in Wallace A. Brice, *A History of Fort Wayne, from the Earliest known Accounts of this Point, to the Present Period*, p. 297, and Henry M. Brackenridge, *Recollections of Persons and Places in the West*, Chapter ix, *passim*.

[16]Also, it was common for farmers and others living near such institutions to supply those working there with food, wood, building materials, soap, clothing, candles, and other items of necessity and comfort. Illustrating this fact is Quaife, ed., *op. cit.*, p. 163.

prairie hay, and for the transportation of men and supplies. The twin blessings which the army posts offered nearby communities—economic opportunity and security from Indian attack—cannot easily be differentiated in importance.[17]

Finally, other construction projects—roads, schools, courthouses, bridges, to cite only a few—employed sizeable bodies of men on full-time and part-time bases.

The presence of government also stimulated journalism. Journalists on the frontier published newspapers, usually weeklies, and either in them or separately they printed land claims, laws, public notices, other legal information, and political literature.[18] Those wishing to file a land claim needed the services of a printer, those running for offices found the press crucial, and those trying to enforce laws found it advantageous to inform the public of the nature of the laws. Whatever the demands on the press—and there were many—they were often heavy enough to attract to even nameless hamlets some type of a press.[19] William Blane, observing the frontier, wrote that after settlers made roads the next task accomplished

is to establish a newspaper; which probably is at first only issued weekly and is small in size. Besides matters of local interest, it contains abstracts of the debates in Congress, most of the new laws, &c; but always has a considerable portion filled up with abstracts from books and magazines.[20]

It was probably true that "It was a very tiny town that could not boast its local newspaper."[21]

Innkeepers, millers, governmental officials, and journalists, in addition to clergy and men of medicine were among the earliest non-agrarian people attracted to the frontier. Short of an adequate sample of settlers indicating dates of arrival and exact occupations, however, the order in which the various occupations trickled into the West remains somewhat murky. Essentially, those occupations associated with *immediate* and *basic* needs of the frontiersmen were first on the scene, and then the long-range

---

[17]*Francis Paul Prucha, Broadax and Bayonet: The Role of the United States Army in the Development of the Northwest, 1815-1860*, p. 150.

[18]Numerous examples are found in Boorstin, *op. cit.*, pp. 124-34. See also Karl Trever, "Wisconsin Newspapers as Publishers of the Federal Laws, 1836-1874," *Wisc. Mag. of Hist.*, XXXI, pp. 305-25 and Gayle Thornbrough, ed., "The Indiana Gazetteer or Topographical Dictionary, 1826," by John Scott, *Ind. Hist. Soc. Pubs.*, XVIII. Additional glimpses into the history of frontier newspapers are found in Horsman, *op. cit.*

[19]See Martineau, *op. cit.*, II, p. 5; Michaux, *op. cit.*, p. 270; Gayle Thornbrough, *op cit.*, pp. 7-8, 12-13; and Clark, *Frontier America*, p. 368.

[20]Blane, *op. cit.*, p. 180.

[21]Horsman, *op. cit.*, pp. 143-44.

and more abstract needs were met. And so, the tavern owner preceded the teacher, the blacksmith arrived before the jewler, the soldier cleared the way for the lawyer, the operator of the saw mill provided shelter to the newly-arrived hatter, the general storekeeper blazed the way for the specialized merchant, and the sheriff tried to make it safe for the banker.

Numerous accounts of the early occupations in settlement illustrate the point. Morris Birkbeck, traveling in early Illinois, came to the conclusion that "Carpenters, smiths, shoemakers, brickmakers, and bricklayers, are among the first requisition for a new settlement: others follow in course;—tanners, saddlers, tailors, hatters, tin-workers, &c, &c."[22] In frontier Indiana, towns grew as follows: "first a blacksmith and wagon shop for the convenience of travelers along the road, then a tavern and a general store, in which the post office was located. From this store peddlers' wagons went forth to the more remote settlements."[23] Among the first twenty-two families in Vermontville, Michigan, were people who engaged in the following occupations: farmer, wheelwright, cooper, cabinetmaker, printer, blacksmith, doctor, surveyor, machinist, merchant.[24] The first occupations of Flint, Michigan, included realtor, postmaster, lumberman, carpenter, wheelwright, blacksmith, sheriff, physician, wildcat banker, grocer, clerk, laborer, and millers operating both saw and grist mills.[25] Some

---

[22]Birkbeck, *Letters from Illinois*, p. 14. In other frontier communities, tanners and others were among the first arrivals. Samuel R. Brown wrote of early Brookville, Illinois: "There are within the precincts of the town, one grist mill and two saw mills, two fulling mills, three carding machines, one printing office [which published a weekly, *The Plain Dealer*], one silversmith, two saddlers, two cabinet makers [cabinet makers sometimes doubled as coffin makers], one hatter, two taylors [sic], four boot and shoe makers, two tanners and curriers, one chairmaker, one cooper, five taverns and seven stores. There is also a jail, a market house, and a handsome court house nearly finished." Samuel R. Brown, *The Western Gazetteer*, p. 54. The presence of a silversmith on the frontier was unusual, perhaps indicating the presence of wealth and desire for refinement usually associated with the court house crew. The lack of any mention of a blacksmith and wheel wright is also unusual. Such an absence was also noticed in frontier Onondaga County, New York. There, however, horses were very scarce in the early 1800s. Carroll E. Smith, *Pioneer Times in the Onondaga Country*, pp. 80-105, 204-11, *passim*.

[23]Kate Milner Rabb, ed., *A Tour Through Indiana: The Diary of John Parsons of Petersburg, Virginia*, p. 138.

[24]Holbrook, *op. cit.*, p. 80. This assortment of occupations appears to have been very typical of frontier settlements.

[25]George H. Hazelton, "Reminiscences of Seventeen Years Residence in Michigan, 1836-1853," *Mich. Hist. Colls.*, XXI, pp. 382-83. The presence of "wildcat" banks on the frontier plagued the settler and kept the local currency in a state of turmoil. Perhaps the bank in Wooster, Ohio, was sound. In any case, the town also sported a land office, along with the usual assortment of occupations found in pioneer villages. Blowe, *op. cit.*, p. 541. For descriptions of two new settlements—Ann Arbor, Michigan, and Mount Pleasant, Ohio—see Stephenson, *op. cit.*, pp. 44-79 and *Niles Weekly Register*, X (June 8, 1816), respectively. (Many towns serving the settlers sported cabinet makers; cabinets and other heavy, bulky objects were more often than not left behind.)

economic activities springing up in the early days of the National Road in Indiana were blacksmiths, wagon shops, taverns, general stores (often combined with post offices). Peddlers operated from the general stores, plying their wares to the more isolated inhabitants in the vicinity.[26] This evidence, while by no means conclusive, does reflect the occupational development in a number of frontier areas over the years.

AGRICULTURE ON THE SOUTHERN FRONTIER AND IN THE SOUTHEAST

Unlike the northern frontier and the northern settled area, the two regions in the South displayed no signs of convergence. In 1820 farmers constituted 96% of those employed in the new lands of the South. In the settled area the figure stood at 88%. The percentage of southern pioneers active in commerce in 1820 approximated that of the northern pioneers, 1%. This compared to 2% in the South's settled area. In terms of manufacturing, the discrepancy between the wilderness and the settled area was even greater: three per cent of the work force in the southern backwoods in 1820 made their living in manufacturing, 10% in the southern settled area.

Two decades later the percentage of southern settlers whose primary work lay in agriculture slipped only 1%, reaching 95%; in the settled Southeast, the same two decades witnessed a drop to 84%. During the two decades, therefore, the settled area lost its predominantly agrarian nature more rapidly than the southern backwoods. By 1840 the percentage of southern settlers making their living by commerce rose to 2%, a tremendous relative increase. Comparatively, the Southeast enjoyed an even sharper spurt, bringing the percentage in 1840 to 5%. Relatively and absolutely, the Southeast turned to commerce more rapidly than the southern frontier. As was the case with agriculture, divergence—not convergence—was the salient occupational trend between the two areas of habitation in the South. This trend was strongest in the field of manufacturing. Over the two decades, the number of southern frontiersmen active in manufacturing experienced no change, holding steady at 3% of the work force. This stood in contrast to the moderate increase on the northern frontier between 1820 and 1840.

Very possibly, many of the factors responsible for the dearth of non-agrarian occupations on the northern frontier also created on the southern frontier an even greater dearth. Like the northern frontier, the southern frontier usually contained no more than six people per square mile, a density hardly great enough to support piano tuners, jewelers, bakers, or many others in specialized and non-essential vocations. Compounding low population density was the fact that by 1840 transportation in the southern

---

[26]Lee Burns, "The National Road in Indiana," *Ind. Hist. Soc. Pubs.*, VII, p. 225.

wilds was, from all appearances, vastly inferior to that in the northern wilderness.[27] Lacking good transportation to urban centers and villages, southern settlers possibly patronized merchants, professionals, and manufacturers to a lesser extent than their northern counterparts.

Both frontiers in 1820 lay on water routes easily navigated by shallow-draft steamboats and other types of water transportation. By 1840 the northern backwoodsman still enjoyed fine water transportation on the Mississippi and its tributaries, and Great Lake vessels were binding together the numerous settlements dotting the shores of the Great Lakes. The heady age of the great canal boom was rudely punctured by the economic turmoil of the late 1830s, but the completed canals and improved waterways helped slip the migrant part of the way west, ply him with some eastern necessities and luxuries after he settled, enmesh him ever deeper into the national market, and relieve him of his burgeoning cash crop.[28] Moreover, railroads began to lace the countryside in the central parts of the Old Northwest, making within a decade or two daring Chicago the hub of rail transportation. These far-reaching strides in northern transportation, both products and causes of the emerging interdependent economy, provided the northern settler with great economic and social advantages over what his predecessor had known twenty years before. The settler of 1840 was, compared to his counterpart of 1820, much more plugged into the national scheme of things; he was dealing with an economy that was rapidly becoming national in nature and tightly bound together. This fact certainly did much to promote the convergence of the occupational composition of the northern frontier toward that of the Northeast.

In sharp contrast, the southern settler of 1840 was in a grim geographical position, especially when compared to his predecessor in 1820. Settlers in the Southwest in 1820 were well served by the Tennessee, Alabama, Tombigbee, and Pearl rivers.[29] The southern frontier of 1840, however, consisted in large measure of counties located in western Arkansas and

---

[27]Illinois, both immediately after statehood and through the frontier era, had *relatively* good transportation, both on land and on water. Examples are found in Edmund Dana, *A Description of the Bounty Lands in the State of Illinois*, pp. 4-5 and Quaife, ed., *op. cit.*, p. 109. At the very time the southern frontier was pushing into western Arkansas, one writer noted "It may be asked, 'If Arkansas be so fine a country, why has it not been settled faster?' There are perhaps three reasons;—a fear of the Indians, a fear of sickness, a fear of bad roads." Peck, *op. cit.*, p. 327. Since much of the northern back country, perhaps especially Illinois, knew the first two fears, many of the differences between at least Arkansas and Illinois appear to hinge on the matter of transportation.

[28]The chapter on household size and household composition in the North contains numerous examples of the developing systems of transportation in the North. For a fine treatment of this topic see George Rogers Taylor, *The Transportation Revolution, 1815-1860*, pp. 15-175, *passim*.

[29]Good descriptions of steamboat travel on southern waters are in Basil Hall, *op. cit.*, III, pp. 309-13 and Tyrone Power, *Impressions of America During the Years 1833, 1834, and 1835*, II.

western Missouri, rugged areas that included the Ozarks and other rather inaccessible places. These counties in 1840 were served by very few navigable waters and even fewer good roads, canals, or railroads. Perhaps as a consequence, occupational developments in the southern wilderness from 1820 to 1840 failed to approach the developments in the Southeast.

The essentially agricultural nature of the Dixie frontier may have stemmed from yet another cause: it is likely that the southern settler, white or black, had less wealth, especially in the form of disposable cash, than the northern settler.[30] Another factor may help to explain the absence of non-agricultural types from the southern frontier. It is related to the question of wealth but stems from more than relative poverty. From 1800 to 1840 the percentage of southern pioneers who were slaves fluctuated between approximately 10 and 30%.[31] Slave labor created much of the wealth on the southern frontier, but the slaves never controlled the wealth they had created. Masters controlled the wealth, determining what was bought and how much was spent. And the amount spent on slaves was usually hardly enough to keep them functioning. Had slaves received just payment for their work and had they spent it without restriction, the occupational composition of the southern wilds might have more closely resembled that of the rest of the nation.[32] The purchasing power of slaves, including what the masters spent on them, was minimal, and the presence of slaves produced little economic demand for certain occupations. This undoubtedly combined with other factors, such as the low density of whites and stunted transportation development in the South, to retard the growth of a strong middle class.

William Blane, a sharp-eyed observer of the frontier process, noticed that

Slavery is a complete check to the building of towns and villages, because it almost entirely prevents any demand for labour or merchandize. Say a man possesses forty slaves. All of these unhappy beings are clothed and fed in the coarsest and cheapest manner, generally on a little salt-fish and Indian corn. They live in huts on the estate of their master, and having nothing to sell, *can buy nothing*. Each proprietor has his shoemaker, tailor, carpenter, &c., on his own estate—all slaves.

---

[30]Perhaps the relative isolation of the southern frontier, a product of rugged terrain and poor transportation, contributed to the relative poverty.

[31]See the Chapter VI, "Race and the Condition of Blacks" and Table 18.

[32]The fact that there were proportionately more slaves in the southern settled section than on the frontier does little to detract from this conclusion. The settled areas contained relatively many slaves *and* relatively many non-agrarian workers. The simultaneous occurrence of these seemingly contradictory phenomena is readily explained by such facts as the comparatively dense population in the Southeast, nearness to northern and European markets, and the date of settlement of most of the Southeast.

Blane added "Hence, in the slave States, the *towns*, as they are called, consist of little more than a tavern, a small store, and a blacksmith's shop."[33] More recently, two historians, closely examining counties in the Old Northwest, were "struck by something which is not duplicated on . . . [the] Southern frontier: the appearance of teaming numbers of *small towns*."[34] They added "there were *five to six times* as many such towns per capita here [in the old Northwest] as in Alabama or Mississippi."[35] Southern society was more stratified than northern frontier society, squatters were less able to obtain land, the average white took far less interest in politics, and as a result compared to the northern settlers fewer farmers of the middling sort were rooted in the soil. The economy and society, including non-agrarian activities, suffered in the new lands of the South.

Another influence may have restricted non-agrarian occupational development in the southern backwoods, especially when compared to developments in the northern backwoods. As was seen in the three chapters on household size and composition, there was a markedly greater tendency for cohesive group migration to occur in the North than in the South. Accordingly, instant communities tended to appear on the northern frontier, not on the southern frontier. These communities were sometimes attempts to reproduce a bit of life from New England, the middle states, or northwestern Europe. As such, they frequently included such non-agrarian specialists as a teacher, clergyman, and other similar people.

Convergence in the North and in the South

Between 1820 and 1840 there were few signs of occupational convergence between the southern wilderness and the southern settled area. Instead, there were some indications that the occupational compositions of the two regions in the South became dissimilar over time. This development in the South was, significantly, very much the opposite of what occurred in the North. Compared to the northern backwoods, that of the South retained for a longer time those occupational traits typical of the West. Of the two frontiers, the southern either attracted comparatively fewer merchants, manufacturers, artisans, and professionals over the years or the region gave rise to comparatively fewer such people, or both. In any

---

[33]Blane, *op. cit.*, p. 202. Agreeing with this basic idea is Basil Hall, *op. cit.*, III, pp. 278-79. A product of low white density is discussed in Flower, *op. cit.*, pp. 337-38. Even so, southern towns did contain occupations similar to those of towns in the northern wilderness. This is evident in several sources: Jonas Viles, "Old Franklin: A Frontier Town of the Twenties," *The Mississippi Valley Historical Review*, IX, pp. 270-72; John Melish, *A Geographical Description of the United States*, p. 375; Alphonso Wetmore, *Gazetteer of the State of Missouri*, p. 44; and Jordan, *op. cit.*, p. 22.
[34]Stanley Elkins and Eric McKitrick, "A Meaning for Turner's Frontier, Part 1: Democracy in the Old Northwest," *Pol. Sci. Qtly.*, LXIX, p. 341. Italics in the original copy.
[35]*Ibid.* Italics added.

event, the occupational differences between the two areas of habitation in the North diminished somewhat between 1820 and 1840; differences in Dixie failed to diminish. Of considerable importance, the northern wilderness was markedly more occupationally similar to the rest of the nation than the southern frontier. This demographic condition attracted some people to the northern frontier and away from the southern wilds, and vice versa.

Compared to the southern wilds in 1820, the northern wilds boasted two and one-half times as many people who made their living from non-agrarian pursuits. Ten per cent of the pioneer work force in the North worked in non-agrarian jobs; in the southern wilderness the figure was 4%. By 1840 the difference had swollen to well over a factor of three. Over 16% of employed northern frontiersmen were engaged in non-agricultural work; the corresponding figure in the South was 5%. As far as employment was concerned, the northern frontier over the two decades became less dependent upon agriculture than the southern frontier, suggesting a higher agricultural efficiency and productivity among northern settlers. This higher efficiency, in turn, did nothing to discourage the growth of many non-agrarian specialized activities.

FURTHER COMPARISONS

There is another way to emphasize the increased dissimilar occupational compositions of the two frontiers: to compare the number of counties in which those engaged in non-agrarian work exceeded one-twentieth the number engaged in agriculture, one-tenth the number engaged in agriculture, and one-fifth the number engaged in agriculture (see Table 20.) In 1820, 59% of the counties forming the northern wilderness contained a non-agrarian work force in excess of 5% of agrarian work force. By 1840 the figure was 89%. In the southern backwoods, the two decades brought but slight change, an increase from 35 to 36%. Forty-one per cent of the northern frontier counties in 1820 housed a non-agrarian work force larger than 10% of the farm work force. Twenty years later 73% of the wilderness counties in the North were in this category. Once again, over the decades the southern backwoods experienced only meager change, creeping upwards from 13 to 14%. (In two lead-mining counties in southwestern Wisconsin, Grant and Iowa, the tillers of the soil in 1840 were actually outnumbered by miners and other non-farming workers. In no southern frontier county in either 1820 or 1840 did non-agrarian workers ever come close to a majority of those employed.) In the northern wilds in 1820, 14% of the counties saw the number of workers engaged in non-agrarian pursuits exceed 20% of those working on the farms. By 1840 the figure stood at 46%. At no time in the southern wilderness did the figure for non-agrarian workers ever top 20%. Hence, in terms of occupational traits, the point radically separating the two frontiers lies somewhere between 10 and 20%. Wherever it lies precisely, the northern backwoods changed greatly between 1820 and 1840; the southern backwoods barely changed at all.[36]

All of the data elicit the conclusion that the northern and southern frontiers were relatively more agrarian than their respective settled areas, the northern frontier becoming less so between 1820 and 1840. The southern frontier was much more agrarian than the northern in 1820, and became relatively more so by 1840.

However, at least three factors vitiated many of the apparent differences between East and West, giving to the wilderness certain non-farming characteristics not manifest in the federal census records: (1) Many pioneers dabbled in non-farming work to augment their incomes; (2) A great deal of non-agrarian work on the frontier was performed by non-professional people, this homespun quality doing much to close the real occupational gap between East and West; (3) Much western commerce was in the form of barter, a fact not apparent in the census returns. Taken together, these factors worked to diminish some of the occupational differences between the backwoods and the settled areas. These warrant further consideration.

JACKS-OF-ALL-TRADES

Instead of trying to remain wholly or largely tied to the soil, many settlers eagerly turned to non-agricultural pursuits. Numerous heads of pioneer households supplemented their incomes by various means, others engaged simultaneously in two or more occupations, and still others flitted from job to job or managed to avoid work altogether. Pioneer households, North and South, added to their incomes by hunting, gathering, fishing, mining, logging, trapping, and by extracting wealth from their surroundings by other means. Others worked on roads, canals, the construction of public buildings, and still others supplied necessities to military posts. For numerous households, non-agrarian activity provided economic security as additional income, a means of diversifying household income, and an economic cushion in the event of crop failure or disasterously low prices. These facts encourage a wary approach to the census data. The data, however accurate, lacked detailed occupational classifications and failed to take into account those who held two full-time jobs and those who were able to supplement their incomes to a considerable extent with a second job.

---

[36]Again, the location and resulting nature of the southern frontier of 1840 appear to have been of great importance in explaining the rather negligible changes occuring in occupations between 1820 and 1840.

Inns and taverns, though numerous, often failed to keep pace with the advancing edge of settlement, and those that did often cost the weary traveler dearly. Practically every frontier household took advantate of this condition, housing the tired and frugal.[37] Patrick Shirreff observed that in the frontier in northern Illinois "as in some parts of Canada, there are few taverns, but *almost every* inhabitant entertains for payment."[38] Basil Hall, a frequent, if unenthusiastic, lodger at frontier houses, had more so say about payment in frontier Georgia:

> In that part of America, where there is no regular travelling, and indeed little travelling of any kind, no taverns, properly so called, are kept up. But in their stead, some houses near the road are always open to any one who calls, and the best fare the inhabitants have, is cheerfully set before their guests. Of course, a charge is made, which varies, as might be expected, inversely as the quality of the entertainment.[39]

Very often such arrangements were completely satisfactory to the traveler and to the accommodating household, the local innkeeper being the only unhappy party. Again, these activities went unrecorded in the censuses, and their net effect was to make the West more like the East than was suggested by the census data.

The extent to which some households diversified their economic pusuits, often with considerable success, is evident in Fortescue Cuming's account of his trip through Ohio in August 1807. He stopped at Beymer's tavern, four miles east of Cambridge, and there he met the Hutchinson household, a household which had migrated from Massachusetts to Franklinville, Ohio, four years previously. There they had operated a store, a distillery, a saw mill, and a farm simultaneously and, when Cuming met them, were returning triumphantly eastward to settle near Albany, New York. The household consisted of Hutchinson, his wife, two teenage daughters, an adult son, another son of some ten years, and a young man who operated

---

[37]Primary sources contain innumerable accounts of weary travelers finding refuge from the rigors of travel in private homes. Most travelers seemed to believe that payment for such accomodation was modest and the services adequate, if not impressive. Among numerous illustrations are Stuart, *op. cit.*, II, p. 376; Fordham, *op. cit.*, p. 95; Michaux, *op. cit.*, p. 190; and Blane, *op. cit.*, pp. 140-41. Blane, after grumbling that the settlers with whom he lodged were often not very civil or outwardly hospitable, admitted that to be charged something for a bed, fire, and venison-steaks was better than spending a hungry night in the woods. He concluded that "Surely the traveller must acknowledge, that the paying about the value of eighteen pence or two shillings, by no means cancels the obligation which he owes to the landlord." *Ibid.*, pp. 140-41. Additional information on this subject is found in Edward Zimmermann, "Travels into Missouri in October, 1836," *Mo. Hist. Rev.*, IX, p. 39.

[38]Shirreff, *op. cit.*, p. 233. Italics added.
[39]Basil Hall, *op. cit.*, III, p. 272.

the saw mill.[40] Perhaps the Hutchinson household was more versatile than most, but certainly a fair proportion of backwoods folk made their living from several sources.[41]

Great numbers of farmers supplemented their incomes by acting as sub-contractors in the construction of roads, railroads, other private and public projects, and in the fueling of steamboats and trains. James Hall stressed the profits to be had by hauling wood to steamboats: "we know of no branch of business in which the farmer could engage more profitably, than in supplying them with fuel."[42] An acre of woods easily provided a farmer with a net profit of $150.00, a sum equal to about a year's wage for some people.[43] One eyewitness to the frontier experience calculated that a boat of 100 tons consumed in twenty-four hours roughly eighteen cords of wood, and Basil Hall wrote, "Sometimes, when we were pushing hard, we burnt 30 cords a day. Each cord cost from 2½ to 3 dollars."[44] Trains, too, by the 1830s consumed western wood. William Nowlin, an early settler of Dearborn, Michigan, supplied cordwood to the early trains puffing through the village.[45] When the National Road cut its way through the dense forests of Indiana, local farmers furnished teams and labor for its construction.[46] Attracted by opportunity or driven by necessity, many pioneer households sought non-agrarian employment to supplement income from farming.

Conversely, it is not unreasonable to assume that many non-agrarian easterners held two jobs, and many reduced food expenses with produce from small gardens. Others stalked vanishing game, gathered wild food, and fished. The federal censuses were unable to take these secondary economic activities into detailed account, thereby failing to encompass the true occupational efforts of many households throughout the nation. This was certainly more true of the frontier than the settled area, where

---

[40]Cuming, op. cit., p. 229.

[41]For more on diversified efforts, see Stuart, op. cit., II, pp. 392-93 and Francis Hall, Travels in Canada and the United States in 1816 and 1817, p. 196. Teachers were urged to diversify their occupational activities: They could "teach school all their lives, which is, or ought to be, a most honourable business, and will not prevent them from carrying on farming to such an extent as to support a family." Robert Baird, View of the Valley of the Mississippi, or Emigrant's and Traveller's Guide through the Valley of the Mississippi, p. 177. Additional aspects of the economic fate of teachers are in Riegel and Athearn, op. cit., p. 137.

[42]James Hall, Notes on the Western States, p. 144. Steamboats, it was observed, "generally stop twice a day to take in wood for the engine, when fresh milk and other necessities are procured." W. Bullock, Sketches of a Journey through the Western States of North America, p. xii. By the 1840s wood was becoming scarce and expensive and technical problems in the burning of coal had been solved, resulting in a reduced demand for wood for steamboat fuel. Taylor, op. cit., p. 60.

[43]James Hall, Notes on the Western States, pp. 144-45.

[44]Rabb, ed., op. cit., p. 71; Basil Hall, op. cit., III, p. 348. See also Howard, op. cit., p. 105.

[45]Nowlin, op. cit., pp. 189-91.

[46]Burns, op. cit., p. 221.

occupations were more highly specialized. Consider the problems the census taker faced when he tried to classify some pioneers on the New York frontier:

> Sluman Wattles . . . was not only a farmer, but a road builder, tailor, shoemaker, lumberman, butcher, hatter, bricklayer, teacher, lawyer and county judge. Another example was Joseph Sleeper, farmer, Quaker preacher, surveyor, millwright, carpenter, stone-mason and blacksmith; and still another, Jedediah Peck, who was farmer, lawyer, millwright, preacher, politician and county judge.[47]

Clearly, the vast majority of these activities never found their way into state or federal censuses. Consequently, the true occupational compositions of the frontier and the settled areas were somewhat more alike than indicated by the census returns, the frontier being less agrarian than the returns indicate and the settled area more agrarian.

Giving great encouragement to those who wanted to be jacks-of-all-trades was the fact that the thresholds—in terms of capital investment, formal training, effort, and knowledge—for most occupations, and most professions, were very low. Individual settlers fluttered freely from job to job and profession to profession, sampling a variety of activities and perhaps settling in several. Incredibly low thresholds were noted by a Swede, Gustaf Unonius:

> The speed with which people here change their life calling and the slight preparation generally needed to leave one calling for another are really surprising, especially to one that has been accustomed to our Swedish guild-ordinances. If liberty in the one case seems too circumscribed, it may well be thought too unlimited in the other. A man who today is a mason may tomorrow be a doctor, the next day a cobbler, and still another day a sailor, druggist, waiter, or schoolmaster. Certainly distinct inconveniences arise from this situation; yet undeniably this unlimited freedom is exactly one of the important reasons why America has advanced with such tremendous speed. It has indeed given opportunity for many humbugs to flourish, but at the same time it has called forth many able men and has spurred them on to greater efforts.[48]

Stated another way, low thresholds in the West resulted in tremendous occupational fluidity. This fact combined with the tendency for numerous farmers to supplement their incomes with non-agrarian pursuits, and the result was that the census figures were qualified in such a way as to make the frontier be, in reality, more like the East.

---

[47]Francis Whiting Halsey, *The Old New York Frontier: Its Wars with Indians and Tories, Its Missionaries, Schools, Pioneer and Land Titles, 1614-1800,* pp. 398-99.
[48]Unonious, *op. cit.,* I, pp. 243-44.

Homespun and Barter

Equally absent from the census returns was the fact that frontiersmen made much of what they needed.[49] Clothes, tools, houses, toys, furniture, and other household items were hewn out of the western forests and fields.[50] Domestic manufacturing accounted for perhaps two-thirds of all clothing worn in the United States in 1810 and 1820. This was especially pronounced where transportation was still relatively undeveloped.[51] James Hall, visiting the West, was thus quite accurate when he claimed that

> A very large portion of the western people manufacture their own clothing; among the farmers this practice is universal: and it extends so far to other classes that it is not at all unusual to see professional gentlemen in affluent circumstances, and men of high official rank, clad in plain domestic fabrics.[52]

Often no transfer of money occurred during the construction and furnishing of pioneer homes, items being purchased only if the combined exertions of the settler and his neighbors were insufficient to produce them. A high degree of self-sufficiency was much less common in the East, even among eastern farmers, tenant farmers, and rural laborers. The natural resources needed to attain self-sufficiency in the settled area were either increasingly scarce or they were owned by others. Also, many easterners, removed from the soil by generations and working fourteen hours a day in a shop or store, had neither skills nor spare time necessary to attain self-sufficiency. As a result, easterners lived in homes and used household items that were manufactured outside of the home, thereby causing someone to be listed in the census as a manufacturer and perhaps someone else to be

---

[49]The federal census returns did not include homemade items that were produced for home use. For example, the labor and overall value associated with the building of a table by a settler for his own use in his cabin went unrecorded; the labor and value and occupational classification associated with the actions of a professional table maker in the East were recorded.

[50]In Ohio immediately after the War of 1812, "manufacturers are in their infancy, all the handicraft arts of the first necessity are in use. The farmers in a great degree manufacture their clothing." Blowe, *op. cit.*, p. 525. On Jan. 17, 1818, Morris Birkbeck and his son explored their newly-settled area in Illinois looking for possible neighbors and they found one, a Mr. Emberson, "making the most of a rainy day by mending the shoes of his household." Birkbeck, *op. cit.*, p. 132. In northeastern Ohio in 1816 domestic manufacturing occured to such an extent that "there is little commerce; the chief trade is in salt, and a few ornamental imported goods." Blowe, *op. cit.*, p. 545. Further reference to home manufacturing and the tendency toward self-sufficiency is found in Cockrum, *op. cit.*, pp. 158-59; William E. Wilson, *Indiana: A History*, p. 159; Wiley Britton, "Pioneer Life in Southwest Missouri," *Mo. Hist. Rev.*, XVI, pp. 270-77; Mary J. Welsh, "Recollections of Pioneer Life in Mississippi," *Pubs. of the Miss. Hist. Soc.*, IV, pp. 346-47, 349-50; Horsman, *op. cit.*, p. 122; Riegel and Athearn, *op. cit.*, pp. 123-24; Howard, *op. cit.*, p. 11; and D. Griffiths, Jr., *Two Years' Residence in the New Settlements of Ohio, North America, With Directions to Emigrants*, p. 68.

[51]Taylor, *op. cit.*, p. 211.

[52]James Hall, *Letters from the West*. p. 68.

listed as active in commerce. Settlers were surrounded by goods and services fashioned in the home and which were, therefore, not responsible for someone appearing in the census in a non-agrarian capacity. Homespun activities made the real occupational composition of the frontier and settled sections more alike than the census indicated.

Similarly, frontier population density and related economic forces usually precluded very many full-time specialists. Often frontiersmen were specialists only by virtue of the fact that they claimed to be so. For example, blacksmiths repaired wagons, supplied farmers with metal implements, and tinkered with firearms. General store owners tended the post office, and supplied itinerant peddlers with pots and pans and other supplies. The agglomeration of economic activity and economies of scale in much of the settled areas enhanced the trend toward specialized economic activities. There were relatively many specialists in the East who did nothing but make wheels, or ploughs, or rifle barrels, or shoes or render in a specialized manner such services as teaching, office holding, or medicine. These specialists were much more than generalists who performed some specialized tasks in their spare time. However, despite the fact that the economic forces on the frontier gave birth to comparatively few individuals who could properly be listed as specialists in the census returns, specialized goods and services were rendered. Once again, the frontier was, in reality, more similar to the settled area in terms of occupations than was indicated by the census returns.[53] Tucked in among homespun efforts were numerous specialized activities.

Work performed in the home, specialized or not, failed to enter the census records. So did the common practice of bartering. Bartering rendered a service by alleviating or circumventing the effects of a shortage of sound, negotiable currency. The practice of bartering was witnessed by D. Griffiths: "With respect to markets for their produce, the Ohio farmers dispose of a great deal by bartering it away at stores for articles of dress, furniture, &c and the store keepers turn it into money."[54] This shortage of currency, widespread throughout much of the frontier, stemmed from at least three causes: (1) Settlers used the money they had to buy or improve land; (2) Settlers used the money to buy a few necessities from either local sources or the East; (3) The market for agricultural products from the West was not yet stable enough to insure a steady supply of surplus cash.[55] The

---

[53]Many individuals in the wilderness toiled in several different activities, including some which were highly specialized in nature. And yet, unless the specialized activity was the major means of making a living, it went unrecorded in the census. In the East there were many full-time specialists, people who were listed in the census as specialists.

[54]Griffiths, op. cit., p. 74.

[55]Supportive of this position is Peter Fox Smith, "A Granville Cooper's Experience with Barter in the 1820s," Ohio Hist. Qtly., LXIX, p. 59. For additional examples of bartering see Howard, op. cit., pp. 111-12; Riegel and Athearn, op. cit., pp. 127-28; and Wilson, op. cit., p. 159.

lack of hard currency, the resulting desire to barter, and the tendency to conserve cash by producing in the home as much as possible inhibited the growth of manufactories and retail stores in the West.[56] They also insured that home-produced items and bartered items, both generally products of the West and both generally escaping the attention of the census taker, made the frontier somewhat more like the settled area than is otherwise implied by official records. In sum, then, the proclivity of settlers to supplement their essentially agrarian livelihood with part-time work in manufacturing and commerce, the tendency of many pioneers to produce by themselves much of what they needed, and the practice of bartering all gave to the frontier some occupational characteristics correctly associated with the East.

Defending the Garden

Despite recorded and unrecorded non-agrarian activities, farming was still the economic mainstay of most settlers. The idea of owning land was paramount in the minds of those who trekked west, and vast numbers realized their dreams. Whether the settler was largely self-sufficient—and a great many were—or whether he carted or floated most of his goods to a distant market and made heavy purchases with the earned cash, the frontier was conducive to agriculture.

The settlers, themselves, helped to make it conducive. They were on the alert for one type of individual who could spoil the Garden, and the decisive action they took against these individuals helped determine the occupational and perhaps social and political compositions of the frontier, making conditions amenable to the settlers. The individuals against whom they leveled their action "did not wear the plain clothes nor tough manners of the settlers, but a smooth manner, a ruffled shirt during the week and a bit of jewelry."[57] They were speculators! Whatever services the speculators actually performed for the newly-arrived settler by securing for him legally sound parcels of land at moderate prices, they were viewed by many as vicious parasites whose presence injected fear and confusion into the minds of pioneers. Settlement was thereby retarded.[58] Had the settlers not moved decisively against the speculator and the agents of speculators—especially

---

[56]On the other hand, the ensuing bartering—flourishing to a greater extent in the wilderness than in the settled area—had the effect of compensating somewhat for the relative absence of recorded commercial activities.

[57]George C. Duffield, "An Iowa Settler's Homestead," *Annals of Iowa*, VI, p. 212. Not all speculators were anathema to settlers. *Resident* speculators, those who actually lived in the vicinity, were tolerated. Even many poorer settlers tried their hand at speculation, and those who profited boasted of their success. See, for example, Griffiths, *op. cit.*, p. 57 and Riegel and Athearn, *op. cit.*, p. 117.

[58]Earnest Calkins, *They Broke the Prairie*, p. 61. Also, see Ray A. Billington, "The Frontier in Illinois History," *Jour. of the Ill. St. Hist. Soc.*, XLIII, and Livia Appel, ed., *A Merry Briton in Pioneer Wisconsin*, p. 26.

those interested in purchasing either large blocs of land or parcels of land encompassing potential mill and bridge sites—the price of land (and the goods and services needed to extract a living from the soil) might have become prohibitively high for many prospective settlers, and settlement would have been further inhibited.

But the value placed upon the ownership of land and the actual rush for land made pioneers intolerant of non-resident speculators and other real or imagined barriers to settlement, and strong action was taken.[59] Institutions sprang into being to curb the speculator, dampen ardent bidding, promote the just settlement of grievances among settlers—in short, simply effect the widespread distribution of land. The speculator and his cohorts, not the settlers, were frequently elbowed from the new lands; farmers were encouraged to migrate, and through the 1830s the West was resonably safe for the yeoman farmer. After all, in an age in which land was—and, perhaps more importantly, was *thought* to be—largely the basis of wealth for most settlers, the yearning to own land brooked little interference from stifling law, scheming lawyers, or absentee speculators. This was especially true on the northern frontier, perhaps particularly in Iowa; southern settlers, shackled by the restraints of a less fluid society, evidently were less effective in thwarting the actions of non-resident speculators and their agents.[60]

The settler, eager to settle the land and often removed by distance from effective state or federal power, realized that the burden of government was with him. The necessity for self-government quickly elicited a craving for local, easily-understood, easily-controlled, decisive, and participatory government. So strong was the desire, and the ability, of pioneers to insure their own forms of justice that professional lawyers were often explicitly banished from judicial proceedings. And the notion that "lawyers is the most cursedest varmit, I reckon, that's about" was by no means

---

[59]For some of the actions taken against speculators, see Angle, ed., *op. cit.,* pp. 75, 163-64; Calkins, *op. cit.,* 61; Charles Joseph Latrobe, *The Rambler in North America,* II, p. 169; Thomas Hedge, "Installation of the Temple Tablet, June 17, 1913," *Annals of Iowa,* XI, pp. 171-72. Club law, conspiracies, threats, and violence were employed to discourage impulsive bidding and the eviction of squatters, and it was noted that "Many strangers, not understanding this, have found themselves most unpleasantly situated." Latrobe, *op. cit.,* p. 230. One visitor to the frontier cautioned, "It is dangerous to threaten a high spirited people with expulsion from their homes." James Hall, *Notes on the Western States,* p. 175. Basil Hall noted of the squatters that they "are their own law-makers and law-breakers, as the case may be." Basil Hall, *op. cit.,* III, p. 355. And to a very great extent, laws odious to squatters and other settlers were ignored or only sporadically enforced. See Havighurst, *op. cit.,* pp. 115-16. For other evidence of actions against speculators and for accounts of settlers' defense organizations, consult Howard, *op. cit.,* p. 163; Riegel and Athearn, *op. cit.,* pp. 118, 175; James Hall, *Letters from the West,* pp. 191-92. In Lake County, Indiana, a Squatters' Union was formed to protect the interests of some 500 settlers. Holbrook, *op. cit.,* p. 64.

[60]See, for example, Stanley Elkins and Eric McKitrick, "A Meaning for Turner's Frontier, Part II: The Southwest Frontier and New England," *Pol. Sci. Qtly.,* LXIX, pp. 567-77.

uncommon.[61] The *ad hoc* nature of the claim clubs, the fact that lawyers were precluded from the resulting proceedings, and the fact that this proto-populist spirit was quite common are evident. For example, "In the summer of 1838 [in Iowa] a plan was set afloat by settlers whereby it was understood that those occupying lands should not bid against one another at the sales nor suffer bidding by *unknown* [italics added] persons." A meeting of settlers was called near Pittsburg, Iowa, at which it was "*Resolved*, that our government is by the people, of the people, and for the people, *and that we are the people.*"[62] Also, in Iowa in the late 1830s and early 1840s

> Lands were eagerly sought. Claimants were ransacking every corner, to make judicious selections, and it would be unreasonable to suppose there would be no collisions, no disturbing questions. But the regulations of our 'Club Law' early made provisions for their settlement. A committee of three—sometimes called Judges of Club Law—was appointed by common consent to take cognizance of such matters, and more especially questions relative to claim property. In cases of disputes or disagreement, this committee—on application—appointed a day and place of hearing, generally in the open air and on the land in question. The parties appeared. The plaintiff presented his case, introduced his witnesses, and said all he wished to say without let or hindrance, or interruption. When the plaintiff was through the defendant had the same privilege. If the plaintiff had lied, the defendent was at liberty to outrank him with a bigger lie, if he could. The standing committee, or a jury especially appointed, then retired, weighed the case, and returned their verdict, which was *final*, and without appeal. A common interest enforced these decisions without trouble. No professional lawyers were allowed, and no expense was incurred, except the time spent at the trial. Our code was very simple, but effective within its limit to a single class of questions.[63]

It should be stressed that such action was usually taken in the *absence* of effective regular law enforcement, not in the spirit of violation of the law. Also, such "common interest" was indigenous and obvious largely to homogeneous communities, ones that were white, agrarian, and with little sense of class structure or deference. As the frontier faded, so did *ad hoc* informal justice.

Such judicial actions, clearly, influenced the occupational composition of the frontier. In addition, the security derived from club law and popular justice undoubtedly affected some household sizes and compositions

---

[61]Featherstonhaugh, *op. cit.*, I, p. 339.

[62]Duffield, "An Iowa Settler's Homestead," pp. 213-14. Italics in the original copy.

[63]Alfred Hebard, "Recollections of Early Territorial Days," *Annals of Iowa*, II, pp. 214-15. Italics in the original copy.

more than others. In particular, newly-married couples, large households, households in economic difficulties, and other economically marginal units stood to gain most by conspiracies to discourage impulsive bidding. They needed land for a fresh start, and a goodly proportion of them got it. Stated another way, the local committees of justice facilitated for some the acquisition of land. And this undoubtedly engendered selective migration to some extent with the result that the demographic, social, and economic characteristics—perhaps the entire culture—of the frontier was altered. Finally, the wealth, security, and feelings of success resulting from a household's triumphant tussle with the wilderness quite likely modified the demographic, social, economic, and psychological traits and circumstances that triggered migration into the wilderness in the first place.[64]

NEITHER SERVANTS NOR MASTERS

One non-agrarian occupation on the frontier, although greatly desired by the settlers and comparatively well-paying, failed to attract people for sustained employment: hired help. Few females were found who were willing to perform domestic chores, and males were not eager to waste many years toiling on someone else's farm.[65] Men simply would not work for others for any length of time when their own efforts could secure land for themselves; women, too, were not too eager to wait on others when their

---

[64]An atypical, even fanciful, frontier experience was the following account of an isolated settlement in early Missouri and the way in which society there functioned: "The governor of the territory considered them beyond the jurisdiction of his government, and they were consequently thrown upon their own resources. During a period of about four years, the only control exercized over them, civil or military, was patriarchal . . . They were not afflicted with judges, sheriffs, or lawyers . . . Contracts were made, and the conditions fulfilled, without the coercion of laws or the agency of ministerial officers. The force of public sentiment . . . regulated society." Alphonso Wetmore, op. cit., p. 81. A hefty proportion of pioneers shared, at one time or another, some of the conditions present in back country Missouri, and the impact upon those who were "thrown upon their own resources" was for most settlers impressive. Again, the homogeneous nature of many settlements did much to encourage those seeking self-government, there being few people other than blacks who were systematically excluded. Had the communities been very diverse and rent with vast economic, religious, and political divisions, then the opportunities inherent in being cut off from the larger society would have been lost.

[65]This was true in spite of relatively good wages paid to hired help. The situation in central Illinois in 1833 was possibly indicative of the general condition of labor on the frontier—at least the northern frontier—over the years: "Labor is scarce and highly remunerated. A good farming help obtains $120, and an indifferent one $100 a-year, with bed and board. A female help receives in private families a dollar a week. The hotel-keeper at Springfield at this time pays two female helps each $2 weekly in cash." In Springfield butter cost 8 cents per pound, eggs 6 cents a dozen, beef 3 cents, and pork 2 cents per pound. Corn cost 10 cents per bushel. An "indifferent" farm hand, then, could purchase at least 5000 pounds of pork per year if he were inordinately fond of pork. Shirreff, op. cit., p. 250. Seven years later in Indiana the Logansport Herald reported very similar prices, including 3 cent beef, 2 cent pork, 8 cent butter, 10 cent cheese and whiskey at 19 cents per gallon. Rabb, ed., op. cit., p. 220.

own efforts could, with the assistance of the favorable sex ratio on the frontier, secure husbands and security.[66] Many laborers arriving in the wilderness remained in the employ of others only long enough to save enough money with which to buy land; they then bid their bosses farewell.

For example, John Bradbury knew that western lands were within the reach of even laborers, and he noted that "From this cause there is a continued tendency in the labourers to turn to farming as soon as they have accumulated a little property."[67] Thomas Hamilton, writing of newly-arrived servants from Britain and elsewhere, claimed

> with him domestic service is only a temporary expedient. The moment he contrives to scrape together a little money, he bids his master good-morning, and, fired with the ambition of farming or storekeeping, starts off for the back country.[68]

Francis Grund noticed much the same thing, although perhaps holding the American servant in somewhat higher regard. Referring to the American servant, Grund penned the following:

> He knows how to read and write, and is sure to understand arithmetic; he takes an interest in politics, reads the papers, and attends public meetings and lectures. He is a member of the militia, pays poll-tax, and is entitled to vote. His mind is constantly engaged in making plans for the future; and, far from being content to remain all his life a servant, he is earnestly contemplating his chance of success in some trade. With these hopes before him, it could not be expected that he would always be a ready, cringing sycophant; but it does not follow, that he must necessarily be unwilling to do his work . . . I am quite convinced that the American servants work harder, and *quicker* than even the English.[69]

Even highly-skilled and well-paid labor, another observer claimed, was not immune to the lure of the land: "Skilled labor, as ever on the frontier, was scarce, irresponsible, and hard to hold off the land."[70]

The independent nature of hired help stemmed from the scarcity of such

---

[66]Employers were well aware of the labor shortage and counted themselves fortunate if they secured help. J. M. D. Burrows, for example, crowed about being able to obtain a hired girl for his household—the culmination of a protracted search. He also noted with pleasure that the girl stayed seven years before marrying, surely something of a record. Quaife, ed., *op. cit.*, p. 145. Other examples are found in Flower, *op. cit.*, p. 165; Howard, *op. cit.*, p. 110; and Margaret Fuller, *Summer on the Lakes, in 1843*, p. 61.

[67]John Bradbury, *Travels in the Interior of America in the Years 1809, 1810, and 1811*, Vol. V of *Early Western Travels*, p. 286. One product of scarce labor was high wages, and another was successful strikes in the West. Riegel and Athearn, *op. cit.*, p. 128.

[68]Thomas Hamilton, *Men and Manners in America*, p. 61.

[69]Grund, *op. cit.*, II, pp. 67-68. Italics in the original copy.

[70]Viles, *op. cit.*, p. 274.

help, and settlers who had previously enjoyed obedient hired hands
bleated ceaselessly about the paucity of such people in the wilderness and
the surly temperaments sported by a large segment of such help as was
available.[71] In 1817 Elias Pym Fordham entered the frontier and observed
that

> The ease with which property is acquired by the industrious, produces
> an equality unknown in Old Countries. No white man or woman will
> bear being called servant, but they will gladly do your work. Your
> hirelings must be spoken to with Civility and cheerfulness. Domestic
> services, perhaps, could be obtained with difficulty.[72]

It was also noted that "the supply of servants has never yet been equal to the
demand;—the consequence is obvious, not only that wages are high, but
that servants are saucy, and difficult to please."[73] Those who labored for
others did so with the realization and understanding that they were
subordinating themselves only economically, not socially or politically.
Countless western laborers regarded their station in life as hardly more than
a temporary stop on the way to better things. This attitude, while
encouraging great social and physical mobility, also had the ironic effect of
promoting social and political stability:

> Neither is there that envy amongst the labouring classes [in America]
> which characterises the *'canaille'* of Europe, and manifests itself by an
> indiscriminate hatred of all whose fortunes are superior to their own.
> Exemption from labour, the *beau ideal* of the French and Italians, is not
> even *desired* by the industrious population of America; and the poor
> are willing to protect the possessions of the rich because they expect
> themselves to need that protection at some future period.[74]

Hired help commanded good wages, exhibited great independence,

---

[71]Those who permitted themselves to be hired by others took great pains to inform the
world that they were still free citizens. Englishmen were warned of the egalitarian tendencies
abroad in the West: "male and female servants, or as they are called 'helps,' must eat and drink
with the family in the country places of the United States." Holmes, *op. cit.*, p. 144. Many
western laborers were "pests to the ... farmers for whom they work, generally at meals,
haunting the fire-side, to the exclusion of the family, at whom they gaze, expecting to be" fed.
Faux, *op. cit.*, p. 291. It was reported from early Napoleon, Indiana, that there, "servant girls are
very proud, and cannot brook the idea of being called servants." Herbert A. Kellar, ed., "A
Journey Through the South in 1836: Diary of James D. Davidson," *Jour. of So. His.*, I, p. 353. The
women and girls of frontier Princeton, Indiana, were "above assisting in the house at a price
day or week. Wives and daughters must do all." Faux, *op. cit.*, p. 216. A friend of Henry
Bradshaw Fearon trod upon the republican sensibilities of a servant by asking for her mistress.
The rebuke from the "help" was swift and huffy: "In this country there is no mistresses, no
masters; I guess I am a woman citizen." Fearon, *op. cit.*, p. 81.

[72]Fordham, *op. cit.*, p. 125.

[73]Stuart, *op. cit.*, II, p. 338.

[74]Grund, *op. cit.*, II, pp. 70-71. Italics in original copy.

switched jobs without notice, entertained high hopes, and repelled efforts to make them more servile.[75] Such souls called their employers "boss," a term that connoted none of the servile, groveling qualities inherent in the European "master."

Although powerful economic crosscurrents began by the 1840s to sweep an increasingly large number of immigrants and natives into urban centers, many immigrants and Americans—perhaps a majority of both—still held to the physiocratic ideas that true wealth springs from the land. (It seems likely that this notion was stronger in the land of Thomas Jefferson and John Taylor of Caroline than in lands of John Adams and Alexander Hamilton, a factor which was possibly a slight countervailing force in the South against mounting economic pressures to either force people off the land or make it economically attractive for them to leave.) So powerful was the lust for land that many people living in Europe and the settled parts of America voluntarily surrendered familiar surroundings, childhood scenes, and considerable security to venture into the wilderness and become landowners.

SUMMARY AND CONCLUSION

The uncertainties inherent in any study of frontier occupations are numerous and formidable. Census records pertaining to occupations are extant for only 1820 and 1840. And the difficulties of categorizing types of work in the West and throughout the nation add another element of uncertainty. Men engaged in several jobs, often of apparent equal importance, and a great deal of work throughout the nation—but especially on the frontier—was of a homespun quality and therefore unrecorded in official records. Added to this, many westerners resorted to bartering to alleviate the effects of currency shortage, thereby clouding the picture even further.

Still, several aspects of frontier work are fairly clear. The needs of the frontier attracted certain types of occupations, occupations that recognized the nature of the frontier and addressed themselves primarily to the problems of establishing security, certainty, and mobility. Most of

---

[75]On at least one occasion those who had formerly enjoyed humble service from hired help attempted to reinstitute a more traditional relationship between servant and master. William Faux visited George Flower and family in 1818 at the English Settlement in Illinois. There he was informed by the family that few servants were available. They also told of a proud servant by the name of Biddy who did very much what she pleased. A conspiracy was hatched against Biddy in an effort to make her more obedient and humble: "On a certain day many visitors were invited to dinner, at which Biddy was not allowed to rise, even to help herself to any thing [sic], but all present vied with each other in attending on Miss Biddy, who in great confusion, left the room, fully sensible of her folly, and next day determined to be a servant for the future." Faux, *op. cit.*, p. 255. Biddy must have been quite exceptional in order to see her "folly." Most native-born western servants would have found only amusement and pleasure in having their employers and their employers' guests vie for the honor of waiting on them.

these occupations fulfilled the essential and immediate needs of the settlers—government, shelter, food, transportation, and communication. The wilderness, furthermore, was relatively more agrarian than the settled areas, and this was more true for the southern wilderness than for the northern. Equally evident, large numbers of farmers in the wilds supplemented their incomes with non-agricultural work, and nearly all busied themselves in slack weeks producing items for the home and farm, facts which partially explain the scarcity of manufacturers and merchants on the frontier. Most pioneer farmers who dabbled in this supplementary and homespun work were recorded in the census tracts as engaging solely in agrarian work. As a consequence, the true occupational pictures of both the frontier and the settled area were somewhat more alike than indicated by the censuses.

One factor was of utmost importance in the development of the West: land, both the availability of it and the *belief* in the availability of it. Settlers acquired, or *hoped* to acquire, vast amounts of land. To get this land, however, many settlers had to exert themselves far beyond mere migration and settlement. Some had to resort to rather extraordinary means. For example, club law—growing either in the absence of effective law or alongside of effective but unpopular law—secured for sizeable numbers of settlers adequate amounts of good land. The economic attractions of abundant land altered law and custom; law and custom, in turn, influenced demography by simultaneously discouraging the presence of such non-agrarian types as speculators and lawyers and encouraging the presence of farming households. Finally, the fierce political and social republicanism brandished by westerners rested heavily on economic opportunity—or on the *belief* in economic opportunity—and this opportunity in the West originated largely in the land. Land was plentiful and it was distributed widely among white people. As a result, the course of the nation's development was profoundly altered.

CHAPTER VIII

The Frontier Fades

The frontier was never static. It was a jagged line of westward-moving ribbons of humanity—some of which narrowed to just a few miles in width at some places, others of which widened to scores of miles, some of which encountered little opposition and churned rapidly across the land, others of which became snagged temporarily on points of opposition before moving onward—generally running along a north-south axis, but jutting east and west upon meeting severe natural or human opposition, or some combination of the two. These lurching ribbons of settlement covered at any moment an area into which was pouring a steady stream of migrants from recent frontiers, the East, and Europe, and out of which was seeping those who wanted to stay ahead of the edge of the frontier, those who perished on the frontier, and those who sought refuge in the eastern states. Inasmuch as the frontier process constantly attracted settlers, prodded other people deeper into the wilderness, and left others behind, it was a continuous process of creation and renewal.

Some energetic souls, William Gregory among the foremost, kept pace with the advancing wave of pioneer settlement most of their lives. This required enormous energy and several migrations, helping to propel the line of settlement westward. Others, once willing to sail into the sea of wilderness and pit themselves against known and unknown hardships and privations, had managed to carve for themselves comfortable niches in the backwoods and wanted to enjoy the fruits of their labors. They were perfectly content to let the frontier, with all its opportunities and difficulties, slip away from them. They would no longer shoulder the burden of advancing the frontier.

It is to these and others that we now turn. In particular, we turn to those who lived in counties that had been part of the frontier a decade previously.[1] Those involved in the settlement process at the beginning of a

---

[1]For each decade, ten frontier counties, five in the North and five in the South, were selected as a sample for this chapter. Some of their demographic traits were measured. The same counties were then measured ten years later—after they were no longer part of the frontier—and the results were compared. For a list of the counties included in the sample see App. F.

decade were often 150 or 200 miles behind it by the end of the decade. The dynamic, churning process of settlement was only a memory, and the excitement and toil entailed therein lay days to the west. What were some of the demographic characteristics of those who lived in regions that had witnessed pioneer activities just a decade previously? More specifically, in terms of demography, did the occupants of such post-frontier lands differ from those who had earlier swarmed onto the same lands as frontiersmen? The answers provided by this comparison will indicate the extent to which wilderness lands lost their typically frontier demographic characteristics over the years. The answers will help test the claim that "The frontier did not last long—within a decade the population characteristics were moderated rapidly and after two decades census data would hardly bear witness to the frontier experience."[2]

A number of hypotheses were devised concerning the degree to which demographic changes occurred in the ribbons of wilderness from the time they formed part of the frontier to a time ten years later:

1. The proportion of the population consisting of youngsters—children under ten—would decline.
2. The proportionate number of young adults would decline.[3]
3. Proportionately, the number of old people would increase.[4]
4. For everyone above ten, the convergence of sex percentages would be such that those of young adults would be most nearly equal by the end of the decade.
5. The proportionate number of male young adults would slip.
6. The same would be true for the elderly.
7. The percentage of the entire population who were male would decline.
8. So would the percentage who were free black.
9. The opposite would be true of the relative number of slaves in the general population.

It was further expected that the first and the last five hypotheses would pertain especially to the South.

In every instance among all pioneer age groups over the four decades, males formed at least 50% of the group. As was seen earlier, adult females sometimes either shied away from the backwoods or entered it hesitantly after others had blazed the trail and ameliorated living conditions somewhat. Other examples illustrate that some women, weary of life in the wilderness, fled eastward. These women—those in the East whose resolve

---

[2]Eblen, op. cit., p. 412.

[3]Depending upon the census year, the young adult age group began at either age fifteen or sixteen and ended at either twenty-six or thirty.

[4]Depending upon the census year, the age group classified as "relatively old" or "elderly" began at either forty-five or fifty.

to migrate flagged in the face of western perils and those on the frontier who sought sanctuary in the more settled parts of the nation—may have totaled only several per cent of the number of women who successfully withstood the hardships of frontier life. But they certainly account in large measure for the persistent (if surprisingly weak) tendency for males in the wilds to comprise a majority of the various age groups. Clearly, the deliberate decision of whether or not to confront western tribulations altered certain aspects of frontier demography.

However, for approximately one-half the white population, those under sixteen, the decision of whether or not to push west was usually made by adults. No evidence suggests that young girls, any more than young boys, were either deliberately cloistered in the East upon migration or shepherded away from the frontier as part of a calculated effort to spare them the rigors of frontier life. The universal trend for a majority of pioneer children under ten to be male must therefore be attributed largely either to the possibility that more males than females were born and survived through age ten or to the possibility that female children were underenumerated in the censuses. (Among children under ten in both settled areas males always outnumbered females.) Since the sex compositions of those under ten were evidently determined by factors other than a consideration of the unpleasantness of western life, no attempt was made in this chapter to analyze sex characteristics of these youngsters.

Compared to the lands encompassed within the northern and southern frontiers, the same belts ten years later usually contained proportionately fewer people under ten; the area in 1810 that had constituted the northern frontier of 1800 provided the only direct contradiction to this rule (see Table 21). Substantiation was thereby lent to the first hypothesis: the proportion of the population composed of youngsters under ten did, in fact, slip over the decade. Lending great support to the hypothesis was evidence from the South over the four decades where the number of youngsters plumeted much faster than was the case in the North. This provided some corroboration for the idea that the first hypothesis and the last five would be especially true in the South.

Several explanations may account for the relative decline in the number of children under ten in the population. Newcomers flooding into the post-frontier areas usually at least doubled the population within the decade, and the traits of these arrivals may have been quite unlike those of the pioneers. The newcomers may have come from different sections of the nation, engaged in different occupations, traveled westward by different means, and migrated for reasons different from those of the earlier pioneering migrants. These factors, alone, could have accounted for differences in demographic traits. In addition, in most places the capital outlay required of such people was considerably greater than that required of the pioneers, a fact tending to screen out those with several children under the age of ten. Another possible explanation centers on the process of aging: the original settlers in the area—those who still remained—were as much as nineteen years older than when they first arrived, this possibly raising the average age in the area and accounting for fewer children under ten. A fourth possibility lies in the fact that such places generally experienced a comparative increase in women. More women almost certainly resulted in a smaller percentage of them being married, a phenomenon noted earlier, and fewer were mothers. The percentage of people under ten as a consequence may have dropped. Another logical answer to the question may hinge on the fact that throughout the nineteenth century the birth rate was falling in the United States. Hence, almost any area that was measured and then remeasured ten years later might show an appreciable slump in the relative number of youngsters.

Regardless of the reasons and regardless of the relative importance of each reason in the equation, the post-frontier regions were home to comparatively fewer youngsters. This trend, moreover, was considerably stronger in the South than in the North.

Most young adults of the era passed through three momentous events: (1) They assumed full economic responsibility as household members while still in their teens. (2) They married within a few years thereafter. (3) They became parents. (Some young folk scrambled the order a bit.) As a result, changes in the proportion of the population in this age group led to weighty changes in various vital aspects of frontier society, economics, and even politics.

The passing of ten years saw the relative number of people in the young adult age group inch downward slightly. In addition, an examination of only young males indicates that in relative numbers this age-sex category crept downward over the decade. Among only female young adults, the relative number inched upward a bit during the decade. Since the frontier contained somewhat fewer adult females than young adult males, it is hardly surprising that the passing of the decade saw an influx of young females, however slight the influx. The gap between the relative numbers of young adult females and males narrowed, females increasing and males decreasing. This trend was particularly strong in the North. Regardless of changes in the sex ratio among young adults, the important change lay in the relative decline of young adults, a decline that brought support to the hypothesis.

Another hypothesis predicted that the decade of post-frontier development would increase the relative number of older people. Excluding the frontier of 1820 from the comparison due to the change in age categories for older people between 1820 and 1830, the relative number of older people always increased during the decade—the greatest

TABLE 21.—Each Frontier and A Decade of Change: Per Cent of the Total White Population in Various Age Groups

	Male					Female				
	0-10	10-15	16-25	26-44	45+	0-10	10-15	16-25	26-44	45+
Counties Constituting the Frontier of 1800										
North	19	8	10	12	5	18	7	8	9	4
South	21	8	9	10	5	20	7	8	8	4
The Same Counties A Decade Later										
North	20	8	9	10	6	19	7	9	10	4
South	21	9	9	9	5	19	7	9	8	4
Counties Constituting the Frontier of 1810										
North	20	8	10	11	5	19	7	9	8	3
South	20	8	10	11	5	19	7	9	8	3
The Same Counties A Decade Later										
North	19	7	10	10	5	18	7	9	8	4
South	19	8	10	10	5	18	8	9	8	4
Counties Constituting the Frontier of 1820										
North	21	8	11	10	4	20	7	9	8	3
South	21	7	11	10	5	19	7	9	8	3
The Same Counties A Decade Later										
North	20	7	14	8	3	19	6	13	7	2
South	19	7	15	9	3	19	6	13	7	2
Counties Constituting the Frontier of 1830										
North	19	7	16	9	3	19	6	13	7	2
South	21	6	13	10	3	20	6	13	7	2
The Same Counties A Decade Later										
North	19	7	15	9	3	17	6	14	8	2
South	19	7	13	9	3	18	7	13	8	3
Counties Constituting the Frontier of 1840										
North	18	6	16	10	3	16	6	14	8	2
South	21	6	14	9	3	19	6	13	7	2
The Same Counties A Decade Later										
North	17	7	14	11	4	16	6	13	9	3
South	18	7	14	9	3	18	7	13	8	2

increases occurred in the belts of land that had formed the frontiers of 1810 and 1840—and support was thus lent to the hypothesis. Interestingly, although perhaps not surprisingly, the greatest gains were among females.

Undoubtedly, some of the increase in the relative number of elderly was due to the inevitable aging of the original settlers. Also, some middle-aged migrants were reluctant to grapple with the elements of the frontier but were eager to acquire land that had been recently subdued and tilled by the efforts of others. (Most likely, too, middle-aged settlers could best afford to purchase land that others had cleared.) In the North, the greatest relative spurt of the elderly occurred in the decade following the existence of the frontiers of 1810 and 1840, the greatest in the South following the existence of the frontier of 1830. Compared to the southern frontier, the northern enjoyed greater increases of elderly during the post-settlement decade. Of the two frontiers, the northern enjoyed the better transportation, the greater number of immigrants, and the greater tendency to practice group migration, facts which later may have been responsible for comparatively many gray-beards.

Proportionately, only in 1810 did the post-frontier area contain more young adults. (The change in age categories between 1820 and 1830 makes comparison of the frontier of 1820 to the post-frontier area quite meaningless.) In general, there was a slight downward drift in the proportionate numbers of young adults living in the post-frontier areas. The entire downward movement, however, occurred in the North, none in the South. The decline, wherever it took place, gives some support to the hypothesis.

The decade brought a general decrease in the relative number of young adult males, there of course being a corresponding increase in each instance in the relative number of young adult females (see Table 22). This was, surprisingly, especially true in the North. Without exception, northern wildernesses contained a higher percentage of males in the young adult age group than southern wildernesses, but within a decade these differences either faded or diminished. At the end of each respective decade, this diminution made the sex differences among the various age groups above ten decidedly smallest for the young adult age group. (The differences between the sexes for this group when it formed part of the frontier population equalled or surpassed 9% once, in 1800 in the North. Differences equalled or surpassed 8% twice, in the northern wilds of 1830 and 1840. The conclusion of the various post-frontier decades found that the differences exceeded 6% only once—this happened in the area that had been southern backwoods in 1820—and they were generally far less than that.)

The raw nature of the frontier dissuaded some young women from flocking to the West, forced some of those on the frontier to flee eastward,

TABLE 22.—Each Frontier and A Decade of Change: Per Cent of various
White Age Groups Who Were Male

	0-9	10-15	16-25	26-44	45+
		Counties Constituting the Frontier of 1800			
North	51.4	54.8	54.6	56.0	56.0
South	51.1	51.6	51.9	54.4	56.2
		The Same Counties A Decade Later			
North	51.8	53.0	49.8	52.5	57.3
South	52.8	55.1	51.6	51.7	56.8
		Counties Constituting the Frontier of 1810			
North	52.0	53.0	51.8	55.2	59.8
South	51.2	52.6	51.0	57.4	58.2
		The Same Counties A Decade Later			
North	51.4	51.2	50.0	54.6	55.6
South	51.9	49.1	50.6	53.3	55.8
		Counties Constituting the Frontier of 1820			
North	51.7	50.4	53.4	55.1	58.6
South	52.4	50.0	52.6	56.6	59.3
		The Same Counties A Decade Later			
North	51.8	52.0	51.2	56.9	54.8
South	49.8	53.8	53.4	55.7	57.3
		Counties Constituting the Frontier of 1830			
North	51.0	52.5	54.5	55.6	53.3
South	51.2	51.7	50.9	58.2	55.0
		The Same Counties A Decade Later			
North	52.2	52.2	52.5	53.6	56.5
South	51.6	51.3	50.6	53.0	53.2
		Counties Constituting the Frontier of 1840			
North	51.9	51.3	54.2	57.1	58.2
South	53.0	50.8	53.4	58.2	59.4
		The Same Counties A Decade Later			
North	51.5	51.8	51.5	55.6	58.0
South	50.9	50.6	51.1	52.5	58.5

and wisked others away to early graves. Also, if a man in the backwoods lost his wife and was unable to remarry quickly he was possibly more likely to stay on the frontier than a woman whose husband died and who was unable to remarry within a short time. But this changed greatly within the post-frontier decade. After the frontier rolled out a region, the sex percentages were, compared to sex percentages for other adults, very nearly equal. The fact that many young couples went west after getting married may have combined with the willingness of women to enter the now-settled region to produce the rough numerical equality between young adult males and young adult females. In any case, the hypothesis received considerable support.

The post-frontier decades, it was anticipated, would herald a relative decline among the elderly who were male. This was the case the majority of the time, the area constituting the wilds of 1800 being the most notable exception. The largest decrease—a rather modest one, at that—took place in the region that had formed the northern frontier of 1810, it being just over 4%. Unexpectedly, only twice (in 1830 and 1840) was the relative decline greater in the South than in the North.

It was also expected that the post-frontier decades would usher in a general downward trend in the relative number of males in the total population. Except for the area that had formed the southern frontier of 1800, the hypothesis received support. The post-frontier downturn was most pronounced in regions comprising the 1810 and 1840 frontiers, weakest in the southern frontier of 1820 and the northern frontier of 1830. The overall decline was sharper in the North than in the South during the initial years, roughly equal for the counties that had formed the frontier of 1820, and stronger in the South thereafter. No explanation for this trend is readily apparent; it may involve the natures of the two frontiers over the years, the difficulties in settling them, and the changes that occurred in each one during the decade subsequent to settlement. It may also have something to do with the fact that by 1820 migration into the southern wilderness originated almost exclusively in the South, and migration into the northern wilderness originated almost exclusively in the North and Europe.

Another hypothesis stated that in the post-frontier counties the decade would reduce the proportion of the population consisting of free blacks. This occurred only in the southern frontier of 1840 (see Table 23). (The relative numbers of free blacks also remained static in the southern frontiers of 1800, 1820, and 1830.) Relatively large gains were registered in the counties forming the northern frontiers in 1820 and 1830, possibly reflecting the beginnings of the exodus of free blacks from the South. Of the five measurements, the smallest change was found in the region that had been frontier in 1800. The hypothesis concerning free blacks was

TABLE 23.—Each Frontier and A Decade of Change: Percentages by Race, Condition of Blacks, and Sex of Whites

Decade and Section	Race, Condition of Blacks, Sex of Whites			
	White Males	White Females	Slaves	Free Blacks
Frontier of 1800				
North	53.6	45.9	.1	.3
South	46.6	42.4	10.2	.8
Same Area in 1810				
North	52.0	47.4	.2	.4
South	44.5	39.3	15.5	.8
Frontier of 1810				
North	53.1	46.3	.3	.3
South	37.1	33.1	29.7	.1
Same Area in 1820				
North	50.8	48.7	.1	.5
South	32.8	30.5	36.2	.4
Frontier of 1820				
North	52.7	46.8	.0	.5
South	38.2	33.4	28.2	.2
Same Area in 1830				
North	51.4	47.5	.1	1.0
South	31.8	28.5	39.6	.2
Frontier of 1830				
North	53.2	46.7	.0	.1
South	36.0	32.4	31.4	.2
Same Area in 1840				
North	52.3	47.0	.0	.7
South	34.8	32.6	32.5	.2
Frontier of 1840				
North	53.7	46.1	.0	.2
South	45.1	38.5	16.0	.4
Same Area in 1850				
North	52.5	47.2	.0	.3
South	43.3	40.6	15.9	.2

rejected, for although comparatively few free blacks were on the cutting edge of settlement, more arrived once the frontier had rolled westward—especially in the North.

Several factors may account for this: (1) Free blacks may have felt less welcomed on the frontier than in the same area a decade later. For example, laws pertaining to the purchase of new lands in the West blatantly discriminated against free blacks. For many whites, the presence of free blacks in the western wilderness injected yet another unknown factor, and white settlers wanted order and certainty in their efforts to get land. (2) Free blacks may have been more accustomed to the environment afforded by the regions immediately behind the frontier than by the frontier, itself. Many were originally town dwellers and possessed skills and attitudes associated with manufacturing and commerce, a fact which made them less suited to pioneer activities than activities affiliated with more densely settled areas. (3) In these post-frontier northern areas, slavery was on the road to extinction. The post-frontier decade found proportionately fewer slaveowners, and they probably had less influence over the lives of free blacks than did other owners in flourishing slave areas elsewhere in the South. Originally, some slaveowners in the northern backwoods entertained strong hopes concerning the prospects of slavery taking root there, certainly stronger hopes than those held about the areas further east. When these hopes died, some owners freed their slaves, and these newly-freed people then augmented the proportion of the population composed of free blacks. Also, a few owners in the South, sick of the institution of slavery and the worry it inflicted on slave and master alike, brought their blacks north and freed them. (4) A few whites—mostly Quakers, it appears—bought slaves in the South, sent them to the North, and freed them; many of these Quakers lived just to the east of the frontier, and many manumitted blacks chose to live near their benefactors. (5) The South, especially by the 1830s, did nothing to encourage its free blacks to remain there. Free blacks in the South faced frequent and mounting harassment and threats, the most awesome of which was the possibility of being enslaved. Consequently, many fled the South and sought asylum in the North, and some found it in areas of recent—but not current—pioneer activity. (6) Some runaways from the South found homes in such areas, too.

Of the two frontiers, the southern usually contained relatively more blacks who were free from bondage—but not for long. Every decade following the existence of the five northern frontiers witnessed increases in the relative numbers of free blacks. The only time this occurred in the South was following the frontier of 1810. Furthermore, aside from the area that had constituted the frontier of 1800, each ten-year interval found comparatively more free blacks in those areas that had formed the northern wilderness than in similar areas in the South. Since the South received proportionately fewer foreign immigrants than the North, it may have been eager to attract virtually any form of human labor to the labor-starved frontier. As a result, free blacks appear to have been tolerated in the new lands of the South until the advancing institution of entrenched slavery demanded their removal. (Some masters professed a deep fear of free blacks mingling with slaves.) The failure of free blacks in the South to increase during the post-frontier decades possibly resulted from the fact that some unfortunate blacks were either enslaved or driven from place to place by repressive customs and laws, some being hounded out of the South entirely. Regardless of the reasons, the trend in the South was sharply different from that of the North.

According to the hypotheses, the post-frontier decade would experience a general increase in the relative number of slaves. This usually failed to occur in the North; it usually did occur in the South. Only during the decades following the frontiers of 1800 and 1820 were there upsurges of slaves in the post-frontier areas of the North. In fact, the counties constituting the northern frontier of 1810 witnessed during the decade a drastic decline. Except for the region that had been the frontier of 1840, every post-frontier region in the South enjoyed an increase in the relative number of slaves. The heftiest surges occurred in those areas that had been the southern frontiers of 1800, 1810, and 1820, the increase in the area that had comprised the frontier of 1830 being extremely modest. Just over 10% of the settlers in the southern backwoods in 1800 were slaves; a decade later the figure stood at 15.5%. The region forming the southern wilds in 1810 witnessed during the decade an increase from nearly 30% to over 36%. Even greater was the increase of slaves in the lands forming the southern frontier of 1820, spurting from just over 28% to almost 40%. The trend toward brisk increases in slaves clearly slackened after the frontier of 1820, and by 1840 there were actually relatively more slaves on the southern frontier than there would be in the same region a decade later. In all likelihood, the trend after 1820 for the post-frontier regions to remain either quite static in terms of slave population or to experience a relative decline was known to the slave powers. If they knew of it, they were doubtlessly alarmed by it.

The presence of some slaves in the North in the early years stems from several sources. Some families in the North had owned slaves for generations, and continued to do so quite late in the nineteenth century. Some people in the Northeast brought their slaves into the northern wilderness, hoping to squeeze a few extra years out of their slaves, and there they were met by Frenchmen and others in Illinois who had owned slaves since before the area belonged to the United States. Some slaves entered the northern wilderness via the efforts of those who spirited them across the Ohio River and into the hands of those who wanted human labor and were willing to pay for it.

The numbers of slaves involved in the North, however, were usually so miniscule compared to the total population that any analysis of increases and decreases is of questionable value. Furthermore, over time various laws and sections of state constitutions were enacted which tended to conform to the spirit of the Northwest Ordinance, gradually disheartening those who were striving to make slavery a viable institution in the North. Legal restrictions against slavery (and against free blacks) certainly reflected the sentiments of the growing proportion of settlers in the new lands of the North who came from the Northeast and Europe. They wanted little to do with slavery, or blacks, and as they came to outnumber those who favored slavery in the Northwest their views predominated. This sentiment also helped abolish the rather widespread device of keeping blacks in chains in the North under circumstances other than that of outright slavery, a device which enslaved far more people in the new lands of the North than were ever reported in the federal census returns. The advent of determined abolitionist activities further dissuaded attempts to cultivate the growth of slavery in the North. By 1840 virtually no slaves were reported in the northern wilds, and the same area a decade later was still free of enslaved blacks.

It seems likely that a causal relationship exists in the northern wilds between freedom for blacks and the extent of slavery. Generally, the ten-year interval found the post-frontier lands containing many more free blacks but no additional slaves. In fact, this was always true for free blacks and usually true for slaves. Some of the free blacks were recently manumitted slaves; others, perhaps fewer in number, had never been slaves. The demise of slavery led directly to the introduction of free blacks into an area, some being the former slaves and others being free blacks who felt it was wise to enter a region only after slavery was dead. At the same time, the entry of some free blacks into a slave-holding area undoubtedly prodded some masters, and their slaves, into areas in which free blacks were scarce. In any case, as the growth of slavery was retarded and then as the institution began to wither in the post-frontier regions, the free blacks in these regions did rather well—if voluntary population growth is a valid index of well-being.

Except for the region that had formed the southern frontier in 1840, all other former frontier regions in the South were home to comparatively more slaves at the end of the ten-year interval, suggesting at least three traits concerning the institution of slavery. Owners avoided rushing headlong into the wilderness with great numbers of slaves. Perhaps the fear of losing expensive investment prompted caution. The difficult nature of frontier work, the threat of Indian raids, the possible opportunities for escape, and the overall problem of slave control restrained some masters. Also, the numerous free blacks constituted for the owners a factor which added uncertainty. Within a decade, however, the relative number of slaves in these areas usually increased markedly, indicating that many of the concerns dwelling in the minds of owners had dissipated to the extent that masters were now willing to take risks.

The decade following pioneer activity brought change to demographic conditions on the frontier. The post-frontier area contained relatively fewer very young children and more elderly people. Differences in sex ratios among young adults narrowed considerably, the same being true to a lesser degree for older folk. The number of free blacks in the North increased, but not in the South. Conversely, the number of slaves failed to increase in the post-frontier regions of the North, but the opposite was true for the South. In short, some exceptions aside, most of the hypotheses received at least moderate support.

CHAPTER IX

Summary and Conclusions

To close this work by reiterating the findings in great detail is neither necessary nor would it be enlightening. Instead, in lieu of a thorough restatement of the findings, it is instructive to present a concise summary of the salient findings, followed by comments on some other aspects of this work.

Of utmost importance is the fact that the household managed to migrate westward, settle in a fresh environment, and perform most of the essential functions for the survival and growth of not only the household but also the rest of frontier society. (To be sure, this triumph of the household unit did not occur in isolation. Other institutions and conditions—the government, the army, congregations, hospitable climate and soil, technology, and fragmented human opposition, to cite but a few factors—played a supportive role in the household's victorious fracas with wilderness conditions.) In addition, the household emerged from the fray relatively intact; it did not have to contort itself into eerie configurations or distend itself into uncanny sizes in order to plunge into the western lands and there carve for itself a comfortable and secure niche. Still, there were some noticeable differences between eastern households and those in the West.

The decades brought generally modest differences in household size and composition between the northern frontier and the northern settled section. Some differences, especially those of size, were actually the opposite of what was hypothesized. Moreover, between 1800 and 1840 household differences between the two northern regions generally diminished, the bulk of the convergence occurring during the 1830s. In comparison, the differences in size and composition in the South were relatively larger, and the evidence sprang few surprises. However, when the typical southern pioneer household was compared to the northern, it usually failed to exhibit markedly more characteristics traditionally associated with the backwoods. In fact, some evidence indicates the opposite was true, the northern household in several ways conforming more closely to the traditional model.

The age and sex compositions of the frontier furnished rather persuasive support for the hypotheses: the wilderness was, in fact, prone to have proportionately more young people and males than the settled area. As was further expected, the differences in sex composition between the two northern regions were generally greater than differences in the South. In terms of age, however, the opposite usually appeared, the differences between the two southern regions topping those found in the North. In neither North nor South was there a distinctively consistent trend of either convergence or divergence. Compared to the northern pioneer, the southern pioneer was younger, though less frequently male.

The inquiry into the degree to which each wilderness was black and the degree to which black settlers were classified as slaves produced interesting results. One fact looms large: the backwoods was home to relatively few black settlers, and even fewer were free. Although proportionately more black settlers in the North became free over the decades, a trend culminating in virtually no blacks being reported as slaves by 1840, the northern frontier always contained among its blacks a higher proportion of slaves than the Northeast. Somewhat the same situation existed in the South. There, due to the pervasive influence of the institution of slavery, proportionately far more blacks were present in the southern wilds than in the northern wilds. Still, even the southern frontier housed relatively few blacks compared to the southern settled area. Unlike free blacks in the northern wilds, those in the southern wilds never constituted more than a minute fraction of the total black population, and there was no movement whatsoever toward freedom for the enslaved southern pioneer. Compared to the entire East, the length and breadth of the frontier was home to few blacks, especially free blacks, facts which possibly constitute the largest and most profound demographic difference between East and West. Clearly, for blacks the western land (particularly in the South) was no haven, no land of opportunity, no magnet attracting the weary and the ambitious alike. Rather, it was a place in which standard fare for those blacks who were present included the lash, unrewarded toil, and the prospect of an early grave.

The evidence for occupations brought forth little that was startling. Compared to the Northeast, the northern forests and prairies were considerably more agrarian, a difference which faded markedly by 1840. Of the two southern regions, the wilderness was the vastly more agrarian, the difference growing with time. The southern frontier was in 1820 emphatically more agrarian than the northern frontier, and by 1840 the occupational gap had actually increased. In brief, the northern wilds acquired occupational traits more nearly in conformity to the rest of the nation, a fact which stood in sharp contrast to the trends in the southern wilds.

Within a decade after the ring of the settler's axe was heard in the woods, the region lost a number of the demographic features normally associated with the frontier. The post-frontier regions, a decade after pioneer activity, were home to proportionately fewer very young people, more elderly. The male majority largely vanished, this being particularly true among young adults and not so true among older people. The post-frontier regions in the North contained relatively more free blacks, these regions in the South relatively fewer. Somewhat the opposite prevailed for the relative number of slaves, the post-frontier decade seeing no general gain in the North, a hefty gain in the South. Over the years, traditional frontier demographic conditions usually faded more rapidly in the North than in the South.

Although most demographic differences between East and West were moderate—and a few were actually the opposite of what was hypothesized —the conditions, events, deliberate actions, chance occurrences, and attitudes affecting frontier demography were neither few in number nor simple in operation. Rather, a great many factors influenced the demographic characteristics of settlers, and the various factors sometimes operated on each other. Added to this is the fact that certain demographic conditions in the wilds frequently affected other demographic variables, which in turn affected still others. For example, the perennial male majority among young adults, evidence strongly suggests, led to a high percentage of women being married, many at an early age. This, in turn, evidently led to the large component of the pioneer population consisting of children. Whatever the influences on demography—the abundance of fresh land, liberty and license, low economic thresholds, an unsettled society, lack of severe obstacles to expansion, the means of travel, technology, ideas concerning individual and group undertakings, information and misinformation, expectations, thoughts concerning duty, fears and anxieties, customs and laws, to cite only some—the result of the sets of diverse, and sometimes conflicting, influences was such that in most instances frontier demographic patterns were not grossly different from eastern patterns. However numerous the variables affecting demographic traits and however intricate their operation, they apparently largely cancelled themselves out, leaving the demographic traits of the settlers—at least the white settlers—essentially similar to those of easterners.

One additional fact concerning demographic changes and demographic variables: the demographic composition existing throughout the nation was sometimes in such a delicate equilibrium that the introduction into a region of just a few adult males, for example, drastically altered many facets of the demographic composition. These alterations, in turn, affected various aspects of society, including ideas and practices associated with economics and politics. Factors affecting demography, however slight numerically, often had weighty and unforeseen consequences on society.

Aside from blacks and a few other groups, those who benefitted from (or suffered from) the western experience were basically similar to those who remained in the East. The western process had a staggering impact on the settlers, the rest of the nation, and much of the rest of the world. The resources of the West encouraged Americans to romp and revel in abundance, cultivate an insistence on both immediate solutions to tough problems and an orderly and bright tomorrow, entertain notions of omnipotence, deviate for several centuries from the mainstream of European development, and in several fundamental ways to step out of historical time and postpone the future. The West held out promises of wealth, physical security, confidence, self-worth, regeneration, republicanism, adventure, a chance to become alienated from the larger society, and other rewards as well.[1] For those who felt trapped on wobbly farms in New England and elsewhere and for those who were pressured from eastern farms into confining workshops and stores, the frontier offered the means by which to recapture both the dream and often the reality of land ownership.[2] Scores of thousands hastened westward, exerted themselves, and entered into new positions and assumed new roles; thousands more flocked into the newly-vacant positions in the East created by those who streamed west; and others toiled in the shops and mills in the settled sections, confident in the belief that they, too, could pack up and start afresh in the new lands if the jarring economic dislocations in the modernizing economy proved to be too unsettling.

And many who lusted after western land gained much more than mere material success. They gained a fresh environment, a new outlook on life, a different set of standards by which to gauge both their position in life and

---

[1] At least one observer saw that among western migrants "a sense of relative consequence is fostered by their growing possessions, and by perceiving towns, counties, offices and candidates springing up around them. One becomes a justice of the peace, another a county judge and another a member of the legislative assembly. Each one assumes some municipal function, pertaining to schools, the settlement of a minister, the making of roads, bridges, and public works. A sense of responsibility to public opinion, self respect, and a due estimation of character and correct deportment are the consequence." Timothy Flint, The History and Geography of the Mississippi Valley, I, p. 188.

[2] Without doubt, far more Americans and immigrants during the 1800s found opportunity in the booming cities and towns than on the land. The trend was strongly and clearly toward urbanization, some townships in the Midwest losing in absolute terms a third or more of their population just several decades after the settlers cleared the land and broke the soil. Even so, the lure of the land remained powerful to countless city dwellers, successful and failure alike. Perhaps the compelling attraction had something to do with some lingering and modified physiocratic notions, perhaps it sprang from American angst and distrust concerning cities and corrupt "European" influences in general, and perhaps it resulted from a desire to remain at least partially free from remote and increasingly interdependent economic forces, social and political complexities, and oppressive "paper" wealth and "artificial" aristocracy. Whether the land was valued for economic reasons, political reasons, or spiritual reasons, it beckoned even to those who were finding material success in the cities.

the positions of their fellows, and a chance to forge ahead in the scramble for much absolute gain and considerable relative uncertainty.[3] Most Americans wanted a chance to pursue freely the riches nature had stored in the American continent, and most wanted this chance for one purpose: to have a roughly *equal* opportunity to become *unequal*. Concerning the opportunities of the West, one basic conclusion is central: with the major exception of blacks, those who surged westward in search of something better, or at least different, appear to have been a rather fair representation of the eastern population, at least insofar as can be determined by a comparison of demographic traits.

This study, I believe, has rendered several services. It provided a working definition of the term "frontier." It made clear the fact that the frontier was not merely a place in space but also a complicated process in time, a process in which specific demographic events and other events occurred inside of an area within a prescribed time span. The study provided the means by which individual frontier counties can be compared to the entire frontier to determine whether or not they are more or less normal demographically. Counties with abnormal demographic patterns may reflect a set of anomalous conditions produced by unusual economic, social, or other phenomena. Similarly, using data from the study, some comparisons can be made between the demography of the American frontier and that of other frontiers—the Australian, Canadian, Russian, and Chinese, for example. Again, differences in demographic patterns may point to other essential differences. The data from this study can be used to compare the differences between the American wilderness and the American settled sections to comparable differences in other nations with frontiers. Such comparisons may uncover differences in the frontier processes. Adapting the methods and approaches developed in this study, it is possible to compare the American frontiers of the early 1800s to earlier and later American frontiers. In addition, some of the evidence marshalled in this study, especially that bearing on household size and composition, offers demographers the chance to compare pre-industrial households in new lands to industrial households in older lands. Finally, the study attempted to use a mutually supportive combination of relatively "hard" census data and relatively impressionistic primary evidence, both woven together within frameworks constructed by demographers and other scholars.

At present, macrostudies of this type rely heavily upon census data

---

[3]Settlers who trekked west and those who observed the settlers as they moved across the land caught glimpses of the West as a regenerative force, an agent of eternal renewal, the land of endless tomorrows. Timothy Flint, well aware of the psychological impact of an unfolding West, asked, "What mind ever contemplated the project of moving from the old settlements over the Alleghany Mountains ... without forming pictures of new woods and streams, new animals and vegetables, new configurations of scenery, new aspects of men and new forms of society?" Timothy Flint, *op. cit.,* I, p. 184.

available in manageable, computerized quantities. Perhaps the future will bring quantification of adequate samples of evidence from city directories, gazetteers, guides, genealogies, memoirs, newspapers, travel accounts, manuscripts, and public records pertaining to marriage, births, deaths, taxes, wills, occupations, education, persistency, military service, and other aspects of the lives of ordinary people. Then questions having a direct bearing on the western experience could be addressed in macrostudy fashion: motivations for migration, selectivity of migration, sources of migration, reasons for specific destinations, dynamics of the actual journeys westward, attitudes toward the West, expectations accompanying migration, the number and lengths of moves of migrants, the reasons for success and failure, comparisons of the lives of both those who trekked westward and similar non-migrating easterners. Perhaps such quantification could result in the formulation of reliable and valid theories governing the westward thrust. Certainly, the dynamic nature of the thrust would become clearer, and it would be easier to filter out some of the extraneous "noise" accompanying the settlement process, which neither influences it nor is influenced by it. All in all, if adequate samples of the various form of evidence which presently lend themselves so well to microstudies were made available for comparative macrostudies, many thorny questions concerning the entire western process could be answered reasonably well.

Demographic developments do not occur in vacuums. Instead, household patterns and other demographic forms pulsate, changing shape and size and function, in response to a host of stimulants. The stimulants include such varied influences as economics and politics, customs and popular beliefs, perceptions of reality and perceptions of self, and hopes, fears, and expectations. They alter demographic traits by influencing such events as age of marriage, decisions to have or not have children, visions of greener pastures elsewhere, availability of hired help, social and economic opportunity, possible need to include in the household such people as grandparents, and the overall well-being of the individual, the household, and institutions and other props supporting the household. At the same time, the nature of the household and other demographic conditions exert a profound influence on outside institutions, laws and customs, economics, expectations, and the overall health, direction, and mechanics of society. The values, mores, institutions, power arrangements, goals and concerns, and degree of social cohesion in society are intrinsically bound causally to demographic patterns found within society. Whether demographic characteristics are viewed as reflections of the forces at work in society or whether they are regarded as influences on society—or, more correctly, some combination of both—a study of demography can reveal and illuminate fundamental and sweeping truths about society and ongoing changes within society.

Appendices

APPENDIX A

Additional Constraints

Great amounts of federal census data were obtained on computer tape from the Inter-University Consortium for Political Research, University of Michigan. All of the data came from the printed federal censuses for the years 1800 through 1850 and included every county in the nation. With the data on tape, the Osiris computer program made it possible to work with whole populations across decades, analyzing the age, sex, racial, and occupational characteristics of the frontier and the settled section. The data forced only one important constraint: the county was the smallest political unit containing such data, and it thus became the basic spatial unit for this study.

Greater difficulty attended efforts to secure data pertaining to household size and household composition. The federal printed censuses do not contain information on individual households; only the manuscript censuses do. The best collection of manuscript censuses for the nation is in the National Archives. Three trips to the Archives were made, and each time specially prepared forms were used to collect and categorize vast amounts of data. Using these forms, it was possible to collect data pertaining to over 8,000 frontier households (nearly 50,000 pioneers) for the five census years from 1800 through 1840. In addition, approximately 9,500 households in the settled sections were recorded, thereby establishing a control group against which to compare the frontier households.

Even the use of such forms, however, did not permit the collection of data from every frontier county. (And the collection of household data from every county in the settled sections was clearly out of the question.) Therefore, a sample of twenty counties was selected from each census year—averaging approximately five each from the northern frontier, the northern settled area, the southern frontier, and the southern settled area (see App. D). And then a sample of white households was taken from each of these counties, a sample that was proportionately larger with counties containing the smallest populations: if a frontier county contained under 1,000 people, every household was included; between 1,000 and 2,000, 50%

of the households; between 2,000 and 5,000, 33% of the households; 5,000 to 10,000, 20% of the households; 10,000 to 30,000, 10%; 30,000 to 50,000, 6%; over 50,000, 2%. A similar sampling technique was used for the settled counties over the decades, but the percentages were reduced for each of these counties because so many had populations in excess of 25,000. Altogether, the samples of households in the settled areas contained almost 54,000 people.

An additional constraint was created by a problem with manuscript censuses for the early southern frontier counties: many of the manuscripts for 1800 and 1810 have vanished over the years. As a result, it was not possible to include in this study households from the southern frontiers of 1800 and 1810.

The fading of the frontier was also investigated by means of a sample of counties (see App. F). A sample was used because the number of computer jobs required to manipulate the data in Chapter VIII did not warrant the use of the computer. Time, too, was saved.

APPENDIX B

Frontier Counties in the Study[1]

Northern Frontier of 1800 (8 counties)
New York: Chenengo, Onondaga, Tioga
Ohio: Hamilton
Pennsylvania: Armstrong, Beaver, Crawford, Mercer

Southern Frontier of 1800 (12 counties)
Georgia: Montgomery
Kentucky: Barren, Cumberland, Green, Hardin, Logan
Muhlenberg, Pulaski, Warren
North Carolina: Ashe
Virginia: Lee, Wood

Northern Frontier of 1810 (22 counties)
Indiana: Clark, Harrison
New York: Genesee, Niagara, Ontario, Steuben
Ohio: Adams, Athens, Clinton, Fayette, Franklin, Gallia,
Geuga, Guernsey, Licking, Muskingum, Preble, Scioto,
Stark, Trumbull, Tuscarawas
Pennsylvania: Erie

Southern Frontier of 1810 (20 counties)
Georgia: Camden, Pulaski, Telfair, Twiggs
Kentucky: Christian
Mississippi: Wilkenson
Tennessee: Bledsoe, Dickson, Franklin, Giles, Hickman,
Humphries, Lincoln, Maury, Montgomery, Roanne,
Rutherford, Stewart, Warren, White

Northern Frontier of 1820 (22 counties)
Illinois: Edwards, Franklin, Gallatin, Jackson, Madison,
Pope, Union, White

---

[1]There are exactly 252 frontier counties in this study. Their boundaries, and their spellings, are as they appeared for the dates indicated. Many of the counties have since been divided into several counties.

Indiana: Davies, Dubois, Fayette, Lawrence, Orange, Pike,
Vigo
Ohio: Darke, Delaware, Huron, Logan, Richland, Shelby,
Union

Southern Frontier of 1820 (23 counties)
Alabama: Bibb, Clark, Conecuh, Dallas, Greene, Jackson,
Lauderdale, Lawrence, Marengo, Monroe, Perry,
Washington, Wilcox
Georgia: Habershaw, Hall
Mississippi: Green, Lawrence, Marion, Pike
Missouri: Montgomery
Tennessee: Hardin, Perry, Wayne

Northern Frontier of 1830 (20 counties)
Illinois: Adams, Fayette, Fulton, Marion, Montgomery,
Pike, Shelby, Wayne
Indiana: Bartholomew, Decature, Hancock, Hamilton,
Hendricks, Johnson, Marion, Monroe, Morgan, Rush
Michigan: St. Joseph, Washtenaw

Southern Frontier of 1830 (39 counties)
Alabama: Butler, Fayette, Franklin, Walker
Florida: Gadsden, Leon, Nassau
Georgia: Carroll, Coweta, Decatur, DeKalb, Fayette,
Harriss, Marion, Merriweather, Monroe, Muscogee,
Pike, Thomas, Troup, Upson
Kentucky: Graves, McCracken
Mississippi: Madison, Rankin, Yazoo
Missouri: Boone, Howard, Simpson
Tennessee: Dyer, Fayette, Gibson, Hardeman, Henry,
McNairy, Obion, Shelby, Tipton, Weakly

Northern Frontier of 1840 (70 counties)
Illinois: Boone, Bureau, Carroll, Clay, DeKalb, DeWitt,
Effingham, Kane, LaSalle, Lee, McHenry, McLean,
Macon, Marshall, Mercer, Ogle, Putnam, Rock Island,
Stark, Stephenson, Whiteside, Will, Winnebago
Indiana: Adams, DeKalb, Elkhart, Fulton, Huntington, Kosciusko,
La Grange, Marshall, Noble, Steuben, Wells
Iowa: Cedar, Des Moines, Henry, Johnson, Lee, Louisa,
Muscatine, Scott
Michigan: Allegan, Berrien, Branch, Calhoun, Cass, Clinton,
Eaton, Genesee, Hillsdale, Ingham, Ionia, Kalamazoo,
Kent, Lapeer, Livingston, St. Clair,
Shiawassee, Van Buren

Ohio: Henry, Mercer, Van Wert, Williams
Wisconsin: Grant, Iowa, Milwaukee, Racine, Rock, Walworth

Southern Frontier of 1840 (14 counties)
Arkansas: Benton, Clark, Hempstead, Lawrence, Madison
Missouri: Barry, Benton, Caldwell, Johnson, Miller, Pettis,
Rives, Shelby, Van Buren

APPENDIX C

Populations of the Various Frontiers

	Northern Frontier	Southern Frontier
1800	43,710	43,572
1810	140,024	94,434
1820	94,718	104,377
1830	76,704	191,922
1840	253,375	49,744
Frontier Totals	608,531	484,049

It should be noted that these figures do not represent all of the frontiersmen throughout the frontiers at the indicated times. Many frontiersmen, perhaps most, lived in counties not included in this study, counties which had frontier characteristics in only *part* of the county and not throughout the county. For example, counties such as Cook County, Illinois, and Wayne County, Michigan, were excluded from this study.

APPENDIX D

Frontier Counties Used in Chapters II & III

Northern Frontier of 1800 (4 counties)
   New York: Chenengo, Onondaga
   Pennsylvania: Armstrong, Beaver

Southern Frontier of 1800 (1 county)
   North Carolina: Ashe*

Northern Frontier of 1810 (5 counties)
   New York: Genesee, Niagara, Ontario, Steuben
   Pennsylvania: Erie

Southern Frontier of 1810 (1 county)
   Kentucky: Christian*

Northern Frontier of 1820 (5 counties)
   Illinois: Pope
   Indiana: Fayette, Lawrence, Vigo
   Ohio: Darke

Southern Frontier of 1820 (5 counties)
   Georgia: Hall
   Mississippi: Lawrence, Marion, Pike
   Tennessee: Hardin

Northern Frontier of 1830 (4 counties)
   Illinois: Adams, Montgomery
   Indiana: Hamilton
   Michigan: Washtenaw

Southern Frontier of 1830 (6 counties)
   Georgia: Fayette, Pike, Upson
   Mississippi: Madison
   Missouri: Boone
   Tennessee: Hardeman

---

*Due to the fact that each of the southern frontiers for 1800 and 1810 has just one manuscript census from which data pertaining to household size and household composition can be obtained, no attempt was made to determine the household characteristics for these two frontiers.

Northern Frontier of 1840 (7 counties)
 Illinois: Stephenson
 Indiana: Adams, Noble
 Iowa: Louisa
 Michigan: Clinton, Genesee, Kalamazoo

Southern Frontier of 1840 (3 counties)
 Arkansas: Hempstead
 Missouri: Barry, Pettis

APPENDIX E

Frontier Counties: Free Blacks and Slaves

On the northern frontier of 1800, only Armstrong County, Pennsylvania, and Hamilton County, Ohio, contained no free blacks. Hamilton County was the only county on the northern frontier not to have slaves; Armstrong County avoided this honor by having one slave.

On the southern frontier of 1800, every county had at least one slave—Wood County, Virginia, having just one. Only Barren County, Kentucky, had no free blacks.

On the northern frontier of 1810, no county in Ohio contained slaves and every county outside of Ohio did contain slaves. All frontier counties contained at least four free blacks and four counties in Ohio had over 100 each.

On the southern frontier of 1810, every county housed slaves. Three counties—Dickson, Giles, and White in Tennessee—numbered no free blacks among their populations. Telfair County, Georgia, and Franklin County, Tennessee, each had just one free black.

On the northern frontier of 1820, only eight counties possessed slaves—none of which were in Ohio. With the exception of Pike County, Indiana, all of the counties in which slaves were located were in Illinois, there being just one frontier county in Illinois without slaves. Two counties in Illinois, Jackson and Union, were the only two counties in the northern wilderness without free blacks.

On the southern frontier of 1820, every county had slaves. Five counties—Bibb in Alabama, Marion in Mississippi, Perry and Wayne in Tennessee, and Habershaw in Georgia—did not contain a single free black.

On the northern frontier of 1830, just four counties had slaves. All of these were in Illinois: Fayette, Marion, Montgomery, and Shelby. Just two counties, Fulton in Illinois and Hancock in Indiana, contained no free blacks.

On the southern frontier of 1830, all of the counties were home to slaves. Four counties—Coweta and Marion in Georgia and Fayette and Walker in Alabama—had no free blacks.

On the northern frontier of 1840, Grant and Iowa counties in Wisconsin and Winnebago County in Illinois were the only counties in which slavery existed, Winnebago and Iowa counties having only one slave each. Thirteen counties had no free blacks: Boone, DeKalb, McHenry, Marshall, Mercer, Stark, and Whiteside in Illinois; Kosciusko and Noble in Indiana; Ceder in Iowa; Clinton and Eaton in Michigan; Van Wert in Ohio.

On the southern frontier of 1840, slaves were present in every county. Free blacks were missing from four: Clark and Madison in Arkansas and Benton and Caldwell in Missouri. Four other counties, all in Missouri, had fewer than five free blacks each.

APPENDIX F

Sample of Counties Used in Chapter VIII

Northern Frontier of 1800 (5 counties)
   New York: Chenango, Tioga
   Pennsylvania: Armstrong, Crawford, Mercer

Southern Frontier of 1800 (5 counties)
   Kentucky: Green, Logan, Pulaski
   North Carolina: Ashe
   Virginia: Wood

Northern Frontier of 1810 (5 counties)
   New York: Niagara, Steuben
   Ohio: Adams, Fayette, Guernsey

Southern Frontier of 1810 (5 counties)
   Georgia: Telfair
   Mississippi: Wilkenson
   Tennessee: Bledsoe, Giles, Montgomery

Northern Frontier of 1820 (5 counties)
   Illinois: Pope
   Indiana: Fayette, Lawrence, Vigo
   Ohio: Darke

Southern Frontier of 1820 (5 counties)
   Alabama: Bibb, Greene, Lauderdale
   Mississippi: Marion
   Tennessee: Perry

Northern Frontier of 1830 (5 counties)
   Illinois: Adams, Wayne
   Indiana: Hamilton, Marion
   Michigan: St. Joseph

Southern Frontier of 1830 (5 counties)
   Alabama: Fayette
   Georgia: Monroe, Thomas

Missouri: Boone
Tennessee: Henry

Northern Frontier of 1840 (5 counties)
 Illinois: De Witt, Stephenson
 Indiana: Adams, Marshall
 Michigan: Kalamazoo

Southern Frontier of 1840 (5 counties)
 Arkansas: Hempstead, Madison
Missouri: Barry, Caldwell, Rives

Bibliography and Index

Bibliography

PRIMARY SOURCES

Andrew, James O. *Miscellanies: Comprising Letters, Essays, and Addresses; to which is Added a Biographical Sketch of Mrs. Ann Amelia Andrew.* Louisville: Morton and Griswold, 1854.

Appel, Livia, ed. *A Merry Briton in Pioneer Wisconsin.* State Hist. Soc. of Wisc., 1950.

Atherton, Lewis, ed. "Life, Labor and Society in Boone County, Missouri, 1832-52, as Revealed in Correspondence of an Immigrant Slave Owning Family from North Carolina, Part 1," *Missouri Hist. Rev.,* xxxviii, no. 3 (Apr. 1944).

Baird, Robert. *View of the Valley of the Mississippi, or Emigrant's and Traveller's Guide Through the Valley of the Mississippi.* Philadelphia: H. S. Tanner, 1834.

Beck, Lewis. *A Gazetteer of the States of Illinois and Missouri.* Albany, N.Y: Charles and George Webster, 1823.

Bell, Margaret Dwight. *A Journey to Ohio in 1810 as Recorded in the Journal of Margaret Van Horn Dwight Bell,* ed. Max Farrand. New Haven: Yale Univ. Pr., 1913.

Birkbeck, Morris. *Letters from Illinois.* London: Taylor and Hessey, 1818.
_____. *Notes on a Journey in America, From the Coast of Virginia to the Territory of Illinois.* 2d ed. London: Severn, 1818. Stresses transportation across the west to southern Illinois and the economic and social conditions in the West.

Blane, William. *An Excursion Through the United States and Canada During the Years 1822-23.* London: Baldwin, Cradock, and Joy, 1824.

Blowe, Daniel. *A Geographical, Historical, Commercial, and Agricultural View of the United States of America; forming A Complete Emigrant's Directory Through Every Part of the Republic.* Liverpool: Edwards & Knibb, 1820.

Brackenridge, Henry M. *Recollections of Persons and Places in the West.* Phila: James Kay, Jr. and Brother, 1834.

Bradbury, John. *Travels in the Interior of America in the Years 1809, 1810, and 1811.* Vol. v of *Early Western Travels,* ed. Reuben Gold Thwaites. 32 vols, Cleveland: Arthur H. Clark, 1904-07. Hereafter cited as *E.W.T.*

Brown, Samuel R. *The Western Gazetteer.* Auburn, N.Y: H. C. Southwick, 1817.

    Many fine accounts of frontier towns and western economic activities.

Brush, Daniel Harmon. *Growing Up with Southern Illinois, 1820-1861,* ed. Milo M. Quaife. Chicago: R. R. Donnelley & Sons, 1944.

Bullock, W. *Sketches of a Journey through the Western States of North America.* London: John Miller, 1827.

Burlend, Rebecca. *A True Picture of Emigration,* ed. Milo Quaife. Chicago: R. R. Donnelley & Sons, 1936.

Buttrick, Tilly, Jr. *Voyages, Travels and Discoveries.* Boston: Putnam, 1831.

Clark, John A. *Gleaning By the Way.* Phila: W. J. & J. K. Simon, 1842.

Cuming, Fortescue. *Sketches of a Tour to the Western Country, Through the States of Ohio and Kentucky; A Voyage down the Ohio and Mississippi Rivers, and A Trip through the Mississippi Territory, and part of West Florida.* Vol. iv. *E.W.T.*

Dana, Edmund. *A Description of the Bounty Lands in the State of Illinois.* Cincinnati: Locker, Reynolds & Co., 1819.

Dean, John C., ed. "Journal of Thomas Dean: A Voyage to Indiana in 1817," *Ind. Hist. Publ.,* vi, no. 2 (1918).

Dickens, Charles. *American Notes for General Circulation.* N.Y: Harper and Brothers, 1842.

    Highly interesting. Contains several references to demographic characteristics of the frontier.

Dorr, Harold M., ed. *The Michigan Constitutional Conventions of 1835-36, Debates and Proceedings.* Ann Arbor: Univ. of Mich. Pr., 1940.

Drake, Daniel. *Discourse on the History, Character, and Prospects of the West.* Gainesville, Fl: Scholars' Facsimilies & Reprints, 1955.

Esarey, Logan, ed. "Pioneers of Morgan County: Memoirs of Noah J. Major," *Ind. Hist. Soc. Publ.,* v, no. 5 (1915).

Farnham, Eliza W. *Life in the Prairie Land.* N.Y: Harper & Brothers, 1846.

Faux, William. *Memorable Days in America; being a Journal of a Tour to the United States, principally undertaken to ascertain, by positive evidence, the condition and probable prospects of British emigrants; including accounts of Mr. Birkbeck's Settlement in Illinois: and intended to show Men and things as they are in America.* Vols. xi and xii of *E.W.T.*

Fearon, Henry Bradshaw. *Sketches of America: A Narrative of a Journey of Five Thousand Miles through the Eastern and Western States of America.* London: Longman, Hurst, Rees, Orme, and Brown, 1818.

    Notes interaction among migrants. Astute observations on Americans and the West.

Featherstonhough, George W. *Excursion through the Slave States.* 2 vols. London: John Murray, 1844.

Ferrall, Simon A. *A Ramble of Six Thousand Miles through the United States.* London: Effingham Wilson, 1832.

Flint, James. *Letters from America, containing Observations on the Climate and Agriculture of the western States, the Manners of the People, and the Prospects of Emigrants, &c., &c.* Edinburgh: W. & C. Tait, 1822.

Flint, Timothy. *The History and Geography of the Mississippi Valley.* 2 vols. Cincinnati: E. H. Flint and L. R. Lincoln, 1832.

Flower, George. *History of the English Settlement in Edwards County, Illinois, Founded in 1817 and 1818 by Morris Birkbeck and George Flower.* Chicago Hist. Soc., Coll., Vol. I.
    Numerous references to demography.

Fordham, Elias Pym. *Personal Narrative of Travels in Virginia, Maryland, Pennsylvania, Ohio, Indiana, Kentucky; and of A Residence in the Illinois Territory, 1817-1818,* ed. Frederic A. Ogg. Cleveland: Arthur H. Clark, 1906.

Fuller, Margaret. *Summer on the Lakes, in 1843.* Boston: Charles C. Little and James Brown, 1844.

Green, Fletcher M., ed. *The Lides Go South . . . and West: The Record of a Planter Migration in 1835.* Columbia: Univ. of So. Car., 1952.
    Fine descriptions of the act of migration.

Griffiths, D., Jr. *Two Years' Residence in the New Settlement of Ohio, North America, With Directions to Emigrants.* March of America Series, 73. Ann Arbor, Mich: Univ. Microfilms, 1966.

Grund, Francis. *The Americans in Their Moral, Social, and Political Relations.* 2 vols. London: Rees, Orme, Brown, Green & Longman, 1837.
    Contains several references to demography and related topics.

Hall, Basil. *Travels in North America in the Years 1827 and 1828.* 3 vols. Edinburgh: Cadell, 1829.
    Contains a number of references to occupations, race, and the condition of blacks.

Hall, Baynard Rush. *The New Purchase: or, Seven and A Half Years in the Far West,* ed. James Albert Woodburn. Princeton: Princeton Univ. Pr., 1916.

Hall, Francis. *Travels in Canada and the United States in 1816 and 1817.* London: Longman, Hurst, Rees, Orme, & Brown, 1818.

Hall, James. *Letters from the West, containing Sketches of Scenery, Manners, and Customs; and Anecdotes connected with the First Settlements of the Western Sections of the United States.* London: Henry Colburn, 1828.

————. *Notes on the Western States; containing descriptive sketches of their soil, climate, resources and scenery.* Phila: Harrison Hall, 1838.

Hamilton, Thomas. *Men and Manners in America*. London: William Blackwood and Sons, 1843.

Hawarth, J. D. "Early Recollections of Keokuk County," *Annals of Iowa*, II, no. 1 (Apr. 1895).

Hazelton, George H. "Reminiscences of Seventeen Years Residence in Michigan, 1836-1853," *Mich. Hist. Collections, XXI (1892)*.

Hebard, Alfred. "Recollections of Early Territorial Days," *Annals of Iowa*, II, nos. 2-3 (July-Oct. 1895).

Hoffman, Charles F. *A Winter in the West*. N.Y: Harper & Brothers, 1835.
    Several references to demography and related matters.

Holmes, Isaac. *An Account of the United States of America*. London: Caxton Press, 1823.

Howells, William Cooper. *Recollections of Life in Ohio, from 1813 to 1840*. Cincinnati: Robert Clarke, 1895.
    Contains several references to demography, especially occupations.

Hulme, Thomas. *A Journal Made During A Tour of the Western Countries of America: September 30, 1818-August 7, 1819*. Vol. x of *E.W.T.*

Johnson, Howard. "A Home in the Woods: Oliver Johnson's Reminiscences of Early Marion County," *Ind. Hist. Soc. Publ.*, XVI, no. 2 (1951).

Jones, Abner D. *Illinois and the West*. Boston: Weeks, Jordan and Company, 1838.

Kellar, Herbert A., ed. "A Journey Through the South in 1836: Diary of James D. Davidson," *Jour. of So. Hist.*, I, no. 3 (Aug. 1935).

Latrobe, Charles Joseph. *The Rambler in North America*. 2 vols. N.Y: Harper & Brothers, 1835.

McConnel, John C. *Western Characters, or Types of Border Life in The Western States*. N.Y: Redfield, 1853.

McKenney, Thomas L. *Sketches of a Tour to the Lakes*. Baltimore: Fielding Lucas, Jr., 1827.

Marryat, Frederick. *A Diary in America*. 3 vols. London: Longman, Orme, Brown, Green and Longmans, 1839.

Martineau, Harriet. *Society in America*. 3 vols. London: Saunders and Otley, 1837.
    Provides much information on the physical aspects of the nation, customs, activities of the people, and demographic characteristics. Notes on the traits of young people and women.

Melish, John. *A Geographical Description of the United States*. Phila: John Melish, 1818.

Michaux, Francois A. *Travels to the West of the Alleghany [sic] Mountains, in the States of Ohio, Kentucky, and Tennessea [sic] and back to Charleston, by the Upper Carolines . . . undertaken in the Year 1802*. Vol. III of *E.W.T.*

Morse, Jedidiah. *The American Gazetteer*. Boston: S. Hall, and Thomas and Andrews, 1797.

Murray, Charles A. *Travels in North America during the years 1834, 1835, & 1836*. 2 vols. London: Richard Bentley, 1839.

Niles Weekly Register. VIII (Apr. 15, 1815); X (June 8, 1816); XXIX (Nov. 26, 1825); XLVII (Nov. 8, 1834).

Nowlin, William. *The Bark Covered House; Or, Back in the Woods Again*, ed. Milo M. Quaife. Chicago: R. R. Donnelley & Sons, 1937.
      Contains numerous references to economic factors prompting migration and affecting settlement.

Ogden, George W. *Letters from the West; Comprising a Tour through the Western Country, and a residence of two Summers in the States of Ohio and Kentucky*, Vol. XIX of *E.W.T.*

Patterson, Isaac, ed. *The Constitutions of Ohio, Amendments and Proposed Amendments*. Cleveland: Arthur H. Clark, 1912.

Peck, John Mason. *A New Guide for Emigrants to the West, containing sketches of Ohio, Indiana, Illinois, Missouri, Michigan, with the Territories of Wisconsin and Arkansas, and the adjacent parts*. Boston: Gould, Kendall & Lincoln, 1836.

Philbrick, Francis S., ed. *Pope's Digest, 1815*. II. Springfield: Ill. State Hist. Library, 1940.

Power, Tyrone. *Impressions of America During the Years 1833, 1834, and 1835*. 2 vols. London: Richard Bentley, 1836.

Quaife, Milo., ed. *Fifty Years in Iowa: Being the personal Reminiscences of J. M. D. Burrows*. Chicago: R. R. Donnelley & Sons, 1942.

Rabb, Kate Milner, ed. *A Tour through Indiana: The Diary of John Parsons of Petersburg, Virginia*. N.Y: Robert M. McBride, 1920.

Richardson, William. *Journal from Boston to the Western Country and down the Ohio and Mississippi Rivers to New Orleans, 1815-1816*. N.Y: Ltd. ed. priv. printed for Value Pilot Corporation, 1940.

Rochefoucault-Liancourt, Duke de La. *Travels through the United States of America, the Country of the Iroquois, and Upper Canada, in the Years 1795, 1796, and 1797*. 3 vols. London: R. Phillips, 1800.

Scott, Franklin D., ed. and trans. *Baron Klinkowstrom's America, 1818-1820*. Evanston: Northwestern Univ. Pr., 1952.

Sealsfield, Charles. *The Americans as they Are; Described in a Tour through the Valley of the Mississippi*. London: Hurst, Chance, and Co., 1828.

Shirreff, Patrick. *A Tour through North America*. Edinburgh: Oliver and Boyd, 1835.

Steel, [Eliza R.] *A Summer Journey in the West*. N.Y: John S. Taylor, 1841.

Stuart, James. *Three Years in North America*, 2 vols. Edinburgh: Robert Cadell, 1833.

Sutcliff, Robert. *Travel in Some Parts of North America in the Years 1804, 1805 & 1806*. Phila: B. & T. Kite, 1812.

Thomson, William. *A Tradesman's Travels in the United States and Canada in the Years 1840, 41 & 42*. Edinburgh: Oliver & Boyd, 1842.

Thornbrough, Gayle, ed. "The Indiana Gazetteer or Topographical Dictionary, 1826," by John Scott. *Ind. Hist. Soc. Publ.*, xviii, no. 1 (1954).

Tillson, Christiana Holmes. *A Woman's Story of Pioneer Illinois*, ed. Milo M. Quaife. Chicago: R. R. Donnelley & Sons, 1919.

United States Census, 1800-1850. All of the census data for the years 1800 through 1850 were put onto tape. All of the data for the years through 1840 were used in this study with the exception of data dealing with citizenship, data found only in the censuses of 1830 and 1840.

With the passing of time, the amount and variety of information found in the censuses increased a bit. The censuses for 1800 and 1810 were identical and yielded data on age, sex, race, and the condition of blacks. The census of 1820 added a category on occupation. The census of 1830 dropped this category but added a category on citizenship and expanded the classification of age. The census of 1840 retained the citizenship category and re-introduced the one dealing with occupations.

In addition, over ninety federal manuscript censuses were sampled in order to secure data on household size and household composition. Fifty were sampled in order to obtain information for Chapter viii.

Unonius, Gustaf. *A Pioneer in Northwest America, 1841-1848: The Memoirs of Gustaf Unonius*, ed. Nils William Olsson. 2 vols. Minneapolis: The Swedish Pioneer Hist. Soc., 1950.

Vigne, Godfrey T. *Six Months in America*. London: Whittaker, Treacher, & Co., 1832.

Vonnegut, Emma S., ed. "The Schramm Letters: Written by Jacob Schramm and members of his Family from Indiana to Germany in the Year 1836," *Ind. Hist. Soc. Publ.*, 11, no. 4 (1935).

Wade, Mason, ed. *The Writings of Margaret Fuller*. N.Y: The Viking Press, 1941.

Warden, David B. *A Statistical, Political, and Historical Account of the United States of North America*. 3 vols. Edinburgh: A. Constable, 1819.
Contains much useful information concerning demography, agriculture, commerce, manufacturing and transportation.

Welsh, Mary J. "Recollections of Pioneer Life in Mississippi," *Publ. of Miss. Hist. Soc.*, iv, 1901.

Wetmore, Alphonso. *Gazetteer of the State of Missouri*. St. Louis: C. Keemle, 1837.

Windell, Marie George, ed. "Westward Along the Boone's Lick Trail in 1826, the Diary of Colonel John Glover," *Mo. Hist. Rev.*, xxxix, no. 2 (Jan. 1945).

Woods, John. *Two Years' Residence in the Settlement on the English Prairie in the Illinois Country, United States.* Vol. x of *E.W.T.*

Yoseloff, Thomas, ed. *Voyage to America: The Journal of Thomas Cather.* N.Y: Thomas Yoseloff, 1961.

Secondary Sources

Abernethy, Thomas Perkins. *The Formative Period in Alabama, 1815-1828.* Southern Hist. Publ. No. 8. University, Ala: Univ. of Ala. Pr., 1965.

Abrahamsen, David. *Our Violent Society.* N.Y: Funk & Wagnalls, 1970.

Allen, H. C. *Bush and Backwoods: A Comparison of the Frontier in Australia and the United States.* Sydney: Angus & Robertson," 1959.

Almack, John C. "The Shibboleth of the Frontier," *Hist. Outlook,* xvi (May 1925).

Andrews, John, ed. *Frontiers and Men.* Canberra: F. W. Cheshire, 1966.

Angle, Paul M., ed. *Prairie State: Impressions of Illinois, 1673-1967,* by Travelers and Other Observers. Chicago: Univ. of Chicago Pr., 1968.

Anthony, Elliott. *The Constitutional History of Illinois.* Chicago: Chicago Legal News, 1891.

Barnhart, John D. "Sources of Southern Migration into the Old Northwest," *Miss. Valley Hist. Rev.,* xxii, no. 1 (June 1931).

Bartlett, Richard A. *The New Country: A Social History of the American Frontier, 1776-1890.* N.Y: Oxford Univ. Pr., 1974.

Berwanger, Eugene. *The Frontier Against Slavery: Western Anti-Negro Prejudice and the Slavery Extension Controversy.* Urbana: Univ. of Ill. Pr., 1967.

Betts, Edward Chambers. *Early History of Huntsville, Alabama, 1804 to 1870.* Montgomery: Brown Ptg. Co., 1916.

Billington, Ray Allen. *America's Frontier Heritage.* N.Y: Holt, Rinehart and Winston, 1966.

_____. "The Frontier in Illinois History," *Jour. of the Ill. State Hist. Soc.,* xliii, no. 2 (Spring 1950).

_____, ed. *The Frontier Thesis: Valid Interpretation of American History?* N.Y: Holt, Rinehart and Winston, 1966.

Boggess, Arthur Clinton. *The Settlement of Illinois, 1718-1830.* Chicago: Chicago Hist. Soc., 1908.
    Relates many of the laws, political decisions, technological developments, and other factors that influenced demography.

Bogue, Donald J. *Principles of Demography.* N.Y: John Wiley and Sons, 1969.

Boorstin, Daniel J. *The Americans: The National Experience.* N.Y: Vintage Books, Random House, 1965.

Bossard, James H. S. *The Large Family System: An Original Study in the Sociology of Family Behavior.* Phila: Univ. of Penn. Pr., 1956.

Bowman, Isaiah. *Limits on Land Settlement: A Report on Present-Day Possibilities.* N.Y: Council on Foreign Affairs, 1937.

Branch, E. Douglas. *Westward: The Romance of the American Frontier.* N.Y: D. Appleton, 1930.

Brice, Wallace A. *A History of Fort Wayne, from the Earliest known Accounts of this Point, to the Present Period.* Fort Wayne, In: D. W. Jones & Son, 1868.

Britton, Wiley. "Pioneer Life in Southwest Missouri," *Mo. Hist. Rev.,* XVI, no. 2 (Jan. 1922).

Buck, Solon Justus. *Illinois in 1818.* Introductory vol. of *The Centennial History of Illinois,* ed. Clarence Walworth Alvord. 5 vols. Springfield: The Ill. Centennial Comm., 1917.
  Many references to household size, sex, race, conditions of blacks, population density, and the origins and movements of settlers.

Burns, Lee. "The National Road in Indiana," *Ind. Hist. Soc. Publ.,* VII, no. 4 (1919).

Calhoun, Arthur W. *A Social History of the American Family.* 3 vols. N.Y: Barnes and Noble, 1918.

Calkins, Earnest. *They Broke the Prairie.* N.Y: Charles Scribner's Sons, 1937.

Caruso, John Anthony. *The Great Lakes Frontier: An Epic of the Old Northwest.* N.Y: Bobbs-Merrill, 1961.

———. *The Southern Frontier.* Indianapolis: Bobbs-Merrill, 1963.

Channing, Edward. *A History of the United States.* Vol. V. *The Period of Transition, 1815-1848.* N.Y: The Macmillan Company, 1938.

Chilman, Catherine. "Some Psychological Aspects of Fertility, Family Planning, and Population Policy in the United States." *Psychological Perspectives on Population,* ed. James T. Fawcett. N.Y: Basic Books, 1973.

Clairborne, J. F. H. "A Trip through the Piney Woods," *Publ. of Miss. Hist. Soc.,* IX (1906).

Clark, Dan Elbert. *The West in American History.* N.Y: Thomas Y. Crowell, 1937.

Clark, Thomas D. *Frontier America: The Story of the Westward Movement,* 2d ed. N.Y: Charles Scribner's Sons, 1969.

———. *Rampaging Frontier: Manners and Humors of Pioneer Days in the South and the Middle West.* 2d ed. Bloomington: Ind. Univ. Pr., 1964.

Clarke, John I. *Population Geography.* 2d. ed. N.Y: Pergamon Press, 1972.

Clausen, John A. and Suzanne R. "The Effects of Family Size on Parents and Children." *Psychological Perspectives on Population,* ed. James T. Fawcett. N.Y: Basic Books, 1973.

Cockrum, William M. *Pioneer History of Indiana.* Oakland City, Ind. Pr. of Oakland City Jour., 1907.

Cole, Arthur Charles. *The Era of the Civil War, 1848-1870.* Vol. III of *The Centennial History of Illinois,* ed. Clarence Walworth Alvord. 5 vols. Springfield: The Ill. Centennial Comm., 1919.

Coleman, Peter J. "The Woodhouse Family; Grant County Pioneers," *Wisc. Mag. of Hist.*, XLII, no. 4 (Summer 1959).

Daniels, John J. "The Earliest Settlers of Linn County," *Annals of Iowa*, VI, no. 8 (1905).

Demos, John. *A Little Commonwealth: Family Life in Plymouth Colony.* N.Y: Oxford Univ. Pr., 1970.

_____ "Families in Colonial Bristol, Rhode Island: An Exercise in Historical Demography," *The Wm. and Mary Quar.*, XXV, no. 4 (Oct. 1968).

Dick, Everett. *The Dixie Frontier: A Social History of the Southern Frontier from the First Transmontane Beginnings to the Civil War.* N.Y: Alfred A. Knopf, 1948.

DuBose, Euba. "A History of Mount Sterling," *Ala. Hist. Quar.*, XXV, nos. 3 and 4 (Winter and Fall, 1963).

Duffield, George C. "An Iowa Settler's Homestead," *Annals of Iowa*, VI, no. 3 (Oct. 1903).

_____ "Frontier Mills," *Annals of Iowa*, VI, no. 6 (July 1904).

Eblen, Jack. "An Analysis of Nineteenth-Century Frontier Populations," *Demography*, II (1965).
    Deals with 1840-1860. Indicates few demographic differences between frontier & settled areas.

Elkins, Stanley M. *Slavery, A Problem in American Institutional and Intellectual Life.* Chicago: Univ. of Chicago Pr., 1959.

Elkins, Stanley and McKitrick, Eric. "A Meaning for Turner's Frontier, Part 1: Democracy in the Old Northwest," *Pol. Sci. Quar.*, LXIX, no. 3 (Sept. 1954).

_____ "A Meaning for Turner's Frontier, Part II: The Southwest Frontier and New England," *Pol. Sci. Quar.*, LXIX, no. 4 (Dec. 1954).

Enloe, Louisa D. "Silas Drake of Marion County, Mississippi, and His Descendants," *Jour. of Miss. Hist.*, XXVII, no. 3 (Aug. 1965).
    Mentions household size, household composition, age, and spacing of children.

Evans, Priscilla Ann. "Merchant Gristmills and Communities, 1820-1880: An Economic Relationship," *Mo. Hist. Rev.*, LXVIII, no. 3 (Apr. 1974).

Ewbank, Lewis B. "A Real Pioneer," *Ind. Mag. of Hist.*, XXXVIII, no. 2 (June 1942).

Faris, John T. *On the Trail of the Pioneers: Romance, Tragedy and Triumph on the Path of Empire.* N.Y: George H. Doran, 1920.

Flanders, Ralph. *Plantation Slavery in Georgia.* Chapel Hill: Univ. of No. Car. Pr., 1933.

Fogel, Robert W. and Engerman, Stanley L. *Time on the Cross.* Boston: Little, Brown & Company, 1974.

Forster, Colin and Tucker, G. S. L. *Economic Opportunity and White American Fertility Ratios, 1800-1860.* New Haven: Yale Univ. Pr., 1972.

Glick, Paul C. *American Families.* Census Monograph Ser. N.Y: John Wiley and Sons, 1957.

Goodsell, Willystine. "Housing and the Birth Rate in Sweden," *Amer. Soc. Rev.*, II, no. 6 (Dec. 1937).

Gordon, Douglas H. and May, George S., eds. "Michigan Journal, 1836, *John M. Gordon,*" *Mich. Hist.*, XLII, no. 3 (Sept. 1959).

Grabill, Wilson; Kiser, Clyde; and Whelpton, Pascal. *The Fertility of American Women.* Census Monograph Ser. N.Y: John Wiley and Sons, 1958.

Greven, Philip J., Jr. *Four Generations: Population, Land, and Family in Colonial Andover, Massachusetts.* Ithaca: Cornell Univ. Pr., 1970.

Gutman, Herbert G. *Slavery and the Numbers Game: A Critique of Time on the Cross.* Urbana: Univ. of Ill. Pr., 1975.

Halsey, Francis Whiting. *The Old New York Frontier: Its Wars with Indians and Tories, Its Missionaries, Schools, Pioneer and Land Titles, 1614-1800.* N.Y: Charles Scribner's Sons, 1901.

Hansbrough, Vivian. "The Crowleys of Crowley's Ridge," *Ark. Hist. Quar.*, XIII, no. 1 (Summer 1954).

Harlan, A. W. "Slavery in Iowa Territory," *Annals of Iowa*, II, no. 8 (Jan. 1897).

Harris, N. Dwight. *The History of Negro Servitude in Illinois and of the Slavery Agitation in that State, 1719-1864.* Chicago: A. C. McClurg & Co., 1904.

Hart, Jesse, et. al. "Pioneer History of the Settlement of Eaton County," *Mich. Hist. Coll.*, XXII (1894).

Havighurst, Walter. *The Heartland: Ohio, Indiana, Illinois.* N.Y: Harper & Row, 1956.

Hedge, Thomas. "Installation of the Temple Tablet, June 17, 1913," *Annals of Iowa*, XI, nos. 2 and 3 (July-Oct. 1913).

Heer, David M. *Society and Population.* Englewood Cliffs: Prentice-Hall, 1968.

Holbrook, Stewart H. *The Yankee Exodus: An Account of Migration from New England.* Seattle: Univ. of Wash. Pr., 1950.

Hollingsworth, T. H. *Historical Demography.* Ithaca: Cornell Univ. Pr., 1969.

Hollon, W. Eugene. *Frontier Violence: Another Look.* N.Y: Oxford Univ. Pr., 1974.

Horsman, Reginald. *The Frontier in the Formative Years, 1783-1815.* N.Y: Holt, Rinehart and Winston, 1970.

Horton, John J. *The Jonathon Hale Farm: A Chronicle of the Cuyahoga Valley.* Cleveland: The West. Reserve Hist. Soc., 1961.

Howard, Robert P. *Illinois: A History of the Prairie State.* Grand Rapids, Mich: William B. Eerdmans, 1972.

Howe, Daniel Wait. "Making a Capital in the Wilderness," *Ind. Hist. Soc. Publ.*, IV, no. 4 (1908).

Hunt, Gaillard. *Life in America One Hundred Years Ago.* N.Y: Harper & Brothers, 1914.

Huntington, Ida M. "Willson Alexander Scott," *Annals of Iowa*, XIII, no. 4 (Apr. 1922).

Inglehart, John E. "The Coming of the English to Indiana in 1817 and their Hoosier Neighbors," *Ind. Mag. of Hist.*, XV, no. 2 (June 1919).

Joerg, W. L. G., ed. *Pioneer Settlement: Cooperative Studies by Twenty-six Authors.* N.Y: Amer. Geog. Soc., 1932.

Katzman, Martin T. "The Brazilian Frontier in Comparative Perspective," *Comparative Studies in Society and History*, XVII, no. 3 (July 1975).

Kennedy, David M. *Birth Control in America: The Career of Margaret Sanger.* New Haven: Yale Univ. Pr., 1970.

Keyes, Elisha W. "Early Days in Jefferson County," *Colls. of the State Hist. Soc. of Wisc.*, XI (1888).

Keyes, Nelson Beecher. *The American Frontier: Our Unique Heritage.* Garden City: Hanover House, 1954.

Knollenberg, Bernhard. "Pioneer Sketches of the Upper Whitewater Valley: Quaker Stronghold of the West," *Ind. Hist. Soc. Publ.*, XV, no. 1 (1945).

Laslett, Barbara. "Household Structure on an American Frontier: Los Angeles, California, in 1850," *Amer. Jour. of Soc.*, LXXXI, no. 1 (July 1975).

Lawlis, Chelsea L. "Settlement of the Whitewater Valley, 1790-1810," *Ind. Mag. of Hist.*, XLIII, no. 1 (Mar. 1947).

Leet, Don R. "The Determinants of the Fertility Transition in Antebellum Ohio," *Journal of Economic History*, XXXVI, no. 2 (June 1976).

Litwak, Leon F. *North of Slavery: The Negro in the Free States, 1790-1860.* Chicago: Univ. of Chicago, 1961.

McCorvey, Thomas. *Alabama Historical Sketches.* Charlottesville: Univ. of Va. Pr., 1960.

McLaren, Angus. "Contraception and the Working Classes: The Social Ideology of the English Birth Control Movement in its Early Years," *Comp. Stud. in Soc. and Hist.*, XVIII, no. 2 (Apr. 1976).

McMaster, John B. *A History of the People of the United States from the Revolution to the Civil War*, Vol. IV. N.Y: D. Appleton, 1895.

Martel, Glenn. "Early Days in Northwest Louisiana," *Ark. Hist. Quar.* XII, no. 2 (Summer 1953).

Mikesell, Marvin. "Comparative Studies in Frontier History," *Annals of Assoc. of Amer. Geog.*, L, no. 1 (March 1960).

Modell, John. "Family and Fertility on the Indiana Frontier, 1820," *Amer. Quar.*, XXIII, no. 5 (Dec. 1971).

Nimkoff, Meyer, ed. *Comparative Family Systems.* Boston: Houghton Mifflin, 1965.

Nixon, Herman Clarence. "Precursors of Turner in the Interpretation of the American Frontier," *So. Atlantic Quar.*, XXVIII, no. 1 (Jan. 1929).

Nunis, Doyce B., Jr. "The Sublettes of Kentucky: Their Early Contribution to the Opening of the West," *Register of the Ky. Hist. Soc.,* LVII, no. 1 (Jan. 1959).

Owsley, Frank L. "The Pattern of Migration and Settlement on the Southern Frontier," *Jour. of So. Hist.,* XI, no. 2 (May 1945).

_____ *Plain Folk of the Old South.* Baton Rouge: La. State Univ. Pr., 1949.

Parker, George. *Iowa Pioneer Foundations,* 2 vols. Iowa City: State Hist. Soc. of Ia., 1940.
    Deals with the years 1830-70 and includes many comments about the frontier, including frontier demography, that apply to the national frontier experience.

Parks, Henry Bamfield. *The United States of America: A History.* 2d. ed. N.Y: Alfred A. Knopf, 1963.

Paullin, Charles O. *Atlas of the Historical Geography of the United States,* ed. John K. Wright. N.Y: Amer. Geog. Soc. 1932.

Pease, Theodore Calvin. *The Frontier State, 1818-1848.* Vol. II of *The Centennial History of Illinois,* ed. Clarence Walworth Alvord. 5 vols. Springfield: The Ill. Centennial Comm., 1918.

Perry, Harriet. "The Life History of Harriet Whitney Collins," *N.W. Ohio Quar.,* XXXI, no. 4 (Fall 1959).

Philbrick, Francis S. *The Rise of the West, 1754-1830.* N.Y: Harper & Row, 1965.

Potter, David M. *People of Plenty: Economic Abundance and the American Character.* Chicago: Univ. of Chicago Pr., 1954.

Potter, J. "The Growth of Population in America, 1700-1860." *Population in History: Essays in Historical Demography,* eds. D. V. Glass and D. E. C. Eversley. London: Edward Arnold, 1965.

Prucha, Francis Paul. *Broadax and Bayonet: The Role of the United States Army in the Development of the Northwest, 1815-1860.* Madison: The State Hist. Soc. of Wisc., 1953.

Quaife, Milo M., ed. "An English Settler in Pioneer Wisconsin: The Letters of Edwin Bottomley, 1842-1850," *Publ. of the State Hist. Soc. of Wisc.,* XXV, (1918).

Quillin, Frank V. *The Color Line in Ohio.* Ann Arbor, Mich: George Wahr, 1913.

Ray, Louis L. "Flatboat Letters from Samuel Gibson Brown," *Year Book of the Soc. of Ind. Pioneers,* (1965).

Rice, Otis K. *The Allegheny Frontier, 1730-1830.* Lexington: Univ. Pr. of Ky., 1970.

Riegel, Robert E. and Athearn, Robert G. *America Moves West.* 5th ed. N.Y: Holt, Rinehart and Winston, 1971.

Rodman, Jane. "The English Settlement in Southern Illinois, 1815-1825." *Ind. Mag. of Hist.,* XLIII, no. 4 (Dec. 1947).

Rothman, David J. "Documents in Search of a Historian: Toward a History of Children and Youth in America," *The Family in History: Inter-disciplinary Essays,* eds., Theodore K. Rabb and Robert I. Rotberg. N.Y: Harper & Row, 1971.

Ryle, Walter H. "A Study of Early Days in Randolph County, 1818-1860," *Mo. Hist. Rev.,* xxiv, no. 2 (Jan. 1930).

Schafer, Joseph. *Wisconsin Domesday Book, General Studies,* Vol. ii: *Four Wisconsin Counties, Prairie and Forest.* Madison: State Hist. Soc. of Wisc., 1927.

Sears, Robert R. "Ordinal Position in the Family as a Psychological Variable," *Amer. Soc. Rev.,* xv, 1950.

Severance, Henry O. *Michigan Trailmakers.* Ann Arbor, Mich: George Wahr, 1930.

Sharp, Paul F. "Three Frontiers: Some Comparative Studies of Canadian, American and Australian Settlement," *Pac. Hist. Rev.,* xxiv, 1955.

Sharpless, John B. and Shortridge, Ray M. "Biased Underenumeration in Census Manuscripts: Methodological Implications," *Jour. of Urban Hist.,* i, no. 4 (Aug. 1975).

Silver, Morris. "Births, Marriages, and Business Cycles in the United States," *The Jour. of Pol. Econ.,* lxxiii, no. 3 (June 1965).

Smith, Carroll E. *Pioneer Times in the Onondaga Country.* Syracuse: C. W. Bardeen, 1904.

Smith, Peter Fox. "A Granville Cooper's Experience with Barter in the 1820s," *Ohio Hist. Quar.,* lxix, no. 1 (Jan. 1960).

Smith, T. Lynn and Zopf, Paul E., Jr. *Demography: Principles and Methods.* Phila: F. A. Davis, 1970.

Spencer, Annie L. "The Blacks of Union County," *Ark. Hist. Quar.,* xii, no. 3 (Autumn 1953).

Spengler, Joseph J. and Duncan, Otis Dudley, eds. *Demographic Analysis: Selected Readings.* Glencoe: The Free Press, 1957.

Stampp, Kenneth M. *The Peculiar Institution: Slavery in the Ante-Bellum South.* N.Y: Alfred A. Knopf, 1956.

Stephenson, Orlando. *Ann Arbor: The First Hundred Years.* Ann Arbor, Mich. Ann Arbor Chamber of Comm., 1927.

Swisher, John A. *Iowa: Land of Many Mills.* Iowa City: The State Hist. Soc. of Ia., 1940.

Sydnor, Charles S. "Life Span of Mississippi Slaves," *Amer. Hist. Rev.,* xxxv, no. 5 (Apr. 1930).

————— *Slavery in Mississippi.* N.Y: D. Appleton-Century, 1933.

Taylor, George Rogers. *The Transportation Revolution, 1815-1860.* N.Y: Harper & Row, 1951.

Thomlinson, Ralph. *Population Dynamics: Causes and Consequences of World Demographic Change.* N.Y: Random House, 1965.

Thompson, Charles N. "Sons of the Wilderness: John and William Conner," *Ind. Hist. Soc. Publ.*, xii, (1937).

Thornbrough, Emma Lou. "The Negro in Indiana before 1900." *Ind. Hist. Colls.*, xxxvii (1957).

Thurston, Helen M. "The 1802 Constitutional Convention and the Status of the Negro," *Ohio Hist.*, lxxxi, no. 1 (Winter 1972).

Trever, Karl. "Wisconsin Newspapers as Publishers of the Federal Laws, 1836-1874," *Wisc. Mag. of Hist.*, xxxi, no. 3 (Mar. 1948).

Viles, Jonas. "Old Franklin: A Frontier Town of the Twenties," The *Miss. Valley Hist. Rev.*, ix, no. 4 (Mar. 1923).

Wilson, William E. *Indiana: A History.* Bloomington: Ind. Univ. Pr., 1966.

Woodson, Carter G. *Free Negro Heads of Families in the United States in 1830 together with a Brief Treatment of the Free Negro.* Washington, D.C: Assoc. for the Study of Negro Life and Hist., Inc., 1925.

Worley, Ted. R., ed. "Story of an Early Settlement in Central Arkansas," *Ark. Hist. Quar.*, x, no. 2 (Summer 1951).

Wright, John Ernest and Corbett, Doris S. *Pioneer Life in Western Pennsylvania.* Pittsburgh: Univ. of Pittsburgh Pr., 1940.

Wrong, Dennis H. *Population and Society.* 3d ed. N.Y: Random House, 1967.

Yasuba, Yasukichi. *Birth Rates of the White Population in the United States, 1800-1860.* Baltimore: Johns Hopkins Pr., 1962.

Zimmermann, Edward. "Travels into Missouri in October, 1838," *Mo. Hist. Rev.*, ix, no. 1 (Oct. 1914).

Index